Boys and girls in the primary classroom

Boys and girls in the primary classroom

*Edited by Christine Skelton
and Becky Francis*

Open University Press

Open University Press
McGraw-Hill Education
McGraw-Hill House
Shoppenhangers Road
Maidenhead
Berkshire
England
SL6 2QL

e-mail: enquiries@openup.co.uk
world wide web: www.openup.co.uk

First published 2003

A catalogue record of this book is available from the British Library

ISBN 0 335 21154 2 (pb)   0 335 21155 0 (hb)

Library of Congress Cataloging-in-Publication Data
CIP data has been applied for

Typeset by RefineCatch Limited, Bungay, Suffolk
Printed in the UK by Bell & Bain Ltd, Glasgow

Contents

Notes on contributors

Louise Archer is a senior research fellow at the Institute for Policy Studies in Education, London Metropolitan University. Her research addresses issues of gender, 'race' and social class across educational sectors. She is co-author of *Higher Education and Social Class: Issues of Exclusion and Inclusion* (published 2003, RoutledgeFalmer) and is currently completing a book on Muslim boys and schooling for Open University Press.

Mike Askew is Reader in Mathematics Education at King's College, University of London. He directed the Teacher Training Agency-funded 'Effective Teachers of Numeracy in Primary Schools' and Nuffield Foundation-funded 'Raising Attainment in Numeracy' and 'Mental Calculations: Interpretations and Implementation' projects. He was deputy director of the five year Leverhulme Numeracy Research Programme looking at teaching, learning and progression from Reception to Year 7. When he is not writing up research he enjoys being a conjuror.

Shereen Benjamin has taught for many years in mainstream and special schools. She is currently a lecturer in Difficulties in Learning at the University of Birmingham. Her research focuses on the sociology of special educational needs, and addresses the intersections of disability, gender/sexuality, social class and 'race'. Her book, *The Micropolitics of Inclusive Education* was published by Open University Press in 2002, and she is co-editor of *Gender and Education: Critical Perspectives*, published by Palgrave in 2003.

Margaret Brown is a professor of Mathematics Education at King's College London. She has taught in primary and secondary schools and directed over 20 research projects in the teaching, learning and assessment of mathematics. She was a member of the Numeracy Task Force at the Department for Education and Skills and is a past president of the British Educational Research Association.

Paul Connolly is Senior Lecturer in Sociology at the University of Ulster. His publications include: *Racism, Gender Identities and Young Children* and *Researching Racism in Education*. He is currently directing a Government-funded study on sectarianism and children in Northern Ireland and also working on a book on boys and masculinities in the early years. (Further details are available at: http://paulconnolly.net)

Bronwyn Davies is a professor of Education at the University of Western Sydney and is best known for her books *Frogs and Snails and Feminist Tales: Preschool Children and Gender* and *Shards of Glass: Children Reading and Writing Beyond Gendered Identity*, both of which are in second editions with Hampton Press. She is also widely cited for her work on positioning with Rom Harré. A collection of her theoretical writing has been published as *A Body of Writing* with AltaMira Press. She has also explored writing through her book *(In)scribing Body Landscape Relations* and has extended her preschool and gender research with a study in Japan which is forthcoming with Hampton Press as *Frogs and Snails in Japan: Preschool Children and Gender*.

Hazel Denvir has been a primary teacher and has worked for many years at King's College London on research projects concerned with primary children's learning of number, especially focusing on low attaining children.

Becky Francis is Reader in Education and Deputy Director of the Institute for Policy Studies in Education, London Metropolitan University. Her research interests include the construction of gender identities, feminist theory, and gender and achievement. She is editor of *Gender and Education* journal (with Christine Skelton). Her sole-authored books are *Boys, Girls and Achievement: Addressing the Classroom Issues* (2000, RoutledgeFalmer), and *Power Plays* (1998, Trentham Books). She and Christine Skelton are also editors of the reader *Investigating Gender* (2001, Open University Press).

Helen Lucey is a senior research fellow at South Bank University in the Families and Social Capital ESRC Research Group focusing on sibling practices in different kinds of families. She is co-author of *Democracy in the Kitchen* (1989) and *Growing up Girl: Psychosocial Explorations of Gender and Class* (2001).

Jackie Marsh is a senior lecturer in Education at the University of Sheffield, where she teaches on the MEd in Literacy and the MA in Early Childhood Education. Her research is focused on the role of popular culture in the literacy curriculum and the place of media literacy in children's out-of-school lives. She is co-editor of the *Journal of Early Childhood Literacy*. Her publications include a co-authored book with Elaine Millard, *Literacy and Popular Culture: Using Children's Culture in the Classroom*, published by Paul Chapman/Sage, and a co-edited book with Nigel Hall and Joanne Larson: *Handbook of Early Childhood Literacy*, published by Sage.

Diane Reay is a professor at the Institute for Policy Studies in Education, London Metropolitan University. She taught in inner London primary schools for twenty years before moving into higher education. Since then she has published widely in the areas of gender, social class and ethnicity.

Michael Reiss is Professor of Science Education and Head of the School of Mathematics, Science and Technology at the Institute of Education, University of London, a priest in the Church of England and an accredited psychodynamic counsellor. His research, writing, teaching and consultancy expertise are in the fields of science education, health education and bioethics. He is the editor of *Sex Education* and director of Salters-Nuffield Advanced Biology.

Valerie Rhodes was a research fellow on the Leverhulme Numeracy Research Programme and the Effective Teachers of Numeracy project based at King's College London. Her research interests focus on numeracy and the use of information and communication technology in the primary school curriculum. She has worked as a school teacher in primary schools.

Jean Rudduck is Professor of Education at the University of Cambridge. Her main research interests are the complexities of institutional change and school improvement; teachers' professional development; and students' perspectives on teaching, learning and schooling. Key dimensions of her work are 'dividing practices', gender issues and pupil voice. Her interest in pupil voice grows out of a longitudinal study of young people's perspectives on schooling funded by the ESRC (1991–96) and she is currently coordinating an ESRC Project on Consulting Pupils about Teaching and Learning, as part of its Teaching and Learning Research Programme.

Christine Skelton is a senior lecturer in the School of Education, Communication and Language Sciences at the University of Newcastle. She was a primary school teacher for ten years before taking up a post at Sunderland Polytechnic as a lecturer in early years education. Her research focuses on gender and primary schooling. Her books include *Schooling the Boys: Masculinities and Primary Education* and an edited collection (with Becky Francis) *Investigating Gender*, both published by Open University Press. She is co-editor, with Becky Francis, of the academic journal *Gender and Education*.

Isobel Urquhart is a senior lecturer in Education Studies and Primary English in the Faculty of Education, University of Cambridge.

PART 1
Setting the scene: gender and educational policy

1 Introduction

Boys and girls in the primary classroom

Christine Skelton and Becky Francis

Policy around educational practice has shifted dramatically since the mid-1980s, and one of the clearest examples has been the development of a focus on 'standards' and achievement. 'Standards' have largely been interpreted as relating exclusively to achievement at public exams. And formal, national exams have dramatically increased during this period[1]. The results of these exams are published in 'league tables' which publicly report the record of each school concerning the results of its pupils[2]. One of the results of this pre-occupation with pupil attainment in public testing has been the identification of, and focus on, the apparent 'underachievement' of boys. Popular conjecture on this topic suggests two things:

- primary schoolboys' needs aren't being met – specifically, that greater emphasis should be given to boys' preferred learning styles together with the provision of more male teachers to act as role models in order to enhance their performance; and
- primary schoolgirls are now doing fine and no longer require our concern.

The needs of girls, or any concept of gender issues as irrevocably tied up between *both* genders, have often been side-lined in the popular literature on the issue of 'boys' underachievement'. Yet the assumptions highlighted above have been challenged on a number of levels. In the first place, it has been convincingly shown that not all boys are underachieving and neither are all girls academic success stories (Gorard *et al.* 1999; Myhill 2002). And, as we have argued elsewhere, these populist discourses on boys' underachievement place the needs of girls in danger of being marginalized. Furthermore, boys (or girls) cannot be considered in isolation (e.g. Francis 2000; Skelton and Francis 2002). We see gender as relational (that is where there cannot be masculinity without a notion of femininity to compare it to, and vice-versa), and it is therefore vital that researchers consider girls' *and* boys' behaviour in their work on gender and schooling.

There have been few recent books dedicated to issues of gender in the primary classroom. Rather, there is a tendency in the literature to focus on secondary schooling at the expense of primary and pre-schooling. Yet children's constructions of gender are formulated and developed long before they enter the secondary school – indeed, psychology studies suggest that the strongest period of 'gender role maintenance' takes place at 4–5 years old (see Lloyd and Duveen 1992 for discussion). So, this book represents a welcome contribution to explorations of gender issues in the primary school. In particular, it aims to enable teachers to see beyond media and government 'sound bites' (such as Crace 2001) by providing teachers with overviews of current research findings in specific aspects of gender and primary schooling. The book also intends to return attention to the relationality of gender, and the impact of children's gender constructions on factors such as classroom behaviour and achievement. Each chapter is devoted to a different issue or curriculum area, and draws on research evidence to suggest strategies that teachers can use to address gender constructions in the primary classroom.

However, before we move to explaining the structure of the book and outlining the various contributions, we want to briefly contextualize the reasons why achievement and underachievement dominate government educational policy before spending some time considering the accuracy of the two assertions given above regarding boys and girls in the primary classroom. We also want to outline the ways in which theories about gender construction have impacted and might impact upon classroom organization and management.

Policy, theory and educational practice

Policy and theory around educational practice was changed dramatically at the end of the 1980s and, since that time, has constantly been revised in ways that make the education system increasingly subject to constant government checks and drives. The Education Reform Act 1988 introduced a quasi-market system to schools in England and Wales whereby parents became the 'consumers' of education and pupils the 'clients' (Coffey 2001; for discussions of the reforms in various parts of the United Kingdom see Salisbury and Riddell 2000). Accompanying this marketization was a standardization of the curriculum across all schools (known as the National Curriculum), the application of which is constantly scrutinized through pupil assessment and school inspections. Further surveillance of the primary curriculum has been introduced via the National Literacy and National Numeracy Strategies. This focus on standards was developed initially by a Conservative government but was continued and has been enhanced by New Labour. Crucially, 'standards' have largely been interpreted as relating exclusively to achievement at public exams such as the Key Stage 1 (KS1) and Key Stage 2 (KS2) Standard Assessment Tasks (SATs). As a result, primary schools have been witness to significant changes in discourse. A school's performance in these exams is publicized through league tables, which are simply unable to take account of the social, economic and cultural complexities of how one school secures more pupils achieving required levels in the SATs than its neighbour. This performativity of primary schools is a discourse of a New Managerialist ethos that stresses 'cost effectiveness' and 'value for money'. As Davies (2003) argues so perceptively, the New Managerialist discourse has been extremely effective at placing responsibility for 'failure' or inefficiency on individual employees in the public sector, rather than on financial underfunding or particular policies. Thus, primary schools have witnessed a move away from the child-centred discourses of the 1980s (Walkerdine 1983; Alexander 1984) and towards accountability discourses of the 1990s and 2000s.

Having provided a brief explanation as to why primary schools are expected to centralize standards and achievement, we will now unpack the two presumptions regarding the 'achievement' of boys and girls in the primary classroom.

Boys' underachievement – failing to meet boys' needs?

The oversimplification of the media and government promoted headline that *all* boys are currently underachieving has been challenged widely and not just in this country but across many western states (Epstein *et al.* 1998; Lingard and Douglas 1999; Francis 2000; Foster *et al.* 2001). These arguments indicate a number of ways in which the claim that boys' underachievement is widespread and created by 'laddishness' and/or faults on the part of teachers or the curriculum conceals a far more complex picture. First, statistical differences between boys' attainments in SATs in relation to girls are pointed to by the government as evidence that boys are underachieving (Miliband 2002). However, this masks the fact that exam performance has *increased* for both boys and girls on a yearly basis and that, in any case, this statistical information has been misinterpreted (Gorard *et al.* 1999; Gorard 2000). Having said this, it is generally agreed that the gap between boys' and girls' performance at literacy, English and modern languages remains quite large (as has been the case for decades). Second, an emphasis on 'boys' versus 'girls' attainments precludes any appreciation of the differences between boys and boys and girls and girls. Groups such as middle-class white boys, and Indian and Chinese boys, continue to achieve highly. White working-class, African Caribbean and Bangladeshi boys tend to underachieve in the British education system (Gillborn and Gipps 1996). But then, as Walkerdine *et al.* (2001) and Lucey (2001) demonstrate so clearly, working-class white girls underachieve compared to their middle-class counterparts too. Of far greater significance in determining a pupil's achievement and life chances than either gender or ethnicity is social class (Gillborn 1997; Ball *et al.* 2000). Third, the idea that primary schools have become overly feminized and thus have neglected boys' learning needs appears to have no basis in evidence. While primary schools continue to be predominantly staffed by female teachers – as they have always been historically – the ways in which schools are organized and managed have become *more* masculinized in recent years (Mahony and Hextall 2000; Skelton 2002). That is, there has been a move away from liberal child-centred discourses towards ones whereby the teacher's role has become more concerned with surveillance and accountability. As Haywood and Mac an Ghaill (2001: 28) have stated, 'High status has been ascribed to the "hard masculine" functions of the accountant, the Key Stage tester, the curriculum coordinator, and the Information and Communication Technology expert.'

Finally, there is the issue of boys and 'laddishness'. Some feminist research suggests that boys' constructions of masculinity as competitive, macho and 'laddish' results in their gradual alienation from school as they seek to position themselves as 'hard' and 'cool', and to distance themselves from the image of the 'boffin' who is constructed as effete (e.g. Epstein *et al.* 1998; Raphael-Reed 1998; Francis 2000; Warrington and Younger 2000). It has also been argued that, due to their construction of masculinity as competitive, boys who are not clearly 'winning' in terms of school achievement very quickly find other ways to demonstrate their successful masculinity (for example, by being the 'hardest', 'cheekiest to teachers' or 'anti-heroes in the classroom'. See Power *et al.* 1998; Mills 2001; Swain 2002). Literacy and language subjects have been traditionally positioned as feminine, and it has therefore been argued that boys disengage with, or seek to distance themselves from, these subjects from an early age (Alloway and Gilbert 1997). Communication and emotional expression is seen as the domain of girls, rather than boys (Rowan *et al.* 2001). So feminist researchers have tended to see boys' underachievement at particular subjects as due to their constructions of gender, and indeed due to the dominant constructions of desirable masculinity in society at large.

As was suggested above, many non-feminist commentators have explained primary schoolboys' comparative underachievement differently. Commentators past and present have argued that primary schools are increasingly 'feminized institutions' (Moir and Moir 1998; Pollack 1998) and one of the suggested solutions is to increase the number of male primary teachers to provide boys with role models (Biddulph 1997; Hoff Sommers 2000). As the concern of the government is with the 'laddish culture' in schools (Blunkett 2000; Miliband 2002) then it can be assumed that male teachers are supposed to offer alternative models of masculinity although what these are supposed to look like is not clear. One of the problems with such thinking is that it assumes that men teachers behave and teach differently to their female colleagues (in ways more appealing to boys), and/or that boys perceive their male teachers in a positive light. Yet as we and others have pointed out, there is scant research evidence to support such assumptions (Smedley 1999; Lahelma 2000; Francis and Skelton 2001; Hutchings 2002; Carrington and Skelton 2003). Furthermore, many boys do not identify with their male teachers and, in some cases, they can be marginalized by them (Connolly 1995; Skelton 2001). Similarly Pole's (1999) work with ethnic minority teachers shows that 'role models' are not 'race' specific in every case. Also, there is actually no evidence to suggest that matching the teaching population by gender makes any difference to young people's classroom behaviour and educational achievement. Indeed, quantitative analysis by Thornton and Brichenco (2002) actually suggests a correlation between greater concentrations of male teachers and poorer discipline in schools. They found no positive link between higher numbers of male teachers and increased primary schoolboy attainment. Their research was quantitative, and it is likely that factors such as school size and location may have impacted on these results (as men teachers seem likely to be located in bigger schools with greater numbers of teachers). Yet these findings do question the assumed link between an increase in numbers of male teachers and the improved achievement and behaviour of primary boys.

Of particular concern is the idea that girls in the primary school are doing well both in comparison to boys and in relation to studies undertaken years ago that highlighted their different and unequal experiences in the primary classroom (Belotti 1975; Clarricoates 1978, 1980; Whyte 1983).

Primary girls are doing well?

As we said earlier, not all girls are achieving, just as not all boys are underachieving. Indeed there is a wealth of research demonstrating how factors such as ethnicity and social class are irrevocably intermeshed with gender thus showing the inadequacy of any explanations that generalize about 'the girls' or 'the boys' (Ball *et al.* 2000; Francis 2000; Reay 2002). A review of the literature of the 1980s and 1990s on gender and primary schooling has shown that little has actually changed for girls in the primary classroom (Skelton and Francis 2002). To illustrate the point, we want to focus on two key areas: the perceptions of teachers and other adults regarding girls' abilities and (appropriate) conduct; and, girls' behaviour in the classroom.

Perceptions of girls

In studies of primary schools carried out in the 1970s and 1980s girls and boys tended to be seen as two distinct and coherent groups. Teachers' perceptions of gender images were of 'typical girls' who were nice, cooperative and conscientious workers (Browne and France 1986; Skelton 1989) and 'proper boys' who were dominant, demanding and difficult but rewarding to teach (Stanworth 1981; Clarricoates 1987). Girls were the 'conformist plodders' who were seen as achieving through hard work, whilst boys were seen as lazy but 'naturally talented' (Belotti 1975; Walden and Walkerdine 1985). So although boys were seen as requiring more inducements to get involved in educational work, they were still regarded by many primary teachers as possessing greater academic abilities than girls. Recent research suggests that this differential perception of girls as achieving through hard work and boys as innately clever continues. This work shows how girls and boys who, in effect, occupy the academic position of the other gender are repositioned by adults in relation to what should be their 'appropriate' gendered location. For example, two highly able Year 6 (11–12-year-old) girls in Renold's (2001) study were not seen as talented by their teachers but as 'bossy', 'overconfident' and one of them as 'not as clever as she thinks she is' (p. 580). And teachers in Maynard's (2002) research of a primary school saw underachieving boys as 'having innate if untapped potential' (p. 67)!

Less attention was given in early feminist research to social class and ethnicity in relation to the abilities of girls and boys. However, Clarricoates (1987) considered the differences generated by social class observing that middle-class girls were expected to be academically successful in a way that working-class girls were not. Ethnicity plays a part here too – for example, more recently, Connolly (1998) has shown how all the girls in the Year 2 (6–7-year-old) class he observed were expected to be compliant and hardworking, but that this was particularly emphasized in the case of the South Asian girls. So, in terms of teachers' perceptions of the abilities of pupils, boys continue to be perceived as 'naturally bright but lazy'. Perhaps the counterside to this – the positioning of girls as 'not naturally bright, but hard-working' – may be one of the reasons that girls' apparent educational success is not celebrated. However, it is not only teachers' perceptions of the differential abilities of boys and girls but their expectations of appropriate gendered behaviours which have been shown to have changed little during the period since the 1980s.

Primary age girls were, and are, expected to be appropriately reticent and suitably demure in the classroom. In one of the early studies of primary classrooms, King (1978) identified a gender code whereby (white) girls were told to 'look pretty' and not to 'shout'. Black and South Asian girls were also stereotyped but in such a way that foregrounded their ethnicity before their gender. For example, Black girls have been and continue to be stereotyped as 'assertive' but seen as achieving better in schools than their male counterparts, while South Asian girls are regarded as passive, meek and ruthlessly oppressed by their families (Fuller 1982; Williams 1987; Connolly 1998). Recent work indicates that when girls do not conform to conventional gender behaviours they invite harsh criticism from teachers. In a study by Reay (2001) teachers spoke of girls who were misbehaving as 'a bad influence', 'scheming little madams' and 'spiteful' whilst boys' similar behaviours were seen as 'mucking about'. Similarly, Skelton (2002) found that those girls who adopted behaviours not associated with being 'properly feminine' were described as 'pushy'.

Girls' behaviour in the classroom

Girls did, and do act, as quasi-teachers; are located in and take up marginalized positions in the classroom; and are generally less confident than boys. The ways in which girls constantly service and facilitate boys are highlighted in the past and present literature on gender and schooling. For example, it has been shown how girls provide boys with an endless array of equipment and services from pencils, rulers and food to sorting out arguments and helping out with homework (Belotti 1975; Mahony 1987; Thorne 1993). In addition, in order to construct themselves as 'good, sensible girls', primary school girls often act as 'quasi-teachers', aiding the teacher with tasks. However, as Belotti (1975) noted, this 'quasi-teacher' role often meant that girls simply ended up clearing up after boys; and Walden and Walkerdine (1985) demonstrate that girls' 'helpful', 'sensible' behaviours were actually despised by the teachers that girls sought to please. Two decades later, Francis's (1998) work has demonstrated that girls continue to take up the sensible, selfless, 'quasi-teacher' role in order to delineate their femininity. She shows that, far from gaining power through this positioning, in mixed-sex interaction the girls' 'sensible selfless' constructions often lead to being marginalized and dominated by boys. Likewise, Renold (2001) illustrates how girls defer to boys and seek out their approval – albeit conversely often expressing exasperation at what they perceive to be boys' 'silly' behaviour (Francis 1998; see also Clarricoates 1987; Thorne 1993).

Among the ways in which girls are located in and take up marginalized positions in the classroom are the use of physical space, the use of curriculum materials, and teacher attention. For example, a consequence of 'proper boys' being seen as dominant, demanding and difficult but rewarding to teach was that they received substantially more of the teacher's time and attention (Stanworth 1981; Spender 1982). Some primary teachers were found to base curriculum activities around topics they believed would motivate boys, in the hope that by engaging their interest, good behaviour would result (Clarricoates 1978). Such practices still occur and, indeed are advocated by some of the strategies recommended to tackle boys' underachievement (see Bleach 1998 for examples). One recent study has shown how a male teacher used 'equal opportunities' discourses to justify selecting 'boy-centred' books to read to the class, as well as selecting a play for the school production where the most roles were for boys (Skelton 2001). Views such as these show little awareness, as Deem (1980) and Spender (1982) remarked upon two decades ago, that various subjects represented in the school curriculum, and the topics included within them, have been constructed from male priorities.

A further aspect of girls' behaviour in the classroom that indicates little change since the mid-1970s is that of their continued lack of confidence, and more recently, greater anxieties over performance in exams. Several early studies noted how girls were generally less confident than boys (Fennema 1983; Licht and Dweck 1983; Walden and Walkerdine 1985). It was found that girls were far more likely to underestimate their performance in a given task than boys and interpret failure in different ways. Boys would accord their failings to lack of effort, or blame the apparent inadequacies of external factors such as exams or teachers, whilst girls tended to blame themselves, attributing failure to lack of ability (Stanworth 1981; Kelly 1988; Jones and Jones 1989). Girls were seen to be more sensitive to any negative teacher feedback on their work whilst boys were more sensitive to the positive feedback (Licht and Dweck 1983). Teachers were seen as partly causative in that their actions contributed towards undermining girls' self-confidence. Perhaps the most well-known example of this is Stanworth's (1981) study in which she coined the phrase the 'faceless bunch' to describe the inability of many teachers to remember the names of the girls in their classes.

Recent studies have shown the growing impact on girls of their lower levels of self-confidence. The greater emphasis on academic achievement in public exams is one area where this is having an effect. There is evidence indicating that female pupils are reporting feeling more stressed and greater anxiety amongst those least likely to enjoy academic success (Chaplin 2000). Particular pressure is placed on middle-class girls where there is an implicit asumption that they will succeed by their parents as well as their teachers (Lucey and Reay 2002). In middle-class families very high academic performance has been found to be routinely understood as 'ordinary' and to be expected (Walkerdine *et al.* 2001; Lucey and Reay 2002). As Lucey (2001: 183) has found, middle-class girls begin to worry about their abilities to succeed from an increasingly early age:

> Looking back at various stages in the research it was clear that these anxieties had been around since the middle-class girls were 10 years old when, despite the evidence of their success, feelings of not being good enough began to surface (Walkerdine and Lucey 1989). This is also consistent with findings from research with Diane Reay in which we found similar patterns of anxiety alongside the production of extremely high performance among middle-class 11-year-old girls.

Furthermore, a recent study of highly able, middle-class girls and boys has indicated that although both genders appear to be equally confident, boys maintain their confidence through competitiveness with each other whilst girls maintain theirs through feedback from their teachers (Land 2003). Given girls' internalization of their anxiety, and self-blame, it is perhaps no coincidence that an increasing number of girls noted as self-harmers are from middle-class backgrounds (Lucey 2001).

To conclude this section, it would seem that the suggestion that primary schoolgirls no longer face gender-specific problems or disadvantages is a misguided one. There are many differing constructions of gender identity among girls, yet some tendencies in expectation continue to be applied to all girls regarding their behaviour. Moreover, other issues, such as lack of confidence and facilitating boys in the primary classroom, continue to be expressed by a majority of primary school girls. In spite of their outperformance of boys in areas such as literacy, girls continue to be devalued, and to devalue themselves, in the dominant gender discourses perpetuated by education and in society more broadly. These observations may sound discordant to teachers who are aware that education has received much advice and given attention to equal opportunities issues over the years since the Sex Discrimination Act was passed in 1975 (for example, the Equal Opportunities Commission [EOC] has published many booklets and resources aimed at all sectors of schooling). The question has to be why, given the apparent concern for equal opportunities, has so little apparently changed for girls and boys? To answer this we will look at the ways in which understandings of gender constructions has changed and affected how we approach these issues with primary children.

Constructing gender in the primary classroom

Schools were not expected to actively challenge gender inequalities in education until 1975 when education was included in the Sex Discrimination Act. To say that the then Department of Education and Science (DES) was unenthusiastic about the inclusion of education in the Act and was resistant to implementing major changes in schools to eradicate gender discrimination, is something of an understatement (see Arnot 1987). This resistance on the part of the DES has been used to partly explain why the EOC and some local education authorities (LEAs) chose to adopt 'weaker' i.e. liberal egalitarian approaches rather than the 'stronger' radical anti-sexist stance (Arnot 1985; Weiner 1985, 1994). Thus, although alternative theories on how gender was constructed existed (Walkerdine 1981; McRobbie 1982) these were far more complex and demanded more sophisticated strategies based on addressing power differences than the political, social and cultural climate could deal with – they were simply ahead of their time. Instead 'the EOC encouraged schools and LEAs to review their provision in terms of gender equality and to develop strategies aimed at developing the full potential of boys and girls' (Arnot *et al*. 1999: 71). This meant drawing on sex role theories.

Sex role theories are an extension of role theories which say that children learn ways of relating to the world around them through observing how people act and by being rewarded when they themselves demonstrate appropriate behaviour or punished in some way if they display inappropriate behaviour (Gregory 1969). So in terms of children developing appropriate gender roles such theories suggest that young girls learn how to be a girl by receiving approval for feminine traits such as caring, gentleness and helpfulness, whilst young boys learn that they are expected to be boisterous, rough and energetic (Oakley 1972; Byrne 1978; Seidler 1989). These messages are delivered to children through their interactions with their families, local communities, nursery workers and primary teachers, and the images transmitted through media. It is possible to discern two key views on how children acquired their knowledge of gender. On the one hand there were the social-learning theorists who argued that gender identity was learned by children modelling their behaviour on same-sex members of their family, peer group, local community as well as the gender stereotypes they saw in books and on the television (Sharpe 1976). An alternative stance was put forward by cognitive-development theorists who suggested that a child's understanding of their *gender identity* as opposed to their *biological sex* depended upon their stage of cognitive development; that is, their intellectual age. One such theorist was Lawrence Kohlberg (1966) who accounted for young children's avoidance of opposite sex behaviours, not in terms of punishment received for not conforming to gender stereotype, but by drawing on Piaget's theory of object constancy. Here the argument was that children at the concrete operational stage believed that a piece of plasticine changed weight when it changed shape – in the same way they would also believe that if a child dressed or played in a sex-inappropriate way its sex also changed (Emmerich *et al*. 1977). It is such psychological theorizing on gender constructions that has been used to support the idea that sexism is at its peak in children aged 5–6 years (Sayers 1984).

The advantage of sex role theories was that they marked a shift away from seeing gender as something which was innate – that is, rather than gender being seen as biologically constructed it was understood to be the result of social conditioning. The ways in which schools were expected to prevent children from developing along gender stereotyped lines was to offer and encourage them to become involved in opposite-sex activities. For example, the booklet *Do You Provide Equal Educational Opportunities?* (EOC 1984) urges primary schools to ensure male and female dolls are provided in the home corner; provide non sex-stereotyped images in wall displays and friezes; give girls opportunities to play with constructional toys; and supply boys with materials that would stimulate language development. Many of the practices recommended in schools' equal opportunity policies today that are intended to redress gender inequalities have their roots in sex role socialization strategies. Yet as we have shown earlier, these approaches have done little, if anything, to change the ways in which boyhood and girlhood is perceived and judged by adults as well as acted out by children in the primary classroom. The question has to be asked as to why this is the case. Our response, together with the contributors to this book, is that adults need to work with children, examining their existing conceptions of appropriate gendered behaviours, in order to provide them with ways of 'knowing and seeing' acceptable, alternative forms of gender identities. Before looking more closely at this idea and setting out the strategies that teachers might adopt in working with young children, we need to address the issue of 'brain differences' between boys and girls. This is an area which has re-emerged recently through discussions on boys' underachievement.

In early discussions of gender there was a clear distinction between supporters of sociological and biological explanations for differences between boys and girls (Oakley 1972). However, recent developments in our understanding of human learning processes suggest that asking whether gender differences are caused by socialization or biology is unhelpful as it is almost impossible to disentangle the two (Halpern 1992; Head 1999). A useful insight is provided by Carrie Paechter (1998) when she points out that recent thinking in neuroscience argues that neuronal connections are strengthened as a result of experience. Thus, it follows that different experiences will lead to differences in neural connections. Paechter (1998: 46) goes on to say sex differences in brain structure can be understood when taking into account that males and females 'do experience the world in different ways, both because of their different bodies and because they are differently positioned in society'. While the concern over boys' underachievement has generated a resurgence of interest in biological accounts (Biddulph 1997; Hoff Sommers 2000; Gurian 2001), the significance of 'brain difference' for gendered behaviour continues to be challenged, and there appears to be little new evidence to suggest that gender differences are a result of physiology.

We, and the contributors to this book, support strategies based on the notion that children develop and understand their gender identity as relational. That is, a boy demonstrates publicly he is a boy by acting out behaviours which are the opposite of what he observes is expected from girls. And girls learn and display what it means to be female by being the opposite of boys. Where 'gender as relational' theories differ from sex role socialization perspectives is as follows:

- In sex role theories children are seen as passive respondents who absorb society's messages about how to act in a gender appropriate way. Where gender is seen as relational or oppositional children are seen as being *actively* involved in learning to be 'proper' boys or girls (Davies 1989; Francis 1998).

- Sex role theorists regard gender as something that is fixed and unchanging regardless of the context. Gender relational perspectives see gender as fluid rather than fixed.

- Sex role theories rely on stereotypes of boys and girls. Gender relational theorists contest the notion of stereotyping and do not support generalized ideas that *all* girls are quiet, hardworking and good at writing any more than *all* boys are competitive, assertive and naturally good at science. Gender relational theorists also recognize that whilst children are aware from an early age of their biological sex, the process of bodily inscription, the 'trying out' of the language, attitudes and behaviours associated with 'being a girl' (or boy) is a longer process. And in addition, the context in which gender identities are displayed is of crucial importance. Alison Jones (1993) uses the notion of a 'schoolgirl' to explain this. She says that one school might place value on the notion of schoolgirls as cooperative, quiet and demure so boisterous girls may be seen as 'naughty' or 'difficult'. However, a different school might strive to encourage independence and confidence in its female pupils so see such boisterous girls as admirably 'stroppy' or, at least, competent. In the same way, children themselves draw on specific notions of gender behaviour in different ways in different situations.

What implications do these differences between sex role socialization and gender relational theories have for classroom practices? The contributors to this book outline specific recommendations for specific subject areas and other aspects of primary schooling. Broadly however, the differences mean that teachers need to *actively* intervene. The assumption in sex role socialization theories that providing children with a variety of images of males and females meant that they would, by themselves, recognize and understand it is acceptable (and desirable) to take up attitudes and behaviours traditionally associated with the opposite sex did not take into account children's own constructions and desires. An example of this can be seen in Bronwyn Davies's (1989) work with young children in *Frogs and Snails and Feminist Tales*. She showed how alternative fairytales such as *Rita the Rescuer* (Corbalis 1987) and *The Paper Bag Princess* (Cole 1986), which were intended to introduce boys and girls to images of more assertive females and more sensitive males, fell short of the mark. Young children were not 'hearing' the intended message of the stories.

For example, in *The Paper Bag Princess*, Elizabeth, the princess, takes on the dragon in order to rescue her handsome fiancé Prince Ronald. During the course of her rescue attempt her clothes are burned off by the dragon and all she can find to wear is a paper bag. By the time she reaches Ronald she is dirty and dishevelled and, rather than welcoming Elizabeth and thanking her for saving him, Ronald tells her off for the way she looks. Elizabeth becomes angry with Ronald for his mean mindedness and dances off into the sunset with the accompanying explanation that they didn't get married after all. The young children in Davies's (1989) study had reservations about Elizabeth as someone who was in the 'wrong' because she did not act in a conventional princess-like way, was messy and dirty and, worst of all, was naked except for the paper bag. On the other hand, the cowardly Ronald who did nothing apart from get taken off by the dragon, locked in his castle and then moaned at Elizabeth was seen by some of the boys as clever and some of the girls as handsome and nice. At the end of the story when Elizabeth rejects Ronald, this was 'read' by many of the children as Ronald deciding he did not want to marry Elizabeth. Davies explains this by pointing to the power of pre-existing structures of traditional narratives which prevent new forms of narrative from being heard. The children were well versed in what *should* happen in fairy-tales, with the handsome prince rescuing the grateful and beautiful princess, so when that convention is subverted, the children still judge the character against traditional images. Not least because young children are eager to identify themselves with their 'correct' gender and will go to great lengths to 'fit' what they see into their understandings of appropriate genders. Davies refers to this as 'gender category maintenance work' whereby if a male or female is seen to adopt ways of acting out of type then children will endeavour to 'let the "deviants" know they've got it wrong' (Davies 1989: 29). When the children were confronted with Elizabeth, a character who did not look or behave in the same way that princesses are generally portrayed in the literature, they rejected her as 'deviant'. The important point here, as Davies is at pains to point out, is that young children should be presented with these alternative images of conventional characters but they have to be helped to actively engage with such storylines.

In developing strategies based on gender relational perspectives for working with primary age children we recommend that, first, teachers recognize their own preconceptions of gender as well as those children bring with them into the classroom. Teachers might ask themselves:

- Are children expected to behave differently because they are a boy or a girl?
- Do I *want* children to behave in ways that signal they are 'proper' boys or girls?
- Are there different sets of expectations of pupils' abilities or potentials based on whether they are a boy or a girl? Am I aware that girls and boys are not homogeneous groups; for example, some girls will act in assertive ways and some boys will play cooperatively?

- How do my interactions influence how children practise gender? What aspects of my daily curriculum practices give meaning to children's understanding of themselves and others as gendered beings?

The gendered views children already hold need to be investigated and understood. These can be identified by asking:

- What are the children's favourite games, toys, television and book characters and what do these tell children about the 'correct' way of being a boy or a girl?
- What images of boys/men and girls/women feature in their play activities and stories?
- How do children interact in the classroom – do they produce particular types of behaviour according to gender?
- What roles, functions and careers do men and women occupy in the school and local community? For example, do women work outside the home and in what jobs and what involvement do men have in their children's upbringing?

Having identified what notions of gender both teachers and pupils already hold then strategies can be developed to challenge prevailing images. It is fair to say that many of the equal opportunity tactics adopted by primary schools should still be utilized such as using non-sexist reading materials, providing children with a range of activities, taking care that language does not divide the sexes by gender, and displaying materials which depict men and women in non-traditional roles. These should be used as a backdrop against which adults actively enable children to confront gender stereotypes. The adult is the key person in developing awareness both in terms of behaviours and intervening in children's play.

- Teachers should ensure they involve themselves in the full range of activities and be particularly aware if they are avoiding certain spaces associated with the opposite sex, such as female teachers avoiding the (male) block play area or sand and water activities, or male teachers avoiding the (female) 'home corner'.
- Children should be presented with imaginative play opportunities where they might devise, explore and deconstruct gender images (see Chapter 4).
- Teachers should reflect on children's storylines to identify the ways in which they make sense of themselves and others and to find ways of weaving alternate storylines into children's play which treat the themes of children's stories seriously, but are fun.

- Teachers should take the opportunity to discuss gender stereotypes and expectations with children directly, in classroom debate and discussion of materials (see Chapter 8).
- When boys or girls dominate a play area they should be asked to question their reasons for doing so. This means that any discussion about gender is firmly based on the children's own storylines and pays attention to what they are saying about their rights to play. For example, teachers might ask 'Who can you play with?' 'Can only boys play with blocks?' 'Can boys and girls play together with blocks?'
- If 'girl only' time is set aside for block play then teachers need to become involved in helping children recognize their developing skills. For example, in observing a group of 6- to 7-year-old girls building a magnificent palace, Epstein (1995) says she should have asked the boys about their perceptions of what the girls could or could not do.

Outline of the book

We had two intentions in preparing this book. The first was to provide teachers with an overview of research findings into how gender features in particular curriculum subjects and other aspects of primary schools. The reason for wanting to do this was because both the government and media have succeeded in drawing attention away from *gender* issues in schooling and placed exclusive emphasis on the problems some boys have in the classroom. As we have suggested earlier, this stance is both oversimplified and naive. Not only does it assume a homogeneity amongst boys but ignores the ongoing problems faced by girls in the educational system. A second intention of the book is to provide primary teachers with strategies that they might utilize in their interactions with children based on the evidence of sound, rigorous research findings. Contributors to the chapters in Part 2 have addressed both these aims.

Before looking in specific detail at gender in relation to various aspects of primary schooling, Louise Archer (Chapter 2) provides a warning note about the current drive towards 'evidence-based practice' in educational research. As we have said, the ideas presented in the following chapters of this book are based on high-quality research, and in this sense are 'evidence based'. Yet the notion of 'evidence-based practice' pursued by policy makers in education has some problematic connotations. There is a concern that there is a value system inherent in this discourse which elevates positivist approaches above others, and which seeks to drive educational research in a particular direction. While there is an obvious logic about the idea that teachers deserve to know 'what works' in the classroom, the ways in which this 'knowledge' is reached is highly contestable. Importantly, as Archer points out in her chapter, the high status accorded to so-called 'objectivist' (positivist) research findings and the subsequent low status given to, say, small scale action research projects de-professionalizes teachers' knowledge. It is against this background of what 'counts' as 'sound' educational knowledge that the contributors to Part 2 write their chapters.

In Chapter 3, Lucey *et al.* draw on research findings from the Leverhulme Numeracy Research Programme to show how shifts in classroom practice promoted by the National Numeracy Strategy have affected girls and boys. The authors argue that the strategy encourages those learning styles underpinned by competitiveness and performativity – indeed those characteristics associated with boys' preferred learning styles. In the same way that earlier research into mathematics illustrated how boys and girls worked differently in the maths classroom, their research suggests that these different ways of tackling and responding to maths continues. It may be the case that the differential approaches of primary age girls and boys towards mathematics has received less attention because, on the surface, girls appear to be performing better than boys in KS2 maths tests (DfES 2002). However, as has been discussed earlier, statistics can be misleading, and the fact that primary age girls do well in mathematical tests does not explain why they fail to take maths at degree level or embark on careers involving maths. While there has been less concern in recent years for girls and maths, there has been considerable alarm over boys' achievements in and attitudes towards literacy. Jackie Marsh argues in Chapter 4 that rather than concentrating on strategies to improve boys' attitudes we should be trying to find approaches that make the primary literacy curriculum appealing to both boys and girls. She reports the findings of a research project highlighting the importance of taking into account children's out-of-school literacy experiences, particularly those related to popular culture. Like maths, science has been regarded as a traditionally male subject and here again, KS2 SAT tests indicate that girls are now outperforming boys (DfES 2002). Yet, as Michael Reiss indicates in Chapter 5, the science curriculum delivered in schools, both in terms of content and pedagogy, is narrowly conceived. He considers the learning demands made upon pupils by current constructions of science and science pedagogy and reflects upon the assumptions made as well as identifying alternative practices that teachers might adopt.

Gender and pupils with special educational needs (SEN) is the topic discussed by Shereen Benjamin in Chapter 6. As Benjamin indicates, surprisingly little attention has been paid to the ways in which SEN issues are gendered. Perhaps the most often noted link between gender and SEN is that more boys than girls are identified as having special needs. However, this is just the headline to the story which the author unfolds in order to explain why SEN provision is distributed unequally between boys and girls and what the potential consequences of this might be. Here Benjamin alerts us to the need to pay attention to current constructions of masculinities and femininities and how these relate to our understandings of special needs.

The discussion in this chapter on constructions of masculinities and femininities is taken up in Chapters 7 to 9. Each author of these three chapters pays particular attention to power disparities in the constructions of masculine and feminine identities. Paul Connolly in Chapter 7 takes gender and children's play as his theme. The centrality of play in the education of very young children occupies a key role in developmental learning theories. Yet, as Connolly shows, the implications of this on children's constructions of their gender identities has been much neglected. He looks at the ways in which masculine and feminine identities are literally 'played out' on primary school playgrounds. The picture emerges of playgrounds as dangerous spaces for young children and the need for adult intervention to enable them to transcend the struggles over power relations they encounter on a daily basis. In Chapter 8, Bronwyn Davies explores how – through storylines in a variety of texts from photographs and films through to traditional and feminist fairytales – boys and girls become gendered beings. Her research shows how both girls and boys consistently return to the ways they have learned to 'be' in the world with the former adopting powerless discourses and the latter, powerful discourses. Davies shows in her work how children can be encouraged to confront and challenge these gendered ways of engaging with the world by adults actively intervening to make these processes visible to them. Diane Reay brings our attention back to the 'gender problem' of the current period: boys and schooling. In Chapter 9 she reflects on her many years of experience as a primary teacher working with disaffected boys. Here she not only explores the attitudes and actions of the boys themselves but questions her own involvement and responses as a female primary teacher to them. Reay identifies how 'the problem' of boys has changed over the last decade or so and suggests ways that teachers, as part of the fabric of society, might play a part in addressing these current concerns.

Finally, in Chapter 10, Jean Rudduck and Isobel Urquhart consider issues of identity, status and gender at points of transfer (for example from infant to junior or primary to secondary school) or transition (e.g. from Year 2 to Year 3). Their research indicates that the responses of boys and girls at these crucial times are far more similar than different. Yet, Rudduck and Urquhart point out that in dealing with the vulnerabililty and insecurity generated at these critical stages, boys and girls tend to reinvest in traditional gender stereotypical behaviours. They, together with all contributors to this book, conclude by noting the importance of the teacher in supporting both boys and girls in understanding and addressing the ways in which gendered identities are constructed and played out in primary classrooms.

Notes

1 For example, 'SATs' formally test children at periods throughout their compulsory school life.
2 For a discussion of the motivations behind the introduction of these league tables, and the impact on schools, pupils and parents, see Ball *et al.* (2000) and Reay and Wiliam (1999).

References

Alexander, R. (1984) *Primary Teaching*. Eastbourne: Holt, Rinehart and Winston.

Alloway, N. and Gilbert, P. (1997) Boys and literacy: lessons from Australia, *Gender and Education*, 9(1): 49–59.

Arnot, M. (1985) *Race and Gender*. Oxford: Pergamon Press.

Arnot, M. (1987) Political lip-service or radical reform? in M. Arnot and G. Weiner (eds) *Gender and the Politics of Schooling*. London: Unwin Hyman.

Arnot, M., David, M. and Weiner, G. (1999) *Closing the Gender Gap*. Cambridge: Polity Press.

Ball, S.J., Maguire, M. and Macrae, S. (2000) *Choices, Transitions and Pathways: New Youth, New Economies in the Global City*. London: Falmer Press.

Belotti, E. (1975) *Little Girls*. London: Writers and Readers Publishing Co-op.

Biddulph, S. (1997) *Raising Boys*. London: Thorsons.

Bleach, K. (ed.) (1998) *Raising Boys' Achievement in Schools*. Stoke-on-Trent: Trentham.

Blunkett, D. (2000) Press Notice, 2000/0368, DfEE.

Browne, N. and France, P. (eds) (1986) *Untying the Apron Strings*. Milton Keynes: Open University Press.

Byrne, E. (1978) *Women and Education*. London: Tavistock.

Carrington, B. and Skelton, C. (forthcoming) Re-thinking 'role models': equal opportunities in teacher recruitment in England and Wales, *Journal of Education Policy*, 18(3): 1–13.

Chaplin, R. (2000) Beyond exam results? Differences in the social and psychological perceptions of young males and females at school, *Educational Studies*, 26(2): 177–90.

Clarricoates, K. (1978) Dinosaurs in the classroom – a re-examination of some aspects of the 'hidden curriculum' in primary schools, *Women's Studies International Quarterly*, 1: 353–64.

Clarricoates, K. (1980) The importance of being Ernest . . . Emma . . . Tom . . . Jane. The perception and categorization of gender conformity and gender deviation in primary schools, in R. Deem (ed.) *Schooling for Women's Work*. London: Routledge and Kegan Paul.

Clarricoates, K. (1987) Child culture at school: a clash between gendered worlds, in A. Pollard (ed.) *Children and their Primary Schools*. Lewes: Falmer.

Coffey, A. (2001) *Education and Social Change*. Buckingham: Open University Press.

Cole, B. (1986) *Princess Smartypants*. London: Hamish Hamilton.

Connolly, P. (1995) Boys will be boys?: Racism, sexuality, and the construction of masculine identities amongst infant boys, in M. Blair and J. Holland (eds) *Equality and Difference: Debates and Issues in Feminist Research and Pedagogy*. Clevedon: Multilingual Matters.

Connolly, P. (1998) *Racism, Gender Identities and Young Children*. London: Routledge.

Corbalis, J. (1987) *The Wrestling Princess and Other Stories*. London: Knight Books.

Crace, J. (2001) Girls 1, boys 0: can football help boys draw level in the classroom? *Guardian Education*, 30 January.

Davies, B. (1989) *Frogs and Snails and Feminist Tales*. Sydney: Allen and Unwin.

Davies, B. (2003) Death to critique and dissent? The policies and practices of new managerialism and of 'evidence-based practice', *Gender and Education*, 15(1): 91–103.

Deem, R. (ed.) (1980) *Schooling for Women's Work*. London: Routledge and Kegan Paul.

Department for Education and Skills (2002) *Gender and Achievement*. www.standards.dfee.gov.uk/genderandachievement/understanding/ nationaldata/ (accessed 25 January 2003).

Emmerich, W., Goldman, S., Kirsh, B. and Sharabany, R. (1977) Evidence for a transitional phase in the development of 'gender constancy', *Child Development*, 48: 930–6.

Epstein, D. (1995) 'Girls don't do bricks': gender and sexuality in the primary classroom', in J. Siraj-Blatchford and I. Siraj-Blatchford (eds) *Educating the Whole Child*. Buckingham: Open University Press.

Epstein, D., Elwood, J., Hey, V. and Maw, J. (eds) (1998) *Failing Boys? Issues in Gender and Achievement*. Buckingham: Open University Press.

Equal Opportunities Commission (1984) *Do You Provide Equal Educational Opportunities?* Manchester: Equal Opportunities Commission.

Fennema, E. (1983) Success in mathematics, in M. Marland (ed.) *Sex Differentiation and Schooling*. London: Heinemann.

Foster, V., Kimmel, M. and Skelton, C. (2001) 'What about the boys?' An overview of the debates, in W. Martino and B. Meyenn (eds) *What About the Boys?* Buckingham: Open University Press.

Francis, B. (1998) *Power Plays*. Stoke-on-Trent: Trentham.

Francis, B. (2000) *Boys, Girls and Achievement*. London: Routledge/Falmer.

Francis, B. and Skelton, C. (2001) Men teachers and the construction of heterosexual masculinity in the classroom, *Sex Education*, (1)1: 1–17.

Fuller, M. (1982) Young, female and black, in E. Cashmore and B. Troyna (eds) *Black Youth in Crisis*. London: Allen and Unwin.

Gillborn, D. (1997) Racism and reform: new ethnicities/old inequalities, *British Educational Research Journal*, 22(3): 345–60.

Gillborn, D. and Gipps, C. (1996) *Recent Research on the Achievements of Ethnic Minority Pupils*. London: Ofsted.

Gorard, S. (2000) One of us cannot be wrong: the paradox of achievement gaps, *British Journal of Sociology of Education*, 21(3): 391–400.

Gorard, S., Rees, G. and Salisbury, J. (1999) Reappraising the apparent under-achievement of boys at school, *Gender and Education*, 11(4): 441–54.

Gregory, R. (1969) *A Shorter Textbook of Human Development*. Maidenhead: McGraw-Hill.

Gurian, M. (2001) *Boys and Girls Learn Differently!* San Francisco, CA: Jossey-Bass.

Halpern, D. (1992) *Sex Differences in Cognitive Abilities*, 2nd edn. New Jersey: Lawrence Erlbaum.

Haywood, C. and Mac an Ghaill, M. (2001) The significance of teaching English boys: exploring social change, modern schooling and the making of masculinities, in W. Martino and B. Meyenn (eds) *What About the Boys?* Buckingham: Open University Press.

Head, J. (1999) *Understanding the Boys*. London: Falmer.

Hoff Sommers, C. (2000) *The War Against Boys*. New York: Simon and Schuster.

Hutchings, M. (2002) A representative profession? Gender issues, in M. Johnson and J. Hallgarten (eds) *From Victims of Change to Agents of Change: The Future of the Teaching Profession*. London: IPPR.

Jones, A. (1993) Becoming a 'girl': Post-structuralist suggestions for educational research, *Gender and Education*, 5(2): 157–66.

Jones, L.G. and Jones, L.P. (1989) Context, confidence and the able girl, *Educational Research*, 31(3): 189–94.

Kelly, A. (1988) The customer is always right . . . girls' and boys' reactions to science lessons, *School Science Review*, 69(249): 662–75.

King, R. (1978) *All Things Bright and Beautiful*. Chichester: John Wiley.

Kohlberg, L. (1966) A cognitive-developmental analysis of children's sex role concepts and attitudes, in E. Maccoby (ed.) *The Development of Sex Differences*. Stanford: Stanford University Press.

Lahelma, E. (2000) Lack of male teachers: A problem for students or teachers? *Pedagogy, Culture and Society*, 8(2): 173–85.

Land, J. (2003) Attitudes and perceptions of high ability boys and girls in independent schools. Unpublished EdD thesis, University of Newcastle Upon Tyne.

Licht, B. and Dweck, C. (1983) Sex differences in achievement orientations: consequences for academic choices and attainments, in M. Marland (ed.) *Sex Differentiation and Schooling*. London: Heinemann.

Lingard, B. and Douglas, P. (1999) *Men Engaging Feminisms*. Buckingham: Open University Press.

Lloyd, B. and Duveen, G. (1992) *Gender Identities and Education*. Hemel Hempstead: Harvester Wheatsheaf.

Lucey, H. (2001) Social class, gender and schooling, in B. Francis and C. Skelton (eds) *Investigating Gender: Contemporary Perspectives in Education*. Buckingham: Open University Press.

Lucey, H. and Reay, D. (2002) Carrying the beacon of excellence: social class differentiation and anxiety at a time of transition, *Journal of Education Policy*, 17(3): 321–36.

McRobbie, A. (1982) Jackie: An ideology of adolescent femininity, in B. Waites, T. Bennet, and G. Martin (eds) *Popular Culture: Past and Present*. London: Routledge and Kegan Paul.

Mahony, P. (1987) Sexual violence and mixed schools, in C. Jones and P. Mahony (eds) *Learning Our Lines: Sexuality and Social Control in Education*. London: The Women's Press.

Mahony, P. and Hextall, I. (2000) *Reconstructing Teaching*. London: Routledge/Falmer.

Maynard, T. (2002) *Exploring the Boys and Literacy Issue*. London: Routledge/Falmer.

Miliband, D. (2002) quoted in *Teachers*, Nov. 2002. www.teachernet.gov.uk/teachers/November2002/Bridgingthegap_Secondary/(accessed 25 January 2003).

Mills, M. (2001) *Challenging Violence in Schools*. Buckingham: Open University Press.

Moir, A. and Moir, B. (1998) *Why Men Don't Iron*. London: Harper Collins.

Myhill, D. (2002) Bad boys and good girls? Patterns of interaction and response in whole class teaching, *British Educational Research Journal*, 28(3): 339–52.

Oakley, A. (1972) *Sex, Gender and Society*. London: Temple Smith.

Paechter, C. (1998) *Educating the Other: Gender, Power and Schooling*. London: Falmer.

Pole, C. (1999) Black teachers giving voice: choosing and experiencing teaching, *Teacher Development*, 3(3): 313–28.

Pollack, W. (1998) *Real Boys*. New York: Owl Books.

Power, S., Edwards, A., Whitty, G. and Wigfall, V. (1998) Schoolboys and schoolwork: gender identification and academic achievement, *Journal of Inclusive Education*, 2(2): 135–53.

Raphael-Reed, L. (1998) Zero tolerance: Gender performance and school failure, in D. Epstein, J. Elwood, V. Hey and J. Maw (eds) *Failing Boys?* Buckingham: Open University Press.

Reay, D. (2001) 'Spice Girls', 'Nice Girls', 'Girlies', and 'Tomboys': gender discourses, girls' cultures and femininities in the primary classroom, *Gender and Education*, 13(2): 153–66.

Reay, D. (2002) Shaun's story: troubling discourses of white working-class masculinities, *Gender and Education*, 14(4): 221–34.

Reay, D. and Wiliam, D. (1999) 'I'll be a nothing': structure, agency and the construction of identity through assessment, *British Educational Research Journal*, 25(3): 343–53.

Renold, E. (2001) 'Square-girls', femininity and the negotiation of academic success in the primary school, *British Educational Research Journal*, 27(5): 577–88.

Rowan, L., Knobel, M., Bigum, C. and Lankshear, C. (2001) *Boys, Literacies and Schooling*. Buckingham: Open University Press.

Salisbury, J. and Riddell, S. (eds) (2000) *Gender, Policy and Educational Change*. London: Routledge.

Sayers, J. (1984) Psychology and gender divisions, in S. Acker, J. Megarry, S. Nisbet and E. Hoyle (eds) *World Yearbook of Education 1984: Women and Education*. London: Kogan Page.

Seidler, V. (1989) *Rediscovering Masculinity*. London: Routledge.

Sharpe, S. (1976) *Just Like a Girl*. Harmondsworth: Penguin.

Skelton, C. (ed.) (1989) *Whatever Happens to Little Women?: Gender and Primary Schooling*. Milton Keynes: Open University Press.

Skelton, C. (2001) *Schooling the Boys: Masculinities and Primary Education*. Buckingham: Open University Press.

Skelton, C. (2002) Constructing dominant masculinity and negotiating the 'male gaze', *International Journal of Inclusive Education*, 6(1): 17–31.

Skelton, C. and Francis, B. (2002) 'Clever Jack and Conscientious Chloe': naturally able boys and hardworking girls in the classroom. Paper presented at the British Educational Research Association Annual Conference, University of Exeter, 12–14 September.

Smedley, S. (1999) 'Don't rock the boat': men student teachers' understanding of gender and equality. Paper presented to the British Educational Research Association Conference, University of Sussex, 2–5 September.

Spender, D. (1982) *Invisible Women: The Schooling Scandal*. London: Writers and Readers.

Stanworth, M. (1981) *Gender and Schooling*. London: Hutchinson.

Swain, J. (2002) The resources and strategies boys use to establish status in a junior school without competitive sport, *Discourse*, 23(1): 91–107.

Thorne, B. (1993) *Gender Play: Girls and Boys in School*. Buckingham: Open University Press.

Thornton, M. and Bricheno, P. (2002) Staff gender balance in primary schools. Paper presented at the British Educational Research Association Annual Conference, University of Exeter, 12–14 September.

Walden, R. and Walkerdine, V. (1985) *Girls and Mathematics*. London: Institute of Education, Bedford Way Papers.

Walkerdine, V. (1981) Sex, power and pedagogy, *Screen Education*, 38: 14–24.

Walkerdine, V. (1983) It's only natural: rethinking child-centred pedagogy, in A.M. Wolpe and J. Donald (eds) *Is There Anyone Here from Education?* London: Pluto Press.

Walkerdine, V. and Lucey, H. (1989) *Democracy in the Kitchen: Regulating Mothers and Socialising Daughters*. London: Virago.

Walkerdine, V., Lucey, H. and Melody, J. (2001) *Growing Up Girl: Psychosocial Explorations of Gender and Class*. London: Macmillan.

Warrington, M. and Younger, M. (2000) The other side of the gender gap, *Gender and Education*, 12(4): 493–507.

Weiner, G. (1985) *Just a Bunch of Girls*. Milton Keynes: Open University Press.

Weiner, G. (1994) *Feminisms in Education*. Buckingham: Open University Press.

Whyte, J. (1983) *Beyond the Wendy House: Sex Role Stereotyping in Primary Schools*. York: Longman.

Williams, J. (1987) The construction of women and black students as educational problems, in M. Arnot and G. Weiner (eds) *Gender and the Politics of Schooling*. London: Unwin Hyman.

2 Evidence-based practice and educational research
When 'what works' doesn't work . . .

Louise Archer

The relationship between educational 'research' and 'practice' has gained ever-increasing prominence within the world of education policy, and is the topic of heated debate and argument. This chapter charts recent developments and discusses the implications for teachers/educators and educational researchers of these struggles. The first section of the chapter charts the development of the current dominant education policy movement towards 'evidence-based practice' (EBP). EBP is then considered from the perspective of educational researchers and teachers, where it is argued that the current obsession with 'what works' runs counter to ideals of professionalism, autonomy and equality. Illustrations are provided from a recent 'systematic review' of evidence in relation to gender equal opportunities interventions and the primary school. The chapter concludes with suggestions of ways in which we, as teachers and researchers, might usefully re-frame and re-conceptualize a more fruitful relationship that enables research to inform practice.

The evidence-based practice movement

Recent years have witnessed a shift within policy discussions and educational policy making. A number of high profile criticisms were made of educational research, accusing it of being irrelevant, 'woolly', of limited scope, poor quality and of little, or no, practical relevance to teachers working in the classroom. Simultaneously, government departments and commentators called for more 'rigorous', 'systematic' research to identify 'what works' to make schools more effective and to raise attainment. As detailed by Ball (2001) and others, these key criticisms were encapsulated in a lecture and articles by Hargreaves (1996, 1997, 1999), reports by Tooley (1998; Tooley and Darby 1998) and Hillage *et al.* (1998) and by statements made by the then Secretary of State for Education, David Blunkett (e.g. 2000).

In his address to the Teacher Training Agency, David Hargreaves launched an attack against 'the frankly second rate educational research which does not make a serious contribution to fundamental theory or knowledge; which is irrelevant to practice . . . and which clutters up academic journals that virtually nobody reads' (Hargreaves 1996: 7). He went on to propose instead an outcomes-based view of education, in which 'research should provide decisive and conclusive evidence that if teachers do X rather than Y in their professional practice, there will be a significant and enduring improvement in outcome' (Hargreaves 1997: 413).

Issues of 'quality' and 'rigour' were also raised in the (largely damning) reviews of educational research conducted by Tooley for Ofsted (1998; Tooley and Darby 1998) and Hillage *et al.* (1998) for the Department for Education and Employment. Following in the wake of these reports, the then Secretary of State for Education, David Blunkett, issued a press release (2000) in which he outlined a vision for a 'revolution', in which research evidence is overhauled and brought into the heart of policy making, through a tightened focus on 'what works and why'. The theme of *coherence* was foregrounded amid concerns that existing research was too 'piecemeal' to be useful to policy makers as well as teachers. Thus Blunkett set out a research agenda, under the 'what works' umbrella, that privileged the evaluation of policy and systematic reviews of research evidence alongside a circumscribed notion of 'blue skies' research (research with no immediate, direct application).

Since then, the impetus for evidence-based policy has continued to gain momentum, spawning new developments such as the National Educational Research Forum's (NERF) consultation paper regarding a national strategy for educational research (see Ball 2001 for a critique). Another key organization involved in pushing forward the EBP agenda has been the EPPI-Centre (Centre for Evidence-informed Policy and Practice In Education), a unit sponsored by the Department for Education and Employment (DfEE)[1] to develop 'systematic reviewing' of educational research. Whilst fuller details of the EPPI methods and procedures for conducting systematic reviews can be found in Peersman *et al.* (1999), the general guiding principles of systematic reviewing can be defined as entailing

> a series of techniques for minimising bias and error, primarily through the use of protocols which state, prior to the review being undertaken, what the criteria are which will guide the review, search strategies, inclusion and exclusion criteria, standards of methodological adequacy, the precise definition of the intervention in question, unbiased estimation of aggregate effect, and so on.
>
> (MacDonald 2000: 131, cited in Evans and Benefield 2001: 529)

Thus, proponents of systematic reviews claim that they are centrally concerned with 'transparency' of method, and purport to use 'an explicit and reproducible methodology' (Evans and Benefield 2001) in order to reduce 'bias' and thus create a 'substantial, quality-assured and accessible evidence base' (Johnson 2002). Thus the assumption is made that if it is made clear how a piece of research has been organized and conducted, then it is easier to decide how valuable or useful it might be to teachers and policy makers.

Such reviews are held up as more 'objective' bases for policy decisions in that, through their objectivity, it is possible to build upon, or be useful to, 'user' perspectives. As Ann Oakley (2001: 576) has written:

> all professionals are interested stakeholders, and stakeholding is a well-known source of bias. This is one reason why systematic research synthesis offers an engagingly democratic alternative . . . other key players – students and parents, for example – who may well have more to gain from explicit, open, even outcomes-based accounts of educational practices than from an outdated reliance on 'expert opinion' models of how knowledge is best constituted.

Thus proponents of systematic reviews distinguish their work from 'traditional' (or 'academic', Bassey 2000, cited in Evans and Benefield 2001: 529) literature reviews, which they would describe as being smaller-scale and subjective accounts of research evidence.

Critiques of evidence-based practice

As Stronach and Hustler (2001) point out, fundamentally the arguments for and against the EBP movement reiterate age-old debates, albeit in new guises, around 'objectivity' and the attempt to position educational research as science. However, as will be argued in the remainder of the chapter, the dominant force of the EBP drive within mainstream education policy means that this is not merely an intellectual debate or a case of choosing 'which side to follow'. The drive towards EBP has profound implications for the ways in which teachers and researchers teach and research, impacting upon numerous issues such as professionalism, autonomy and equality.

Given the emphasis upon 'objectivity' within EBP rhetoric, it is perhaps unsurprising that proponents tend not to question the underlying politics. For example, Evans and Benefield (2001) suggest, somewhat naively, that the new terminology of EBP 'fits neatly with the current focus on "outcomes" and "value for money" which underpins much government policy' (p. 530). But as Davies (2003) astutely details, it is far more than this; the terminology is all part and parcel of a wider power exercise. Evidence-based practice is the offspring of 'new managerialism' (Trow 1994; Clarke and Newman 1997), a form of governance that is characterized by increasing centralized administrative and managerial control, in which power is shifted away from professionals and practitioners through imposed (and internalized) cultures of surveillance and audit. Thus, drawing on the work of Rose (1999), Davies argues that 'de-professionalization' is a common feature of new managerialism, because the source of knowledge is removed from the practising professional and transferred to 'auditors, policy makers and statisticians, none of whom need know anything about the profession in question' (2003: 91).

Within the new managerialist framework, emphasis is placed upon 'standards' and 'quality', which are monitored through intense testing and benchmarking. These auditing and surveillance regimes, whilst (supposedly) promoting 'quality', actually increase the levels of centralized control/governance by creating cultures of anxiety and fear, carrying the constant threat of revealing the monitored subject as never being 'good enough' (Davies 2003). Higher education research is now tightly controlled through a vast array of performance measures, and these measures create an increased climate of anxiety and insecurity (Ball 2001; Hey 2001). Attempts to engage and 'play the game', to re-make the 'good enough' self within the new system, are also difficult. For example, drawing on the work of Schmelzer (1993), Davies outlines how the 'remade self is extraordinarily vulnerable and peculiarly unable to hold on to the openness of mind so valued within the professional ethics of teachers and scholars' (2003: 93). In other words, it is hard to practise equality within a new managerialist working environment because less value is placed on equality issues, for example 'quality' is often given precedence and seen as more important. It is also harder because staff are often in less secure positions (e.g. due to moves towards fewer permanent job contracts and/or because staff are now constantly being assessed, having to meet benchmarks). All of these factors make it harder for challenging inequalities to be a central activity within everyday teaching practice.

The EBP obsession with objectivity and elimination of bias (through the use of positivistic methods) also overlooks the bias of power and normative assumptions inherent within the approach. As Davies (2003) pertinently notes, within EBP discourses there is little recognition of wider questions of bias concerning which evidence is chosen to 'count' and who selects it. For example, teachers are not meant to rely on their own professional judgement, experience and/or readings of literature to inform their teaching choices and decisions. Rather, the EBP model favours evidence that has been selected, reconstituted and provided by some other (often non-professional) party.

In other words, as a new managerialist practice, EBP assumes an instrumental/technicist relationship between research and policy (Hammersley 2001), also termed the 'engineering' model (Hammersley 1997) of social research. Within this approach, research is conceptualized as *working upon* the social world, whilst not being a *part* of the social world (Ball 2001). The EBP discourse, as encapsulated by the NERF consultation paper, thus 'stands as part of the hyper-rationalisation of late modern government. The attempt to monitor, control and instrumentalize' (Ball 2001: 266). Thus critics argue that the government's approach to educational research is not so much concerned with the content of research, nor is it 'really' about improving classroom practice, rather it is about exercising control and regulating the sector: EBD is just another tool with which to govern. As commentators have also noted, EBD reproduces, rather than challenges, inequalities: it is a profoundly gendered and classed movement which, Hey argues, is clearly linked to a backlash in the wake of the feminization and de/classing of research (see her excellent article on the social production of academic labour in research, 2001). For example, the masculinist assumptions are illustrated in the new managerialist terminology that lauds 'hard' outcomes and 'rigour' over 'soft' and 'woolly' (fluffy?!) research.

As discussed earlier, within an EBP model, emphasis is placed upon the role of 'users', who are held up to be the rightful audience for, and beneficiaries of, (unbiased) research evidence. These 'users' are primarily defined as policy makers (the audience who require the evidence in order to determine strategies and action). More generally, 'users' are also understood as being teachers and 'consumers' of education, such as pupils and parents, who may benefit from the implementation of more effective teaching strategies, or teachers who learn 'better' ways of working.

But the EBP emphasis upon 'users' is contradictory and unbalanced. Politicians, civil servants and other 'top-level' policy makers will certainly have more influence in guiding the agenda of 'what counts as worthwhile', 'whether it is being done in the best possible way' and the definition of 'effective' strategies than, say, teachers or pupils. As will be discussed further in relation to systematic reviews, there will also be imbalances between different groups of 'users' in terms of their ability to access, make sense of, and act upon/ operationalize the evidence. Furthermore, as Davies also notes in her excellent article (2003: 97), user-consultations are built into EBP discourses such that 'the representatives will have acquired the new discourse and so become party to its dissemination'. In other words, Davies suggests that only 'on-message' feedback and views tend to be sought, so that 'users' comment on the topic in question rather than, for example, criticizing the broader approach being taken.

Proponents of EBP, such as Oakley (2001), do acknowledge that they need to do more work with regard to incorporating the perspectives of users, and indeed a recent government invitation to tender reiterated this point[2]. Yet it is highly questionable as to whether it is possible to substantially challenge inequalities whilst working within the unexamined, powerfully normative confines of a new managerialist discourse. As Davies notes, new managerialism is not compatible with emancipatory political perspectives. Yet this incompatibility is often hidden by the use of terminology and 'the language of managerialism cleverly cannibalises liberal humanist terms [such as "quality" or "literacy", for example] that seem, on the face of it, indisputably virtuous and desirable' (Davies 2003: 98). Thus, to paraphrase Davies, who can dispute the desirability of quality or literacy? I would argue that a critical interrogation of EBP conceptualizations of user perspectives is crucial, otherwise there is a danger that (unrepresentative, tightly controlled) 'user perspectives' will be used as a particularly powerful, justifying discourse to bolster whichever argument, policy or strategy that they are selected to provide support for. Similarly, the prevalent rhetoric of 'best practice' and 'good practice' can be viewed as attempts to extract the best value for money (the most productivity from least resources), albeit disguised in seemingly uncontentious language. As Davies (2003) explains, whilst actually incompatible with equal opportunities issues, new managerialism can be invoked as mistakenly serving social justice/minority group interests, as illustrated, for example, by the EPPI-Centre's repeated rhetoric of 'us[ing] the research evidence to provide a better education for our children'[3].

As Bronwyn Davies so crucially argues, the process of actually *using* evidence to *inform* practice is not straightforward either. Considerable investments of time and resources are required in order to enable teachers to become reflexive practitioners who can read both the assumptions and theory underpinning research findings and their own practice. Davies contrasts this scenario with assumptions inherent within the EBP approach, in which teachers are supposedly presented with (digested) 'research findings' which they then (un-problematically, automatically?) 'use' to guide their practice/performance, which is simultaneously intensively monitoring and surveyed. Davies argues however that in the reality of most teachers' lives and working conditions, there is no straightforward method through which such evidence can easily or necessarily inform practice in meaningful ways.

An illustration: EPPI-Centre systematic reviews of education

As indicated earlier, 'systematic reviews' are heavily promoted within the drive towards EBP. In the UK, the EPPI-Centre is being funded by the Department for Education and Skills (DfES) to produce such reviews of research literature within education, building upon the centre's previous reviews in the field of health promotion[4]. The illustrations provided below are based upon the author's involvement as a research fellow working part time to produce one of the 'first wave' of education reviews under the topic of gender and education[5].

EPPI-Centre systematic reviews are unavoidably grounded in positivism, assuming that objectivity is both possible and desirable and privileging scientific methods. These underlying assumptions are clearly reflected in the types of studies that give the highest value and in the way the reviews are conceptualized and produced (Hammersley 2001). Despite Oakley's (2001) defence of the Centre's approach, others have noted that 'what is curious about this dual application of the positivist model to the task of reviewing is that it takes little or no account of the considerable amount of criticism that has been made of that model since at least the middle of the twentieth century' (Hammersley 2001: 545).

Systematic reviews have been identified as one of the weapons in the new managerialist 'discourse of derision' (Ball 2001), as they work to discredit and devalue alternative forms of research review. It has been suggested that even the terminology (*'systematic* review') subtly uses a 'rhetorical sleight of hand' to discredit alternatives through the implication that 'other' reviews are necessarily inferior by virtue of their designation as 'unsystematic' (Hammersley 2001). However, the 'systematic-ness' of such reviews can be questioned; as described earlier in this chapter, systematic reviews assume that all relevant evidence can be identified and collected in an orderly, replicable fashion. Yet my experience of conducting our review suggested that this ideal may be rather different in practice. For example, issues of limited time and funding mean that pragmatic decisions are required to arbitrarily draw cut-off points within searching, location and classification of studies. The intensive, time-consuming method for classifying studies also dictates that arbitrary decisions be made to determine the micro-focus of the review in order to cut down the numbers of studies to be reviewed in-depth.

For example, the scope of the Gender Review (to examine equal opportunities concerning gender in primary schools[6]) was continually restricted during and throughout the review process for purely pragmatic reasons. A mechanistic search and retrieval strategy yields an unmanageable quantity of mostly irrelevant studies, which are then coded, in order to be formally 'excluded', in a time-costly exercise. The intensive bureaucratic process of subjecting remaining studies to standardized coding (both core and specific 'keywording' sheets and later extremely long 'data extraction' brochures, necessarily undertaken by more than one evaluator) meant that we were forced to severely limit the scope of the review. This narrowing was purely to comply with the formalized methodology, rather than for reasons of meaning, value or relevance. For example, we restricted the evidence for the review by location (excluding international research, single-sex schools, non classroom-based interventions etc.), type (only non-research orientated interventions) and date of study (finally reduced to post-1990 studies only, thereby excluding seminal 1980s gender interventions).

A feature of this type of 'systematic' review report is the appending of lengthy lists detailing which databases, journals, etc. were searched using which terminology, but, I would argue, this does not necessarily increase the review's 'reliability' or validity. For example, strict adherence to rigid guidelines for classifying material may mean that less of the evidence, and/or less of the *important* evidence, is actually read or incorporated in a meaningful way than in a more traditional literature review. This issue over *meaning* versus *process* relates to the concern raised by Hammersley (2001) regarding the systematic review method for 'synthesising' research findings. Hammersley cites Freese (1980) to argue that, because of their technicist and evaluative orientation, systematic reviews do not take account of the cumulation of knowledge. In other words, the self-positioning of such reviews as 'objective' and 'outside' theory does not facilitate the development of ideas and thinking. Hammersley (2001: 548) proposes instead that

> what a series of studies should produce is a theory which is continually modified to increase its explanatory power. The findings of studies are not just added together; each one that makes a genuine contribution changes the emerging theory.

So in order to properly 'synthesise' research findings, Hammersley argues that researchers need to '*think* about the substantive and methodological issues, not just . . . apply replicable procedures' (2001: 549).

There were, as Oakley herself has admitted (reported in Budge 2002), numerous 'teething' problems encountered by the education review groups, derived in part from the difficulty (impossibility?) of attempting to transpose a medical model (from health reviews) to education. For instance, some types of study design, such as action research, just did not 'fit well' within the positivistic framework and, in my own experience, the rigid, standardized method-focused methods felt wholly inappropriate for 'getting at the substance/ meaning' of the educational research studies. In this respect, Hammersley (2001: 548), usefully questions 'the assumption . . . that studies can be assessed in purely procedural terms, rather than on the basis of judgements which necessarily rely on broader, and often tacit, knowledge of a whole range of methodological and substantive matters'. This dissonance between technicist/ professional viewpoints was exemplified early on in the review, when at a general 'training' meeting for group members, the proposal of a particularly narrow definition of 'an intervention study' (defining the research element as the primary focus, rather than, for example, an intervention designed primarily to create a change in the classroom) threatened to discount almost the entire field of educational research as 'non-interventions'! Such instances highlight the unavoidable political nature of even the most naive, technicist decisions and classificatory exercises.

The proposal that systematic reviews' adherence to 'explicit' guidelines eliminates bias is also questionable. Critical social scientists and educational researchers have done much to ensure that 'Other' viewpoints are represented and recognized in their research. Sociologists, such as Oliver (1992), have also explored the problems and implications associated with 'expert' opinion, calling for shifts in power within the social production of research. Indeed, there is a considerable body of ever-developing educational feminist reflexive practice that aims to actively engage with issues of power, representation and equity within the production of research. Systematic reviews are as biased and subjective as any other review, and it is revealing to note that the (circumscribed) transparency they achieve in terms of detailing their method, is very much absent in relation to detailing their underpinning politics and normative assumptions.

In my own experience, transparency and systematic-ness were not defining features of the review process. A number of the 'explicit procedures' were actually retrospectively imposed and/or were developed by the EPPI-Centre as the review progressed. Many of the 'real', but 'messy' experiences of doing the review (the details necessary to enable a 'true' replication) were edited out in order to conform to a 'clean' template.

Systematic reviews' claims to transparency, utility and accessibility also require closer examination. The technicist jargon is certainly not accessible to most readers, indeed as a member of the review group I required, and in turn was required to provide, considerable guidance over the opaque and confusing procedures and terms. For many 'users' and non-academic readers the rather dense terminology and method-heavy style of reporting can be inappropriate and irrelevant[7]. For example, detailed accounts of how studies were identified for review (see, for example, Evans and Benefield 2001) may be far less interesting and useful than a clearer focus on the 'substance' of such reviews[8]. I would suggest that professional judgement, appropriate to the aims and topic of a particular review, may actually 'work better' than adherence to standard templates, as one size rarely fits all. Furthermore, the prefacing of a standardized, technicist report with simplified 'user summaries' (saying why the [still inaccessible] report is useful for their particular 'population') does not achieve democratization, or accessibility, of knowledge. It can be alternatively read as rather patronizing, elitist and as a form of normative (typically 'New Labour') social control (see Gewirtz, 2001)[9], especially given that the structural locations of less powerful 'users' will circumscribe their ability to really 'act' upon or 'use' the evidence[10].

Perhaps, however, the most intriguing contradiction within systematic reviews arises from a tension between their aim, to produce 'useful' overviews of 'what works', and the end product. EPPI reviews have been criticized for being too narrow to be useful and for failing to provide any conclusive ideas as to what works (Budge 2002)[11]. As already discussed, the technicist/formulaic reviews cannot adequately review or contribute theoretically to the surveyed topic areas and they are, additionally, rather inaccessible reports. Thus I would suggest, to rather ironically paraphrase one of their champions, that they run the risk of becoming rather obscure reports that nobody reads, and which do not contribute to theory/knowledge (Hargreaves 1996). In short, systematic reviews appear 'not to work'.

Implications for practice

The evidence-based practice movement is also challenged by observations that policy making is not a purely rational process. Research evidence is only ever one of many factors that are considered when forming policies (Weiss 1979; Nutley and Webb 2000, both cited in Evans and Benefield 2001). Within research environments anecdotal stories abound regarding the 'selectivity' with which funders may read/ignore, 'encourage' or 'discourage' particular findings from commissioned research. And of course, the educational problems identified as requiring investigation are rarely (if ever!) divorced from existing politics and predetermined positions. However, the primacy afforded to 'knowledge' and 'evidence' within current governmental discourses does encourage an ever-tightening control over the sanctioning and legitimation of what 'counts' or can be 'trusted', which inevitably raises important issues for researchers and practitioners alike;

> Cultural capital has to be legitimated before it has symbolic power. Capital has to be regarded as legitimate before it can be capitalised upon: what, how and who you know and whether it is worth knowing.
>
> (Skeggs 2000: 14, cited in Hey 2001: 72)

I would suggest therefore that the fierce debates and boundary-building discussed within this article illustrates how an increased emphasis upon 'evidence' is necessarily accompanied by an ever-tighter control over what 'counts' as evidence.

The EBP movement also carries huge implications for the teaching profession. As Davies (2003) cogently demonstrates, new managerialism entails de-professionalization through increasing the control exercised by policy makers, bureaucrats and technicians. The terminology of the movement continually and subtly, undermines practitioners' professionalism and expertise as a valid source of knowledge/judgement. For example, Evans and Benefield (2001) dismiss evidence that is 'known to work' by teachers (dismissed and de-professionalized as 'craft knowledge') as opposed to 'proved to work' under EBP conditions. Whilst they demur that 'bottom-up strategies, developed by practitioners, . . . are a key stimulus for change and innovation' (p. 540), they reserve the need to assess (i.e. control) these strategies, justified through the appropriation of liberal ideals ('to change practice and improve outcomes for children', Evans and Benefield 2001: 540). In other words, EBP has profound implications for the control of teachers and teaching practices.

EBP discourses also contain the potential to proscribe and direct the nature of academia. The normative, narrow emphasis upon method as a means for ascribing 'soundness' or 'validity' to studies threatens the diversity of academic practice. Within prevailing EBP/managerialist policy discourses and the newly commodified academic marketplace (Hey 2001), 'knowledge' and 'knowledge workers' become key sites for control; they are necessary because of their role in the production of 'intellectual capital', yet this role also requires their careful control. Questions of equity also become apparent in relation to who can afford to produce 'good enough' evidence. For example, EPPI reviews were only partially funded and not all review groups had equal access to alternative sources of financial support. Thus although 'the DfES provided £20 000 for each of the first four [reviews] the true cost to the universities involved was nearer £80 000' (Budge 2002).

Conclusions and ways forward

It has been argued throughout this chapter that from a critically-aware, egalitarian perspective, there is little evidence in favour of the EBP movement. Thus the question becomes, which viewpoint to place more trust in? Both 'technicist' and 'academic' approaches are inevitably subjective, both come from particular epistemological positions and both claim their own manner of expertise. However, as identified by Ball (2001), the current policy weight given to evidence-based practice has been accompanied by the 'discourse of derision', that is/has been used to rework what it means to be a teacher/ academic, challenging the legitimacy of more critical and egalitarian practices. Although a proposal for a special issue of the *British Educational Research Journal* (titled 'In Praise of Educational Research') has been advertised as part of a growing movement of resistance.

From either perspective however, it can still be argued that there is a continuing need for educational research findings that can be drawn on by teachers to support and inform their classroom practice. The EBP idealization of positivistic research, and derision of less formal types of 'action research', do not preclude the development of critically-aware interventions and practices. The following chapters attempt to find a way forward within the current climate, detailing various forms of evidence, and ways in which it might usefully inform practice, but doing so from outside the confines of the EBP perspective. For example, illustrations are provided of teachers generating their own evidence (as researchers of their own practices and the institutions they worked in), and developing new practices on the basis of these. In contrast to EBP perspectives, teachers' professional knowledge is understood as fundamental to teaching, and is valued and built upon, rather than undermined and derided as not 'rigorous'. The book thus demonstrates a/n (alternative) view of research as critical discourse producing a range of solutions (Ball 2001). Contributors' 'evidence' aims to inform a practice that allows room for discussion, debate and building of knowledge through suggestions of multiple, sensitive ways of working across and within different contexts, developing ways of thinking around and beyond 'what works'.

Notes

1 The Department for Education and Employment (DfEE) has since changed to the Department for Education and Skills (DfES).

2 *Learning to Listen: A Study of Ways of Involving and Consulting Children and Young People in Central Government Decisions.* Invitation to tender issued by the DfES, August 2002.

3 Diana Elbourne, speaking at the launch of the EPPI-Centre First Wave Reviews, 24 June 2002, Victoria Thistle Hotel, London.

4 See eppi.ioe.ac.uk/EPPIWeb/home.aspx (EPPI-Centre website) for further details.

5 Francis, B., Skelton, C., Archer, L. (2002) A systematic review of classroom strategies for reducing stereotypical gender constructions among girls and boys in mixed–sex UK primary schools (EPPI-Centre review), in *Research Evidence in Education Library*, issue 1. London: EPPI-Centre, Social Science Research Unit, Institute of Education. Available on-line from the EPPI-Centre website.

   It should be made clear here, however, that all the views expressed within this chapter are my own and are not necessarily representative of the other report authors. Nor should my use of the review (to illustrate my criticisms of the EPPI/EBP approach) be read as in any way critical of the work or contributions of any of our Gender Review Group members.

6 This was the original scope, although it was refined through the process of conducting the review.

7 For example, the 'parent summary' for the gender review suggests that in their current format such reviews have little to offer parents.

8 I could propose instead to re-name systematic reviews as 'technicist exercises' or 'rule-bound surveys' or 'administrative/bureaucratic' reviews.

9 For example, the 'parent governor summary' provided via the EPPI-Centre for our review (extract below) illustrates the un-selfcritical, normative middle-class proscriptive rhetoric that has previously been identified by Sharon Gewirtz within DfES 'advice to parents'. The 'summary' excerpts below is

grossly unrepresentative of the report and goes way beyond the reviewed evidence. The summary is actually predominantly personal opinion/bias, dictated from a privileged (middle-class, white normative) perspective, telling 'other' parents what to do, and is unsubstantiated by the review. As such I find it hugely problematic.

'Make sure your child's school is aware of this review . . . Ask to see the resources the school has to tackle gender stereotyping and how they are used. Encourage the school to acquire more if necessary. But don't leave it all up to the school: encourage your child to borrow appropriate resources (e.g. books) and be prepared to discuss the issues they raise . . . Your own family life is unlikely to be free from gender stereotyping or its influences . . . Don't let your own stereotypical views influence your child's choices: rocket science is for girls, and any boy, not just Billy Elliot, can do ballet. You cannot prevent gender stereotypes from being applied to your child by other, especially older, people . . . Humour, as well as understanding, can be a great help in dealing with other people's stereotypes!' Extracts from school parent governor summary, eppi.ioe.ac.uk/EPPIWeb/home.aspx?Page=/reel/review_groups/gender/review_one_summaries_governor.htm

10   As the parent summary suggests, '. . . it is not clear what parents would do with these findings. Even those who are governors do not have the influence to introduce the sorts of interventions evaluated . . .'.

11   Although, of course, some reviews would blame the lack of 'rigorous' research evidence in relation to their highly specific question as the reason for inconclusive findings. However, given the almost infinite number of highly specialized research questions that could be applied within the field of educational research, the inevitably ubiquitous conclusion that 'more evidence is needed' (see published reviews) becomes rather unhelpful.

References

Ball, S.J. (2001) 'You've been NERFed!' Dumbing down the academy: National Educational Research Forum: 'a national strategy-consultation paper': a brief and bilious response, *Journal of Education Policy*, 16(3): 265–68.

Bassey, M. (2000) Reviews of educational research, *Research Intelligence*, 71: 22–9.

Blunkett, D. (2000) Influence or irrelevance: can social science improve government? *Research Intelligence*, 71: 12–21.

Budge, D. (2002) Launch of the first EPPI-Centre reviews, *Times Educational Supplement*, 12 July.

Clarke, J. and Newman, J. (1997) *The Managerial State*. London: Sage.

Davies, B. (2003) Death to critique and dissent? The policies and practices of new managerialism and of 'evidence-based practice', *Gender and Education*, 15(1): 91–103.

Evans, J. and Benefield, P. (2001) Systematic reviews of educational research: does the medical model fit? *British Educational Research Journal*, 27(5): 527–41.

Freese, L. (1980) The problem of cumulative knowledge, in L. Freese (ed.) *Theoretical Methods in Sociology*. Pittsburgh, PA: University of Pittsburgh Press.

Gewirtz, S. (2001) Cloning the Blairs: New Labour's programme for the re-socialization of working-class parents, *Journal of Education Policy*, 16(4): 365–78.

Hammersley, M. (1997) Educational research and teaching: a response to David Hargreaves' TTA lecture, *British Educational Research Journal*, 23(2): 141–62.

Hammersley, M. (2001) On 'systematic' reviews of research literatures: a 'narrative' response to Evans and Benefield, *British Educational Research Journal*, 27(5): 543–54.

Hargreaves, D. (1996) Teaching as a research-based profession: possibilities and prospects. *Teacher Training Agency Annual Lecture*. London: Teacher Training Agency.

Hargreaves, D. (1997) In defence of research for evidence-based teaching: a rejoinder to Martyn Hammersley, *British Educational Research Journal*, 23(4): 405–19.

Hargreaves, D. (1999) Revitalizing educational research: lessons from the past and proposals for the future, *Cambridge Journal of Education*, 29: 239–49.

Hey, V. (2001) The construction of academic time: sub/contracting academic labour in research, *Journal of Education Policy*, 16(1): 67–84.

Hillage, J., Pearson, R., Anderson, A. and Tamkin, P. (1998) *Excellence in Research in Schools*. London: Department for Education and Employment/Institute of Employment Studies.

Johnson, P. (2002) Address given at the Launch of the EPPI-Centre First Wave Reviews, 24 June, Victoria Thistle Hotel, London.

MacDonald, G. (2000) Social care: rhetoric and reality, in H.T.O. Davies, S.M. Nutley and P.C. Smith (eds) *What Works? Evidence-based Policy and Practice in Public Services*. Bristol: Policy Press.

Nutley, S. and Webb, J. (2000) Evidence and the policy process, in H.T.O. Davies, S.M. Nutley and P.C. Smith (eds) *What Works? Evidence-based Policy and Practice in Public Services*. Bristol: Policy Press.

Oakley, A. (2001) Making evidence-based practice educational: a rejoinder to John Elliott, *British Educational Research Journal*, 27(5): 575–76.

Oliver, M. (1992) Changing the social relations of research production? *Disability and society*, 7(2): 101–14.

Peersman, G., Oakley, A. and Oliver, S. (1999) Evidence-based health promotion? Some methodological challenges, *International Journal of Health Promotion and Education*, 37: 59–64.

Rose, N. (1999) *Powers of Freedom*. Cambridge: Cambridge University Press.

Schmelzer, M. (1993) Panopticism and postmodern pedagogy, in J. Caputo and M. Yount (eds) *Foucault and the Critique of Institutions*. University Park, PA: Pennslyvania State University Press.

Skeggs, B. (2000) Rethinking class: class cultures and explanatory power. Keynote address to the Cultural Studies and the Working Class Reconsidered conference, UEL, 29 January.

Stronach, I. and Hustler, D. (2001) Editorial, *British Educational Research Journal*, 27(5): 523–5.

Tooley, J. (1998) *Educational Research: A Review*. London: Ofsted/HMSO.

Tooley, J. and Darby, D. (1998) *Educational Research: A Critique*. London: Ofsted.

Trow, M. (1994) *Managerialism and the Academic Profession: Quality and Control*. Buckingham: Open University.

Weiss, C. H. (1979) The many meanings of research utilisation, *Public Administration Review*, 39: 426–31.

PART 2
Researching gender in the primary classroom

3 Girls and boys in the primary maths classroom

Helen Lucey, Margaret Brown, Hazel Denvir, Mike Askew and Valerie Rhodes

Introduction

In this chapter we will briefly outline developments in the rich and diverse area of research, practice and theory relating to gender and mathematics in the primary classroom as they have progressed since the mid-1970s. We will look at how research concerns have shifted from a relatively narrow focus on girls' alleged underachievement in mathematics to a much broader set of concerns which include asking questions about the construction of girls and boys as learners, feminine and masculine subject positions and pedagogic practice. We will then consider some initial findings from the Leverhulme Numeracy Research Programme in the light of contemporary and past research as well as the implementation of the National Numeracy Strategy.

Since the mid-1970s there has been a shift of focus from research which, in the 1970s and 1980s prioritized the question of *girls'* underachievement in mathematics towards a much broader foci of research questions pertinent to *gender* and mathematics. This widened perspective has also been increasingly sensitive to developments and changes outside the confines of mathematics education itself.

In the 1970s, just as the heavy production base of the UK was being dismantled, industry argued that it needed more skilled labour, especially in science and technology to meet the needs of the new computer-led service, information, finance and 'light' industries. It was perceived that these were needs that could only be filled by increasing the number of girls in those fields. The kinds of questions that were prevalent in the early research of the 1970s were all raised from within a perspective that tended to view gender as a fixed and independent variable (Atweh and Cooper 1995). Questions such as, are there gender differences in achievement and performance in maths and, do girls and boys of comparable ability participate in mathematics to the same degree, also reflected the predominant quantitative 'scientific' paradigms of that time. For instance, Fennema and her colleagues developed attitude scales and formulated arguments about boys' and girls' beliefs about maths, confidence in learning maths and the differential treatment of boys and girls in the mathematics classroom by teachers (Fennema and Sherman 1977; Fennema and Peterson 1985). Numerous studies clearly demonstrated that actual differences between the sexes were much smaller than claimed and could not explain the large differences in girls' and boys' participation in maths at post-compulsory levels. Importantly for current research in maths education it did seem that patterns of teacher behaviour, classroom organization and pedagogic practice influenced girls and boys differently. For example, while boys preferred and did better than girls in repetitive tasks, girls favoured and did better than boys in cooperative tasks (Hanna 1996). Having successfully challenged and disproved the entrenched belief that boys studied maths at a higher level because they were better at it than girls, this early work cleared the path for researchers to consider other questions.

The second kind of approach that Atweh and Cooper (1995) identify is one in which gender is viewed as an intervening variable, and is concerned with questions such as do teachers interact with girls and boys in different ways in the maths classroom; is there differential encouragement of boys and girls to study maths; how do the contexts in which girls and boys learn maths affect achievement and participation; and, what is the effect of role models and career stereotypes on boys' and girls' subject selection? At the same time as these questions were being posed the women's movement was raising awareness of the fact that girls did not have the same educational opportunities as boys (Spender 1983). The late 1970s to mid-1980s then were witness to a surge of anti-discrimination and equal opportunities policy, practice and legislation concerned with removing barriers identified as inhibiting females' participation in those areas traditionally dominated by males (Leder 1996).

Feminist work in the area of maths education and research has continued to be extremely innovative and largely responsible for the development of another approach, whereby gender is viewed not so much as a variable but rather as a *social construct* whose nature and role is under interrogation (Atweh and Cooper 1995). The kinds of questions raised within this approach are centrally connected to issues of power and value – of what does and doesn't 'count' as mathematical knowledge, as ability, as a 'good' learner. This outlook highlighted very quickly that dynamics of power are not only at play in relation to gender, but that social class, 'race' and ethnicity are highly implicated in differences in mathematical attainment. It is work in this vein and the theoretical assumptions underpinning it that we now consider.

Theoretical directions and developments in gender and mathematics research

Up until the mid-1980s, maths education drew mostly on mathematics itself or on psychology as the principle disciplines for the production of knowledge in the field (Kilpatrick 1992). A shift occurred at this time in the UK, as mainly feminist researchers began questioning some of the most basic assumptions about boys and girls in education[1]. Drawing on theoretical developments in postmodernism and poststructuralism, feminist research into gender and maths made powerful challenges to established orthodoxies which presented 'truths' about gender and knowledge (Burton 1986). The dualisms of rational/ irrational, subject/object, masculine/feminine, active/passive and culture/ nature that are the basis of modernist and humanist rationality, and of dominant Western ideology, all came under severe attack from postmodern writers. This work demonstrated that what were previously thought of and presented as clear, unvarying 'facts' about girls and boys, about maths, and about what goes on in mathematics classrooms were neither clear nor stable.

Key research being carried out at that time included the innovative work of the Girls and Mathematics Unit (GMU)[2]. Rather than positing a set of 'truths' which could then be used to make generalizations about boys and girls in mathematics, this work drew on a number of currents within post-modernism, in particular the work of the French poststructuralist Michel Foucault, in order to expose and deconstruct the assumptions that lay behind such taken for granted truths. Although the usefulness of poststructuralist ideas is contested within the field of gender and maths, the concept of 'discourse' which is closely connected to a particular understanding of 'power' is useful in helping us to understand how girls and boys take up gender roles in ways that are multiple and contradictory. A discourse can be defined as a way of thinking, speaking, behaving, writing that presents particular relationships as normal, self-evident, real. Discourses lay such certain claim to unchallenge-able 'truths' that within any given discourse only certain things can be said or thought: they therefore structure the ways in which we can think about things. This points to the regulative element of discourses, for in order to challenge the assumptions, truths and realities contained within them, one must necessarily step outside the discourse itself. To do this is to put oneself beyond that which the discourse prescribes as normal behaviour and therefore to risk being penalized or pathologized (Foucault 1988; Burman 1994). From this perspective the GMU work argued that the characteristics of the ideal child maths learner, as active, exploratory and challenging, are not gender-neutral but in fact closely match the characteristics of an idealized masculinity: the ideal child, it turns out, is in fact the ideal boy (Adams and Walkerdine 1986).

In the late 1980s maths education researchers were moving beyond the limitations of reproduction theory and turning instead to sociology and cultural studies for the intellectual resources to address issues of identity, culture and power as they are manifest in the mathematics classroom. Poststructuralist and postmodern ideas were key in problematizing popular accounts that tended to posit girls as the problem and challenged a number of arguments at that time about how to improve the situation of girls and women in maths and science. For instance, on the back of research from the United States which argued that girls were less confident in maths, suffered greater 'math anxiety' (Dweck and Bush 1976; Dweck and Elliot 1983) and were less competitive than boys, some argued that 'resocialization' was the key to increasing their performance, a strategy that would support the development of attributes more usually associated with boys such as 'competitiveness and risk-taking . . . as a means of achieving their more active participation in class' (Leder 1996: 43). However, the idea that girls could either simply or straightforwardly step outside of gendered discourses which prescribe ideas about what constitutes feminine behaviour to take up subject positions that are more usually associated with boys, and without any negative consequences, is absurd. In the maths classroom, girls who acted like boys in that they took risks and made confident challenges to the teacher were not viewed in the same way as boys: indeed, this behaviour may have courted negative evaluations by teachers. Girls then, may manifest the same behaviour as boys, but within the highly prescriptive, gendered discourses that operate in classrooms, even primary classrooms, it may not *mean* the same thing (Walkerdine and Lucey 1989).

Let us now turn to the Leverhulme Numeracy Research Programme and consider some of their preliminary findings relating to gender in the light of current research of gender and mathematics and recent policy developments in the field of mathematics education.

The Leverhulme Numeracy Research Programme

The Leverhulme Numeracy Research Programme (LNRP) is a longitudinal study of the teaching and learning of numeracy, investigating factors leading to low attainment in primary (elementary) numeracy in English schools, and testing out ways of raising attainment. Two cohorts of children, one starting in Reception (4- and 5-year-olds) and one in Year 4 (8- and 9-year-olds), were tracked through five years of schooling. Schools were selected in four varied local education authorities (LEAs) to give us a sample including schools of different types. Pupil data was collected at several different levels ranging from large scale, twice yearly, assessments on each of the two cohorts (some 1700 children in each cohort) through to detailed case studies of six children from each cohort in five schools, each of whom were observed for two weeks of mathematics teaching each year of the programme (Brown *et al.* 2000, 2001). While the large scale assessment data provides insights into pupil progress at a general level, the case study data enables us to gain insights into how individual children respond to specific teaching. With such a large data set it is difficult to provide more than a glimpse of the findings in this chapter. Although we have selected classroom data from just three children, Meg, George and Oscar, these act as exemplars of much wider themes across the sample (for more detailed findings and analyses from the LNRP see Askew *et al.* 2003; Millett *et al.* 2003; Street *et al.* 2003).

The National Numeracy Strategy

Continuing political concern over standards of basic skills in primary schools led to a National Numeracy Strategy (NNS), introduced in 1999/2000 and although not legally imposed, almost universally implemented. Two of the key features of the NNS are an increased emphasis on number and on calculation, especially mental calculation, including estimation, and selection from a repertoire of strategies; and a three-part template for daily mathematics lessons, starting with 10–15 minutes of oral/mental arithmetic practice, then direct interactive teaching of whole classes and groups, and finally 10 minutes of plenary review (National Foundation for Education Research 1998).

Ruth Merttens and Darrell Wood (2000) compare aspects of pre- and post-NNS classroom strategies and explore what this means in terms of models of learning, changes to pedagogy, beliefs and assumptions about how children learn maths. They note that the implementation of the mental-oral starter is predicated on three interconnected factors:

- *Repetition.* Some skills need to be practised little and often to eventually get to the stage where they become unconscious and certain operations can be carried out 'automatically'. For example counting in tens, number value, etc.
- *Whole class teaching.* This supports the idea that it is more effective to teach some types of skill to the whole class or a large group rather than to individuals, pairs or small groups. Through such practices the NNS subscribes to Lave's view (1988) of learning as an apprenticeship where children join in gradually, a process that she describes as ' "legitimate peripheral participation" where children are instigated into "expert practices" by more competent practitioners' (Merttens and Wood 2000: 15).
- *Performativity.* A particular notion of 'understanding' is employed, one that privileges the idea of children 'making sense' of maths in a number of different contexts.

As part of the LNRP over 1300 children from 35 schools in Year 4 in 1997/8 were tested. The same test was given to the new Year 4 children in the same schools in 2001/2. Both tests were administered in June. This has given us a way of evaluating the effect of the National Numeracy Strategy which was implemented in schools in 1999/2000, halfway between our two testings. The results demonstrate that the average gain is 3 per cent. However there are differences between different genders and children of different attainment.

Table 3.1 indicates that boys' scores were higher than girls' on both occasions and in all ranges. For example, the average score of the top 5 per cent of boys in June 1998 was 92 per cent whereas for the top 5 per cent of girls it was 89 per cent. Over the period of the introduction of the Numeracy Strategy the boys also seem to have improved slightly more (5 per cent, going from 62 per cent to 67 per cent, as opposed to 3 per cent, going from 61 per cent to 64 per cent). When you look at where the improvements have been largest it appears that it is the middle 50 per cent of boys who have gained most (6 per cent), whereas average girls have improved only by 3 per cent. At the lower end there has been little improvement in scores for any children, but low attaining girls seem to have lost out slightly since the strategy was implemented, with the average scores of the lowest 5 per cent of girls decreasing from 22 per cent in 1998 to 21 per cent in 2002. In fact if one further examines the composition of the top 5 per cent in the whole sample in June 2002, there are twice as many boys as girls in this highest attaining group, and there are correspondingly slightly more girls than boys in the lowest attaining 5 per cent.

Possible reasons for this differential effect of the Strategy will be examined in the next section.

Table 3.1 Mean percentage scores for different attainment groups by gender tested in June 1998 and June 2002

	Boys		Girls		All	
	1998	2002	1998	2002	1998	2002
Highest 5%	92	93	89	91	90	92
Highest 10%	88	90	86	88	87	90
Highest 25%	83	86	81	83	82	85
Middle 50%	63	69	61	64	62	66
Lowest 25%	37	40	37	39	37	40
Lowest 10%	29	30	28	28	28	29
Lowest 5%	24	24	22	21	23	23
Overall mean	62	67	61	64	62	65

Masculine and feminine subject positions

Research in the 1980s revealed that girls are put in a 'double-bind'; caught between what is seen as necessary to achieve femininity and be a 'good girl' by doing what the teacher asks and what is necessary to be regarded as good at maths. It was found that even high achieving girls were described by their maths teachers as hard workers, plodders, capable, neat, conscientious and helpful. However, given that these are not the traits that were seen to indicate talent in maths, then girls' early successes were not viewed as a sign of such talent or even of 'real' learning (Walden and Walkerdine 1986). Conversely and somewhat ironically, boys whose performance was far lower and behaviour far poorer than that of girls in the same primary classroom could be said to be 'bright' and have 'flair' though the 'hard' evidence for this was elusive (Walkerdine and Lucey 1989).

In the mid-1990s girls' increased examination success and participation in post-compulsory education signalled for some a 'closing of the gender gap' (Arnot *et al.* 1999). However, in an educational context in which girls were now viewed as doing very well and a social and economic context which had undergone profound change, it was boys' newly perceived underachievement which provoked a moral panic (Sammons 1995; Epstein *et al.* 1998). Current educational research on gender stresses how fears relating to the construction of, and concomitant threat of erosion to, a 'proper' masculine identity circulate constantly in schools and contribute to the production of gendered 'learner identities'. This would suggest that it is boys and not girls who are now put in a 'double-bind'.

How have shifts in classroom practice, as promoted by the NNS, affected girls and boys? Research in the 1980s and 1990s stressed that girls liked to work in different ways in maths lessons than boys; for instance they wanted to be able to understand how things worked, not just get the right answer (Boaler 1997); they worked well in groups, appreciated and responded to being able to clarify their thoughts in the process of working things out collaboratively, 'sharing insights, experience, knowledge, concerns and confusions' (Rogers and Kaiser 1995: 193).

NNS recommendations that stress the use of questioning and the idea that lessons should have 'pace' have introduced a strong 'performative' element. But it is important to consider how this shift in pedagogy demands a corresponding shift on the part of the pupil, requiring them to work out strategies to be seen to actively participate in the lesson in the right way, by producing correct answers to closed questions and appropriate answers to questions inviting explanation (Denvir *et al.* 2000).

The following examples of Meg, George and Oscar, aged 7 years, highlight some of the ways in which pupils present themselves as actively engaged with the mathematics and illustrate how these are closely tied up with presentations of the self including gendered identity. While it is difficult in such a short space to do justice to the complexity and contradictoriness of subject positions available to and taken up by girls and boys in the maths classroom, the examples we give here are illustrative of some trends across the data set from Reception to Year 6.

Meg

As part of a whole class session, the teacher is working on halving numbers. Each child has an individual white board and marker pen with which to display answers.

Teacher: Half of 36?

Meg starts to lift her board up to show the teacher. She has written '15', but before she shows it she notices that others around her have '18'. She quickly changes it; the teacher does not notice and says, 'Well done, Meg.'

Teacher: Half of 72?

Meg puts on an act. She takes the top off her pen, pushes it back again and looks puzzled. She appears to be counting – her lips are moving but it is not clear what she is saying. She turns round and sees what George has written then turns back again and wrinkles her face (as if to say, 'I'm concentrating hard'). Then she looks around at several boards and sees what answer others have got. Next she closes her eyes and screws up her face. After a time her face lights up as if she's just made a big discovery and she writes down '36'.

Over four years, researchers have observed Meg producing post hoc explanations which did not match what she did and were sometimes not even mathematically correct, but always presented with great conviction. Her teachers consistently describe her as able, hardworking and reliable and Meg strives to continue to appear like this to the teacher. This is not a one-off case. Strong trends across the Leverhulme data set suggest that gendered patterns of interaction in the primary school mathematics classroom are similar to those that researchers found in the 1970s and 1980s (Walden and Walkerdine 1986; Burton 1986). For instance, even high achieving girls like Stephanie and Aayesha in Rowan School 'work quietly' and 'get on', whilst average and more able boys are much more apt to challenge, in terms of both challenging the teachers' authority and displaying more challenging behaviour.

However, in relation to other children, Meg behaves differently, enjoying having power and some control over them (Denvir *et al.* 2000), a position that is supported by teachers' giving her responsibilities such as entrusting her with a set of cards for a fraction game for her group. In studies which focus on teachers' behaviour and interactions between girls and boys, girls tend to be seen as passively reacting to the status quo rather than contributing to it, or being the authors of it. Jungwirth (1996) maintains that because teachers are seen as interacting more with boys, this supports the view that it is boys who have the most influence on classroom dynamics. That there is something equally dynamic in interactions between girls and teachers, and girls and boys for that matter, is obscured. From an interactionist and ethnomethodological perspective girls play an active role in the development of relationships to maths and the dynamics of the maths classroom.

Clark (1990) argues that boys and girls have different ways available to them of being powerful. Boys have access to direct forms of power such as sexual harassment or direct challenges to the authority of the teacher. Girls' means are more indirect, for example by being a quiet, cooperative pupil or taking on the role of teacher, a role that does not compromise their femininity: 'by being positioned like the teacher and sharing her authority, girls are enabled to be both feminine and clever; it gives them considerable kudos and helps their attainment' (Walden and Walkerdine 1986: 125). However, the circulation of power is seldom as straightforward as it appears on the surface. Girls may gain power in taking up this position, but being like a teacher also means becoming nurturant, helping others, being sensible and mature. This is a position which Francis (2002) argues may actually mean an abdication of power as she found in her research that 'girls' sensibleness/maturity meant taking a back seat while the classroom interaction and teacher attention was dominated by boys' (p. 61).

George

The teacher and the class are playing a game where the teacher has a hidden shape and the children have to ask questions with a yes/no answer to figure out what it is.

> Teacher: It's a shape. You're going to have to guess what shape. It might be a solid 3D shape or a 2D shape. Put your hands down [*they've already got their hands up, presumably to guess*] and I'll tell you some clues first.
>
> Teacher: It's got, six faces, all square
>
> George: [*immediately, calling out, not loudly but still quite clearly*] Cube
>
> Teacher: It's got eight vertices, 12 edges which are all the same length.
>
> George: [*putting hand up this time*] Is it a cube?
>
> Teacher repeats all this information. There are now six hands up.
>
> Teacher: Lenny?
>
> Lenny: [*who is sitting next to George*] A cube.
>
> Teacher: See if that is right.

She pulls out the cube from under the puppet's body.
George: You gave too many clues.

George is a high performing boy who in this example is engaged with the mathematics and is seeking to engage with the teacher and the class by using his mathematical insight. His motivation to engage comes from his interest in the mathematics as well as a desire to maintain his position as a clever, articulate boy. At this stage, George's subject position as good at maths does not appear to compromise his masculine identity: he has no problem with standing out as very good at maths and in fact seems to have an investment in positioning himself as 'different' to the other children. Unlike many of the high achieving girls, he does not 'get on quietly', but frequently makes challenges to the teacher, to keep up with him, or to provoke more serious intellectual challenges being offered to him.

Connell (1989) maintains that hegemonic masculinity is powerfully invested in autonomy, through authority, aggression and technical competence. This is at odds with discourses about becoming a good learner in primary schools which point to group and teamwork which presume peer codependency. This disjunction leads to boys constructing the nature of their learning differently from girls. Vygotsky emphasized intersubjectivity, functioning of discursive practices including positioning and 'voice' and social relationships in the classroom as crucial to learning. Using key ideas from Vygotsky, Fielding *et al.* (1999: 176) argue that socio-cultural and socio-economic relations position more boys than girls as ineffective learners and that boys are more likely to be 'encultured in the view that they should learn alone or under the guidance of the teacher'. Because one-to-one interactions with teachers are usually brief, being an 'effective learner' for boys requires them to become self-sufficient learners or to seek other ways of bidding for the teacher's attention. Girls, on the other hand, are more likely to seek and offer help to each other. They are more likely to engage in on-task talk about work and, therefore, more likely to be in receipt of appropriate 'scaffolds' for learning.

Although it seems that younger children who are enthusiastic about their learning are less subject to peer sanctions, there is evidence that by the last year of primary school, boys who are seen to work hard and to enjoy it can attract negative responses from their classmates (Skelton 2001). Is it also important for boys to distance themselves from anything viewed as feminine and therefore low-status (Reay 2001)? If this is the case, it may be that maths suffers less from such negative connotations because of its place as *the* status subject in primary school by teachers as well as pupils. It is where children at primary school are most likely to be grouped by ability and therefore where differences in achievement are highlighted most vividly (as well as, of course, in physical education). Nevertheless, research indicates that even very young boys then feel the need to guard against the designation of 'geek' by not being seen to work hard: a disavowal of the importance or even enjoyment of school must somehow be demonstrated in order to be acceptably masculine (Frosh, Phoenix and Pattman 2001; Bartholomew 2001, 2002). In the maths classroom George presents his achievement in maths as effortless.

Oscar

The teacher is asking children to double and halve various numbers. Each time they write down their answers on a white board and show it to the teacher.

Oscar gets all of the answers correct. I can't see how he is doing them, whether he is doing them by himself or copying.

Teacher: Half of 36?

Teacher: Oscar how did you get 18?

Oscar: I don't know.

The teacher asks someone else.

Later in the same lesson the teacher is using a disk of card folded into four segments to stand for a cake.

Teacher: This one is cut into four, into quarters. X comes along and eats a quarter. How much is left? Write it down on your boards.

Oscar writes 1/3.

Teacher sees the researcher looking and looks herself. She says, 'Oscar, How many is it cut into?'

Oscar: Umm, three, . . . no four.

Teacher: Four. So that's the number at the bottom. The other number goes at the top.

Oscar changes his 1/3 to 3/4.

Leverhulme test data indicates that low attaining girls' performance in maths has worsened since the implementation of the NNS. It is not quite clear why this is so, but some low attaining girls have expressed their dislike of the public nature of whole class questioning. Boys may have improved because they like the competitive nature of this, and some like Oscar strive hard to succeed like the more able boys. Alternatively it may be that the emphasis on mental arithmetic rather than written work in the Strategy is more appreciated by boys.

The National Numeracy Strategy stresses the benefits of understanding process rather than getting the right result partly through an emphasis on the idea that there is no one right way of doing things. However, evidence from the Leverhulme Programme suggests that *generally speaking* this practice is more easily taken up by boys than girls and that boys are more prepared than girls to 'do things their own way'. Girls, on the other hand, seem to be more concerned than boys in trying to remember what the teacher has said and following her instructions. In relation to the new pedagogy of maths, boys seem to be able to incorporate or buy into the notion that the same mathematical problem can be addressed in a number of different, although equally valid ways. But this is not always the case; unlike George, Oscar seems to like being fairly unobtrusive in the classroom and keeps a low profile, offering 'safe' answers and, unlike Meg, sticking with 'Don't know' rather than risking an incorrect response when asked to describe his strategy. Initially he was identified by his teacher as 'average' in mathematical attainment. He used to work quite slowly, taking his time, capable and proficient. Now he works in the same group as George, identified as higher attaining throughout. George and Oscar now spend time together as a pair both inside and outside the classroom. The friendship with George is very important to Oscar, who enjoys competitive situations and introduces this element into interactions with other children, and this may be the reason for the culture of speed and competitiveness which is creeping into Oscar's work and which prompts him to fall back on getting the answers from George. Evidence suggests that it is more difficult for girls to respond positively to competitive situations in the classroom and that competitive goal orientation is more compatible with boys' learning styles, being motivated by the collecting of points and winning, whereas girls are more concerned with procedures and processes (Higgins 1995). Oscar may also be motivated by 'winning' but even more important to him is his desire to maintain his position in the class as George's friend.

Leverhulme data suggests that, overall, girls are not doing as well as boys in mathematics. But there is a more complicated story to tell about all pupils' attainment, one which involves social class, 'race' and ethnicity and reveals a positive element of girls' attainment. It would seem that among the working-class children, the only 5 who score in the highest 5 per cent are all girls, and mostly from families from the Indian sub-continent. Indeed, the Leverhulme project figures for attainment and progression between 1997 and 2002 suggest that there is much less difference between the performance of different social groups among girls than among boys (Millett *et al.* 2003). High scoring boys, like George in the above example, are almost all from the middle classes, whereas girls are more evenly spread at both extremes of the attainment range.

Conclusion

Over twenty years after feminist researchers posited the idea that girls were in a 'double-bind' when it came to being successful in maths, we might ask whether or not the conditions of 'proper femininity' have altered and if girls still have to be 'good' in order to be properly feminine? In presenting some data from the Leverhulme Numeracy Research Programme, it would seem that girls' and boys' ways of interacting in maths classrooms, with the maths, with the teacher and with each other, are surprisingly familiar, traditional even.

Perhaps this is one subject area where girls' 'conformist' behaviour and apparent willingness to engage with school discourses may be compatible with normative femininity but are at odds with contemporary pedagogic practices in maths, particularly those favoured by the National Numeracy Strategy, which promote a more performative, competitive learner style.

We would suggest that teachers need to be wary of letting whole class sessions become a public arena for confident children, predominantly boys, to demonstrate their autonomy and creativity, and in which less confident children, mainly girls, dread being exposed. It can be a more productive use of time for children to practise mental calculation at their own level in well-matched pairs or groups. Even in whole class sessions developing new ideas and strategies, pauses for group discussion may take the spotlight off individual performance; allowing less confident children to report the conclusions of their group, rather than their own answers.

Notes

1   Lerman (2001) notes that movements and events across the globe were also influential in broadening the theoretical repertoire of maths educators, in particular the emergence of ethnomathematics (D'Ambrosio 1984) as well as calls for greater democratization of the maths classroom and the devoting of one day at the 6th International Congress on Mathematical Education in 1988 to mathematics, education and society.
2   The Girls and Mathematics Unit, founded by Valerie Walkerdine, conducted research between 1982 and 1989 and was located at the Institute of Education, University of London.

References

Adams, C. and Walkerdine, V. (1986) *Investigating Gender in the Primary School.* London: ILEA.

Arnot, M., David, M. and Weiner, G. (1999) *Closing the Gender Gap.* Cambridge: Polity Press.

Askew, M., Brown, M. and Millett, A. (eds) (2003) *Teaching and Learning About Number: Interactions in Primary Lessons and Pupil Progression.* Canada: Kluwer Academic.

Atweh, B. and Cooper, T. (1995) The construction of gender, social class and mathematics in the classroom, *Educational Studies in Mathematics*, 28: 293–310.

Bartholomew, H. (2001) Learning environments and student roles in individualised mathematics classrooms. Unpublished PhD thesis, King's College London.

Bartholomew, H. (2002) Negotiating identity in the community of the mathematics classroom, *Proceedings of the Third International Mathematics Education and Society Conference*, pp. 133–43.

Boaler, J. (1997) *Experiencing School Mathematics: Teaching Styles, Sex and Setting.* Buckingham: Open University Press.

Brown, M., Askew, M. and Millett, A. (eds) (2003) *Teaching, Learning and Progression in Key Numeracy Topics.* Canada: Kluwer Academic.

Brown, M., Askew, M., Rhodes, V., Denvir, H., Ranson, E. and Wiliam, D. (2001) Magic bullets or chimeras? Searching for factors characterising effective teachers and effective teaching in numeracy. Paper presented at the British Educational Research Association Annual Conference, University of Leeds, 13–15 September.

Brown, M., Denvir, H., Rhodes, V., Askew, M., Wiliam, D. and Ranson, E. (2000) The effect of some classroom factors on Grade 3 pupil gains in the Leverhulme Numeracy Research Programme, in T. Nakahara and M. Koyama (eds) *Proceedings of the 24th Conference of the International Group for the Psychology of Mathematics Education*, 2: 121–8. Japan: Hiroshima University.

Burman, E. (1994) *Deconstructing Developmental Psychology.* London: Routledge.

Burton, L. (ed.) (1986) *Girls into Maths Can Go.* London: Holt, Rinehart and Winston.

Clark, M. (1990) *The Great Gender Divide: Gender in the Primary School.* Melbourne: Curriculum Corporation.

Connell, R. (1989) Cool guys, Swots and Wimps: the interplay of masculinity and education, *Oxford Review of Education*, 15: 291–303.

D'Ambrosio, U. (1984) Socio-cultural bases for mathematical education, in *Proceedings of the Fifth International Congress on Mathematical Education*. Boston: Birkhauser.

Dweck, C. and Bush, E. (1976) Sex differences in learned helplessness 1: differential debilitation with peer and adult evaluators, *Developmental Psychology*, 12(2): 147–56.

Dweck, C. and Elliott, E. S. (1983) Achievement motivation, in E.M. Hetherington (ed.) *Socialization, Personality and Social Development*. New York: Wiley.

Epstein, D., Elwood, J., Hey, V. and Maw, J. (eds) (1998) *Failing boys?: Issues in Gender and Achievement*. Buckingham: Open University Press.

Fennema, E. and Peterson, P. L. (1985) Autonomous learning behaviours: a possible explanation of gender-related differences in mathematics, in L.C. Wilkinson and C.B. Marrett (eds) *Gender-related Differences in Classroom Interactions*. Florida: Academic Press.

Fennema, E. and Sherman, J. A. (1977) Sex-related differences in mathematics achievement, spatial visualization and affective factors, *American Educational Research Journal*, 14(1): 51–71.

Fielding, S., Daniels, H., Creese, A., Hey, V. and Leonard, D. (1999) The (mis)use of SATs to examine gender and achievement at Key Stage 2, *The Curriculum Journal*, 10(2): 169–87.

Foucault, M. (1988) *Politics, Philosophy, Culture: Interviews and Other Writings 1977–1984*. London: Routledge.

Francis, B. (2002) *Boys, Girls and Achievement*. London: Routledge/Falmer.

Frosh, S., Phoenix, A. and Patman, R. (2001) *Young Masculinities*. Basingstoke: Palgrave.

Hanna, G. (ed.) (1996) *Towards Gender Equity in Mathematics Education*. Canada: Kluwer Academic.

Higgins, J. (1995) We don't even want to play: classroom strategies and curriculum which benefit girls, in P. Rogers and G. Kaiser (eds) *Equity in Mathematics Education: Influences of Feminism and Culture*. Bristol: Falmer Press.

Jungwirth, H. (1996) Symbolic interactionism and ethnomethodology as a theoretical framework for the research on gender and mathematics, in G. Hanna (ed.) *Towards Gender Equity in Mathematics Education*. Canada: Kluwer Academic.

Kilpatrick, J. (1992) A history of research in mathematics education, in D.A. Grouws (ed.) *Handbook of Research on Mathematics Teaching and Learning*. New York: Macmillan.

Lave, J. (1988) *Cognition in Practice: Mind, Mathematics and Culture in Everyday Life*. Cambridge: Cambridge University Press.

Leder, G. C. (1996) Gender equity: A reappraisal, in G. Hanna (ed.) *Towards Gender Equity in Mathematics Education*. Canada: Kluwer Academic.

Lerman, S. (2001) Cultural, discursive psychology: a sociocultural approach to studying the teaching and learning of mathematics, *Educational Studies in Mathematics*, 46: 87–113.

Merttens, R. and Wood, D. (2000) Sea changes in mathematics education: an elaboration of aspects of the National Curriculum Strategy, *Mathematics Teaching*, 172: 13–17.

Millett, A., Brown, M. and Askew, M. (eds) (2003) *Teaching, Learning and Progression in Key Numeracy Topics*. Canada: Kluwer Academic.

National Foundation for Education Research. (1998) *National Numeracy Project: Technical Report*. NFER.

Reay, D. (2001) 'Spice girls', 'nice girls', 'girlies' and tomboys: gender discourses, girls' cultures and femininities in the primary classroom, *Gender and Education*, 13(2): 153–66.

Rogers, P. and Kaiser, G. (eds) (1995) *Equity in Mathematics Education: Influences of Feminism and Culture*. Bristol: Falmer Press.

Sammons, P. (1995) Gender, ethnic and socio-economic differences in attainment and progress: a longitudinal analysis of student achievement over nine years, *British Educational Research Journal*, 21(4): 465–85.

Skelton, C. (2001) *Schooling the Boys: Masculinities and Primary Education*. Buckingham: Open University Press.

Spender, D. (1983) *Invisible Women: The Schooling Scandal*. London: Writers and readers Publishing Co-op.

Street, B., Askew, M., Brown, M. and Millett, A. (eds) (2003) *Numeracy Practices At Home And At School*. Canada: Kluwer Academic.

Walden, R. and Walkerdine, V. (1986) Characteristics, views and relationships in the classroom, in L. Burton (ed.) *Girls into Maths Can Go*. London: Holt, Rinehart and Winston.

Walkerdine, V. and Lucey, H. (1989) *Democracy in the Kitchen: Regulating Mothers and Socialising Daughters*. London: Virago.

4 Superhero stories
Literacy, gender and popular culture

Jackie Marsh

Literacy has been at the centre of debates about gender and achievement in recent years. This chapter provides a brief overview of key issues in this debate before moving on to examine ways in which the literacy curriculum needs to be developed if it is to meet the needs of *all* children in contemporary society. It is argued that only by paying attention to the way in which out-of-school literacy practices – which are primarily rooted in popular culture, media and new technologies – impact on children's experiences, can schools ensure that they motivate both boys and girls to engage in schooled literacy practices. The chapter draws from a specific research project which utilized popular culture in the primary literacy curriculum to illustrate this, but also outlines a broad range of work which has served to indicate how traditional gendered constructions of literacy can be challenged effectively in the classroom.

The chapter is written from a theoretical standpoint which recognizes the relational nature of gendered identities (Davies 1989; Millard 1997; Francis 1998, 2000; Orellana 1999). That is, it is acknowledged that gender is socially constructed and the categories of 'masculine' and 'feminine' are developed in relation to one another. As Francis suggests, 'there is one (notional) masculinity and one (notional) femininity constructed as oppositional to one another, and consequently shifting, but flexible, and incorporating contradictions' (Francis 2000: 15). The shifts, contradictions and flexibility, therefore, can account for the diverse range of 'masculinities' and 'femininities' that are performed by individuals. Hegemonic masculinity and femininity incorporate a range of dualistic discourses that children adopt in order to perform their gender and this performance requires them to demonstrate how their particular gender identity is constructed as different from the other (Davies 1989; Francis 1998). Paechter (2003) suggests that children learn these gendered discourses through participating in 'communities of practice' (Lave and Wenger 1991), that is, groups which share particular discourses. Paechter draws on Lave and Wenger's concept of 'legitimate peripheral participation' in communities of practice (Lave and Wenger 1991), a term which describes the process of watching and learning as an apprentice in a group as a means to developing full 'membership', to suggest that the construction of gender is achieved through participation in specific communities of practice. Hegemonic constructions of masculinity and femininity lead to

> a socio-cultural imperative to establish, naturalize and sustain differences between boys and girls, men and women, from an early age, and this naturalization of difference is part of the process by which children are incorporated, from birth, as legitimate peripheral participants in communities of practice.
>
> (Paechter 2003: 71)

Within these gendered communities of practice, children learn particular ways of performing their gendered identities, identities which are constructed in relation to each other and which lead to 'borderwork' (Thorne 1993: 64) or 'category maintenance work' (Davies 1989: 29), the act of clearly defining the borders between masculine and feminine. In terms of becoming literate, therefore, it is clear that children participate in gendered communities of practice in which they learn what it means to be a girl or boy in relation to reading and writing practices (Orellana 1995, 1999; Millard 1997). These differently gendered literacy practices make any simplistic attempt to analyse the ways in which boys and girls develop competence in literacy impossible. However, this does not appear to have prevented a range of reductionist discourses being proffered in recent years in an attempt to explain why boys are apparently underachieving in relation to schooled literacy practices. In the following section, these debates and issues are summarized before the chapter moves on to examine ways in which schooled literacy practices narrow possibilities for both boys *and* girls.

The underachievement of boys in literacy debate

In 1993, an Ofsted report, *Boys and English*, (Ofsted 1993) indicated that boys were underachieving in all aspects of the English curriculum. As Millard (1997) notes, this was not a new phenomenon. The Assessment of Performance Unit (APU) had also identified disparities in attainment in English between girls and boys in reports developed between 1979 and 1983. Indeed, the underachievement of boys in the subject has been an issue for much longer than that; as Cohen (1998) points out, John Locke was ruminating on the issue in 1693.

Millard's (1997) book, *Differently Literate*, was the first major text that examined the issue in any depth and provided a theoretical framework for an analysis of this underachievement. The key thesis of this book, based on an extensive survey of 255 secondary pupils, was that boys and girls like to read and write about different things, have different attitudes towards schooled literacy and do different things with their literacy skills once outside of school. She argued that many of the boys she interviewed were disadvantaged by the limited range of texts on offer in the school curriculum, texts which usually excluded boys' interests. Although Millard makes it equally clear that any analysis of the issue should also identify ways in which girls' literacy is also often limited by their propensity to conform to traditional conceptions of literacy propagated by schools, when success in employment is increasingly predicated on wider notions of literacy (embedded within the technological developments since the 1980s), this message appeared to be ignored in many of the ensuing debates. Boys soon became the victims, to the extent that a controversial illustration accompanying one *TES* article on the subject (Wragg 1997) portrayed a class of boys shackled to large balls and chains which were locked around their ankles.

A number of reasons were proffered for this underachievement in literacy by boys. The key factor appeared to be the construction of a hegemonic masculinity in which 'real boys don't do English' (Millard 1997; Moss 2000; Skelton 2001a). A second suggestion was that the English curriculum offered by most schools is 'feminized' in that it focuses upon narrative genres and the emphasis is on producing personal responses to literature, both of which are not in line with boys' interests (Alloway and Gilbert 1997; Millard 1997). Third, the fact that society in general devalues literacy and literacy instruction as it is framed within school and instead privileges techno-literacies could impact on boys' reluctance towards the subject (Alloway and Gilbert 1997). Other suggestions proffered, which appear to have little evidence in the research literature, included the suggestion that female teachers have lower expectations of boys. (Renold [2001] argues that this is part of a general 'blaming discourse' directed at women teachers in relation to boys' underachievement.) In addition, it has even been argued that there is a lack of male role models in many boys' homes which may lead to a disinterest in competition (Bleach 1998), that there are differences in boys' and girls' cognitive styles (Warrington and Younger 1997) and that there are fundamental differences in boys' and girls' brain development (Moir and Jessel 1998)[1]. It has been difficult for teachers to tread their way through this minefield in order to determine what the key issues at stake really are[2], but suffice to say within this chapter that the causes of boys' underachievement in literacy cannot be clearly traced, because the underachievement pattern itself is very complex.

The actual level of underachievement of boys in literacy in the primary stages is in itself open to debate. The latest available figures for England and Wales[3] appear to indicate that the gap is consistent across Key Stages 1 and 2, with the biggest concern being in relation to the 16 per cent gap in attainment in writing at Key Stage 2 (see Tables 4.1 and 4.2).

Table 4.1 Key Stage 1 results 2002: percentage of pupils at Level 2 or above

	England		Wales	
	Boys	Girls	Boys	Girls
Reading task	81	88	78	86
Writing task	82	90	76	86
Spelling task	73	83	–	–
English	–	–	79	88

Source: DfES National Statistics (www.dfes.gov.uk/statistics) and National Assembly for Wales Statistical Release (www.wales.gov.uk/keypubstatisticsforwalesheadline/content/scholls-teach200 . . .)

Table 4.2 Key Stage 2 results 2002: percentage of pupils at Level 4 or above

	England		Wales	Wales
	Boys	Girls	Boys	Girls
English test (English or Welsh in Wales, according to first language)	70	79	English: 75 Welsh: 84	English: 84 Welsh: 81
Reading test	77	83	–	–
Writing test	52	68	–	–

Source: DfES National Statistics (www.dfes.gov.uk/statistics) and National Assembly for Wales Statistical Release (www.wales.gov.uk/keypubstatisticsforwalesheadline/content/scholls-teach200 . . .)

However, this simplistic attention to numbers has been open to much critique and it has been suggested that figures used to fuel the debate have been misrepresented (Gorard *et al.* 2001) and miscalculated (Gorard 2000). Indeed, Gorard *et al.* (2001) suggest that a close analysis of O level/ GCSE figures from 1974 would suggest that the gender gap is not a new development, nor does it have a consistently clear trajectory in favour of girls. In addition, as data from Gillborn and Mirza (2000) indicate, underachievement in English is a much more complex picture than is often presented. They analyse data in relation to gender, class and 'race' and present a picture that looks very different in nature to the one often proffered as evidence that boys globally underachieve. In their analysis, it is clear that it is only *some* groups of boys who underachieve and that social class is a more significant factor than gender in underachievement, for example, some groups of working-class girls perform less well than some groups of middle-class boys. Gillborn and Mirza's

(2000) data indicate that it is the interaction between 'race', social class and gender which is significant in any analysis of literacy attainment and that lack of attention to this interaction can lead to misunderstanding and further inequities as schools strive to address the issue as a 'failing boys' syndrome. The complex web of social class, gender and ethnicity is reflected in the results of the Key Stage 2 Welsh Tests (2002) in which boys' attainment exceeded that of girls (see Table 4.2).

There have been a large number of initiatives that have sought to address the issue of boys' underachievement in literacy[4], many of which have been predicated on the need to ensure that boys are motivated and engaged in the literacy curriculum. In the following sections, I wish to outline an approach to issues of gender and literacy in the primary classroom that takes a more fundamental look at the nature of the curriculum itself and explores how far the literacy curriculum offered in primary schools is relevant to the current needs of boys *and* girls. In response to this question, I turn first to examine the changing nature of literacy in contemporary society.

The changing nature of literacy

It is clear that, since the 1970s, the nature of literacy has been changing rapidly, primarily due to technological innovations. It is now commonplace to send written messages via mobile phones, to respond to written text on interactive television, to access information from the Internet and to engage in synchronous and asynchronous communication using email, chat rooms and other forms of digital communication. Such activities, by their very nature, challenge established notions of literacy as the boundaries between texts, signs, symbols and images blur and the notion of 'reading' can no longer be applied to printed words alone[5]. Reading has become a process in which we need to decode, encode and make meaning from written and printed letters and symbols alongside still and moving images in ways which were simply not required in the past.

In addition to this technological, seismic shift, the range of texts that many children in the UK now encounter in their daily lives is vast. Children are surrounded by a rich plethora of pleasurable narratives and have access to a wider range of texts than previous generations, such as books, comics, magazines, environmental print, stickers, television, film, computer games and so on. Many of these texts have multiple connections with others. This 'intermedia intertextuality' (Kinder 1991) has a number of implications. First, it means that children can move seamlessly from one kind of text to another, confident in the fact that they will know names of characters, storylines and so on as they meet the same story in different formats. Second, children can engage in a particular narrative even if they cannot afford to buy a large number of the texts. This shared connection with others is important for the development of friendships and peer groups (Dyson 1997). Of course, there are disadvantages to this kind of process in that children can be pressurized into buying goods, or asking parents and carers to buy them goods, through peer pressure and ruthless marketing by multinational companies (Kenway and Bullen 2001). Nevertheless, the implications of this popular cultural network are significant for teachers in terms of the teaching and learning of literacy.

In the 1960s there was a growing concern that the advent of television meant that children were reading fewer books. However, this 'displacement' theory, as it is known, has been discounted by a number of academics who have pointed out that children have, in numerous surveys over the years, consistently read about the same amount, which is on average 15 minutes a day (Neuman 1995; Livingstone and Bovill 1999). The fears that were expressed over television viewing have also been raised in relation to a number of other children's leisure pursuits. These concerns can, in part, be ascribed to the regular resurgence of 'moral panics' in society; panics in which older generations condemn the leisure pursuits of young people, pastimes which are misunderstood and perhaps feared (Cohen 1987). Thus, over the centuries, a number of popular pursuits have been denounced as debased, with the potential to corrupt and mislead. Silent movies, superhero comics, television, video and, more recently, computer games, have all been castigated at some point by educationalists, politicians and the media. It is no coincidence that many of these forms of entertainment are integrally linked with technological development and some commentators have suggested that the moral panics surrounding these pastimes are linked to a fundamental fear of the unknown by an older generation that does not possess the technological capabilities of youth (Luke and Luke 2001). The consequence of this lack of understanding of the changing and complex nature of childhood worlds and, along with that, the revolution which is taking place with regard to literacy is that, in the main, policies and practices in schools do not reflect the contemporary cultural landscape. This is clearly the case if the National Literacy Strategy Framework (DfEE 1998) is analysed in close detail.

National Literacy Strategy: narrow conceptions of literacy?

The National Literacy Strategy (NLS) was introduced in England in 1998. It has since been widely adopted in schools across England. In many schools across Wales, Scotland and Northern Ireland, some elements of the strategy have been adopted and adapted, but its use in its standard form is not usual practice[6]. The NLS developed a framework for the teaching of literacy which sets out what should be taught during each term for each year group in the primary school. Within the NLS Framework for Key Stages 1 and 2 (DfEE 1998), there is a clear set of objectives for word, sentence and text level which set out in detail the skills, knowledge and understanding expected at each stage.

Unfortunately, we have to wait until Year 3 (7–8-year-olds), term 2, to encounter the first mention of 'media texts', despite the extensive evidence that very young children are competent users of a range of televisual and media texts (Browne 1999; Marsh and Thompson 2001). Moreover, this first mention of media in the NLS is nestled within a range of texts and is to be explored in terms of 'limitations'. Children must examine the 'merits and limitations of particular instructional texts, including information technology (IT) and other media texts . . .' (DfEE 1998: 35). Critical analysis of a media form is to be encouraged, but it is unfortunate that the first mention of media texts must be linked immediately to the notion of exploring its 'limitations'. There are only 11 references throughout the NLS framework to media texts. The media texts most frequently referred to are newspapers and the activities related to televisual texts are primarily those that provide opportunities to compare written texts with moving images, which only serves to emphasize the primacy of the written word. However, the significance of any mention at all of media texts within a national literacy curriculum for the primary years should not be overlooked. It is a welcome development from the 1988 National Curriculum Orders for Key Stages 1 and 2, in which media texts were not mentioned at all.

Nevertheless, the National Literacy Strategy Framework clearly privileges particular types of texts and producers of texts. All references to producers of texts use the words 'writer', 'author' or 'poet', and there is no mention of producers, directors or creators. It could be argued that the term 'author' is used in a generic sense to include authorship of televisual and media texts, but the word is most frequently used in conjunction with terms that relate to the written word. This marginalization of media texts could be seen visually, as well as ideologically, in the revised version of the National Curriculum (Qualifications and Curriculum Authority 1999), which was published after the introduction of the National Literacy Strategy Framework in 1998. In the main body of the text, it was suggested that the range of literature used in the Key Stage 2 English curriculum should include:

a a range of modern fiction by significant children's authors;
b long-established children's fiction;
c a range of good-quality modern poetry;
d classic poetry;
e texts drawn from a variety of cultures and traditions;

   f myths, legends and traditional stories;
   g playscripts.

(QCA 1999: 54)

These texts are all part of the traditional primary canon. In a note embedded within the margins, we find the following:

> ICT opportunity: Pupils could use moving image texts (for example, television, film, multimedia) to support their study of literary texts and to study how words, images and sounds are combined to convey meaning and emotion.

(QCA 1999: 54)

In this instance, not only were media texts pushed literally to the side, they appeared only to support the study of 'literary texts'. In the Key Stage 1 National Curriculum orders, media texts did not appear at all. Presumably, policy makers felt that a child needs to reach an age when they can be assumed to be a competent reader of printed texts before being allowed to study media texts.

Thus it is clear that the official exclusion of media texts from the National Literacy Strategy Framework is not based within a contemporary theoretical understanding of the teaching and learning of literacy. Eighty years after the Newbolt Report (Board of Education 1921), we are still enmeshed in a literacy curriculum that promotes a cultural hierarchy in which media texts are on the bottom rung, let in reluctantly as a means of enhancing children's response to more canonical texts. The lack of attention to media texts can also be applied to other forms of multi-modal texts, often located within children's popular culture. This narrow focus on traditional printed texts in national curricula is, as Kress (2000) points out, rather shortsighted:

> In the world of market-dominated consumption, as much in the world of an economy of information and services, meaning resides in commodities of all kinds, both because commodities have been constructed as signs and because commodities are taken as signs by those who construct their identity through choice-in-consumption. Meaning is therefore no longer confined or confinable to 'texts' in a traditional sense, nor is communication. A curriculum of communication which is to be adequate to the needs of the young cannot afford to remain with older notions of text as valued literary object, as the present English curriculum still does, by and large.

(Kress 2000: 145)

An understanding of the narrow conceptions of literacy embedded within current curriculum frameworks is important for any analysis of gender and attainment. Children outside of school engage in a wide variety of literacy activities which are embedded within media, new technologies and popular culture (Livingstone 2002). If the school curriculum fails to reflect these wider interests, then children may become increasingly alienated from schooled literacy practices and less willing to engage in activities which they consider to be out of date. Girls, however, are known to conform more readily to schooled literacy practices (Millard 1997; Moss 2000) and, therefore, the disadvantages may appear on the surface to be less marked for them, as we have seen to be the case with the recent focus on the increasing disengagement with literacy that many boys exhibit. Nevertheless, the disadvantages girls face in engaging compliantly with dated conceptions of literacy in school are just as pressing (Alloway and Gilbert 1997; Millard 1997; Moss 2000). In addition, if issues relating to gender and attainment are to be addressed adequately, then hegemonic constructions of masculinities and femininities need to be analysed and children helped to question how they shape, and are shaped by, these discourses (Francis 2000; Renold 2001; Skelton 2001a; Millard 2003). Popular culture, media and new technologies offer a myriad of opportunities for deconstructing these representations of gender and developing critical literacy skills, skills which are essential in order to challenge the stereotypes which perpetuate literacy myths, including those relating to underachievement (see also Chapter 8 for a discussion of critical literacy). In the following section of the chapter, I will draw on research which has focused on the use of popular culture in the literacy curriculum in order to illustrate how it can both motivate children and provide opportunities for the development of critical literacy skills.

Popular culture, motivation and literacy

If children are to become effective and enthusiastic readers and writers, then they need to be motivated to engage in literacy activities in the classroom (Turner 1995; Turner and Paris 1995; Guthrie *et al.* 1996). Certainly, demotivation appears to be linked to a lack of engagement in the literacy curriculum by particular groups of boys (Maynard 2002). In the following section, I outline a research project conducted in a primary school which aimed to explore the effect on motivation of the introduction of a popular cultural theme into the literacy curriculum (Marsh 1997). In order to illustrate issues relating specifically to gender and literacy, two children are featured and their responses to the project detailed.

The project

The project was conducted in a base which housed two Year 2 (6–7-year-olds) classes. There were 57 children in the two classes combined, 28 girls and

29 boys. Thirty-eight children spoke English as an additional language. A role-play area based on the *Batman* superhero narrative was set up in a space shared by the two classrooms. In order to promote gender equity, the role-play area was entitled the 'Batman and Batwoman HQ'. A range of resources were provided, including costumes, accessories and a wide variety of resources for reading and writing (paper, diaries, notebooks, noticeboards, a computer, pens, pencils, comics and so on). I observed the role-play area for a total of ten days and collected data using video and field-notes, in addition to interviews with the two teachers involved. The number of literacy events children took part in – activities which involved acts of reading and/or writing – were counted, in addition to the number of imaginative play events. In the following analysis, I focus on two children in the classes, Paul and Safeena, in order to draw out key themes.

Paul

Paul was aged 6, a child of African Caribbean and English dual-heritage who lived with his parents and four brothers and sisters. He was a popular, friendly boy who loved to talk with his friends about his favourite television programmes and toys. Although he loved listening to stories and had a vivid imagination, Paul did not like to create his own stories; in fact, he disliked writing altogether. At the beginning of the project, the teachers were asked if they felt children would engage in reading and writing activities in the bat cave. Paul's teacher indicated that, in fact, Paul was her 'benchmark' for the success or otherwise of the project. She said of him:

> I don't think Paul would write in a role play area because he's not inclined to write. He needs a lot of leaning on to write really, and encouragement, and even then it takes him a long time, so he's a bit resistant to things like that. If he does anything as a result of the theme that's an indication that it is very successful, so I'll watch that.

On the first day of the project, Paul was as keen as everyone else in the base to enter the cave, but he did not get an opportunity. On the second day, he entered it with his friend Adam. They immediately put on their Batman capes and then in role as Batmen, they began to look for the Joker (a villain in the Batman narrative). They took two chairs and placed them side by side in the middle of the cave. Paul grabbed some paper and thrust it at Adam. For some time, they sat drawing and writing in the cave, interspersed with dialogue that indicated that they were engaged in role play in which they were also driving the Batmobile, chasing after the Joker, as this transcript from the video data illustrates:

Transcript	**Commentary on action**
Paul: Press that when I'm driving so it'll drive itself . . . Get writing.	Paul points to an imaginary button on the dressing up rack (which they are pretending is the Batmobile). Paul starts to write on one of the pieces of paper. Adam looks on, not certain what to do.
Adam: Are you drawing a picture?	He looks at Paul's paper.
Paul: Yeah. Draw a picture of a man.	They sit alongside each other, drawing and writing, for some time. Later on, they move to huddle around a chair. Paul uses the seat of the chair as a desk to rest the paper on. Adam looks on whilst Paul writes.
Paul: I'm telling the police that the Joker has got all the money. You go and get the 'phones, quick.	Paul continues writing – he is writing a letter to the police and has drawn a picture of the Joker. When Adam returns with the 'walkie-talkies', they leave the writing on the chair and chase round the cave, shouting into the 'phones.

Thus, from his first moment in the cave, Paul had been engaged in writing in role. This may appear on the surface to be an insignificant event, but there is much work that has illustrated how play and literacy are interrelated and how taking part in activities such as this can develop a range of language and literacy skills (Barrs 1988; Roskos and Christie 2001). The field-notes and video data reveal that this was not an isolated incident – almost every time he was in the cave, Paul engaged in literacy activities at some point. These included writing letters to Gotham police, drawing maps to help in the chase for the Joker, making lists of items the Joker had stolen and writing about Batman's adventures in the diary. However, what was even more thrilling than this for his teacher was that Paul became motivated to engage in writing activities in the classroom. The teachers utilized the children's enthusiasm and, throughout the project, set classroom tasks which drew on the Batman theme. Paul volunteered to take part in each of these activities; no encouragement or coercion, usually a necessity in his case, was needed. At the end of the project, Paul's teacher enthused:

> Initially, I met the suggestion of incorporating a role-play area based on popular culture into the classroom with some reservations . . . Each time there is a new TV programme or film, there is a resurgence of kicking games and I thought the same thing (or worse) might happen if these situations were set up in the normally controlled atmosphere of the classroom . . . I found that throughout the period, children clamoured to do writing tasks based on the theme . . . and a child reluctant to write extended pieces would begin with a brief note

to the Joker and end with a page full of writing . . . Having such a popular focus early in the school year gave a 'kick-start' to some children's writing and the benefits are still showing in this group of children, many of whom regard writing as a pleasure.

I asked if this included Paul and, indeed, it did. He was, as this teacher phrased it, '. . . now so turned on to writing, it's amazing'. Paul was not an isolated case. Of the 29 boys in the two classes, teachers predicted at the start of the study that 14 of them would not engage in literacy activities at all once in the cave, based on their previous assessment of the boys. *All* of these boys were observed reading and writing in the role-play area throughout the project. In addition, the 'literacy events' taking place in the cave were counted, i.e. all the events in which reading or writing played a part. There were 371 events initiated by girls and 357 events initiated by boys, thus indicating that the gendered difference in literacy activity was not as great as expected. It would appear that, for this class, using popular culture provided a means of orientating boys towards schooled literacy. However, it is essential to explore what such discourses offer girls, as focusing upon the needs of boys at the expense of girls is not a way forward in terms of gender equity in the classroom (Skelton 2001a, 2001b). A closer look at the experiences of one girl, Safeena, can therefore serve to illuminate ways in which the role-play area offered opportunities to contest hegemonic feminine identities.

Safeena

Safeena was a 6-year-old girl who spoke English and Punjabi fluently and was also learning Arabic at the local mosque. She lived with her parents, paternal grandparents and three older sisters. Safeena was a confident reader and writer and enjoyed all literacy-related activities. However, Safeena's teacher identified her as a girl who would not be interested in a role-play area based on a superhero theme:

> Safeena doesn't spend much time in role-play areas, she isn't part of that friendship group who go in them a lot. Also, I think it's not the sort of topic that would interest her, she likes things that appeal more to girls, you know, topics that are stereotypically girls' themes, if that makes sense. She's really into 'girlie' things such as clothes and pop stars, and so on. So I don't think she will go for the Bat cave.

Safeena demonstrated interest in the cave on the first day it was set up. She and her friend Saira entered the cave, donned cloaks and immediately sat down to write. On that first occasion, they spent over 30 minutes in the cave, writing letters to Batman, writing in the Batwoman diary and reading the

Batman comic. However, they interspersed this fevered activity with bursts of imaginative role play, in which they both assumed the role of Batwoman and chased the Joker, engaging in imaginative play in which they were active and heroic superheroes. This was a common pattern in Safeena's use of the cave and she appeared to be particularly attracted to the sense of agency that donning Batwoman's cloak gave her, as this extract from the field-notes indicates:

> Safeena has a cloak on and is swooping about the rather confined space (two other girls and one boy are also in the cave). 'I'm Batwoman', Safeena announces to no-one in particular. Nisha joins her and soon the two girls are swishing from side to side of the cave, occasionally bumping into one of the others. Safeena stands on a chair and jumps off it, flapping her cloak and shouting, 'I'm Batwoman!' Mena decides to join them and asks the girls to help her dress in role, which they do. Safeena, Nisha and Mena are all dressed up and ready to go. They write a note to the Joker. 'Say, "We're gonna get you" ', Safeena suggests. Nisha runs about, cape spread out, on some private mission. Note completed, they all rush over to the Batmobile. 'You drive, I'll get the map' Safeena tells the others. Marcus enters. 'Who's the Joker?' 'Nobody. Go away', Safeena tells him.

As with Paul, Safeena's experience was not unique amongst the girls. The superhero theme provided them with opportunities to engage in more active role play than was usual, play in which they could take on key roles and become more adventurous in both their play and literacy choices (see Marsh 2000 for a fuller discussion of girls' engagement in superhero play and also Holland 2003). Thus within this study, it was clear that the superhero theme had been very attractive to the boys in the class and had led to increased levels of interest in literacy activities by them. It demonstrated that the inclusion of popular texts and themes within the literacy curriculum could orientate boys towards more traditional texts. But, importantly, it also engaged girls. It is essential not to introduce practices which promote boys' engagement in literacy at the expense of girls (Moss 2000; Skelton 2001a, 2001b). If texts or themes are introduced which have traditionally appealed to boys, then teachers need to work out ways of ensuring that girls can also access the texts. In this project, much time was spent before the role-play area was introduced discussing the possibilities for literacy and the necessity to challenge the usual stereotypes with regard to superheroes. In undertaking work such as this, girls may be offered a wider range of roles than the typecast, narrow ones on offer in many traditional literacy texts. In addition, work on popular culture can enable children to engage in the multi-modal forms of meaning-making referred to earlier in this chapter. In this project, children were involved with analysing films, researching the Batman narrative on the Internet, using related computer games and so on. These multi-modal forms are not confined to popular culture, but popular culture offers a wider range of opportunities for these forms to occur naturally in curriculum work.

There have been a number of other studies which have also indicated how the inclusion of popular cultural texts in the primary literacy curriculum can provide motivation and enhance children's engagement in literacy practices (Dyson 1994, 1997; Marsh and Millard 2000; Millard and Marsh 2001). The emphasis on this work is not to suggest that the inclusion of such texts is an end in itself, or that children should only have access to popular texts. Children need access to the literacy discourses of the powerful if they are to develop the cultural, social and economic capital needed to succeed at school (Luke 1994). But popular culture can provide a means of bridging the gulf that exists between home and school for many children. For example, Dyson (1996) illustrates how work on superheroes led to a study of Greek gods for a class of American children and demonstrates how children can understand a potentially alien text more fully through the lens of their own experiences.

Using popular culture in the literacy curriculum raises a range of important questions relating to the substantive content of many of the texts. The media and popular culture are saturated with racism, sexism, violence and other oppressive discourses and, therefore, the use of these texts in the classroom leaves teachers with difficult decisions to make, which can include censorship in some cases. However, simply banning the use of all contentious texts and media forms will not solve the problem (although, of course, there is a body of material which would not be suitable for use in primary classrooms). Children will still be accessing this material outside of school. Neither would it be productive simply to launch into a project in which children critiqued the texts for their offensive content. This approach can lead to superficial responses from children who have learned how to play the teacher's game and know what to say to demonstrate political correctness, whilst not shifting from their private, pleasurable and often politically incorrect response to the texts. Instead, popular culture and media texts can be part of a literacy curriculum which develops critical readers and writers; children who can interrogate texts at the same time as they can analyse the ways in which such texts provide them with narrative satisfaction (Alvermann *et al.* 1999; Comber and Simpson 2001). In addition, such work can be important in enabling children to critique hegemonic constructions of gender in relation to choices made with regard to literacy practices, and allow them to explore alternative versions in which stereotyped responses to literacy work and restricted choices of texts can be effectively challenged. In the final section of the chapter, I will look briefly at the role that popular culture can play in developing critical readers and writers.

Critical literacy

Critical literacy is predicated on the premise that no text stands alone – literacy is socially and culturally constructed and, within each act of authorship and readership, we can trace intentions, processes and outcomes which are inflected with power and which are historically situated within specific socio-political contexts. Critical literacy involves interrogating texts in order that some of these discourses of power can be identified and deconstructed (see Comber and Simpson 2001).

Freebody and Luke (1990) suggest that a reader can adopt four roles in relation to texts, that of code-breaker (decoding the text), text-participant (constructing meaning), text-user (finding authentic uses for texts), and text-analyst (critically reading the text). Children need to be able to work at all four levels in order to become competent readers and writers. Comber (2003) has argued that, traditionally, the schooling of younger children has focused on code-breaking to the detriment of the other three roles and suggests that schools need to provide opportunities for children to operate at all four levels in order for them to develop as critical readers and writers.

Popular cultural texts can provide a very useful source of material for developing critical literacy in relation to gender roles. Gender stereotypes are deeply embedded within much popular culture material (Marsh and Millard 2000). Using some of these texts to explore hegemonic gender construction can tease out some of the complexities and alert children to the ways in which gender is constructed within texts and how those texts shape their own sub-jectivities. As gender is inextricably related to other aspects of identity such as 'race', social class, sexuality and physical ability, the way in which popular cultural texts address the interface between these can be subject to interroga-tion. In the following example, children were asked to examine critically the superhero discourse in order to determine how related texts mediated par-ticular versions of masculinity and femininity. The activity was framed for the children in terms they could understand; they were invited to look at texts and examine what they said to them about what it meant to be a girl or boy.

Superhero stories

A class of 5- and 6-year-old children were provided with opportunities to inter-rogate a range of texts using a critical literacy framework. This work included children looking at a range of superhero comics and film extracts and answer-ing the following questions:

- What are the people like in these texts?
- What do they look like? Do they look like you, your friends and the children in this class?
- Who are the good people in the stories? What do you notice about them?
- Are they male or female?
- Do males and females do the same kinds of things in the stories?
- Make a list of the actions that males do and the actions that females do in the stories.
- Decide which actions you think are the best in the story. Who does these – males or females?
- Who are the bad people in these texts?
- What do they look like?
- Why do you think the authors have written the stories in this way?
- Who are the stories written for? How do you know?
- Make a list of superheroes who are male. Now make a list of super-heroes who are female. What do you notice?
- Choose three superheroes. Describe what they look like. Are they male/female? Young or old? What colour is their skin? How are they dressed? What do you notice about what you have found out?

The children brought a wide range of knowledge of these kinds of texts to the discussions and were able to identify ways in which gendered patterns were inherent in the superhero stories, in addition to identifying that all of the superheroes were white in the texts they purveyed. At a later stage, children were asked to produce stories in which they could include females and black characters as superheroes. This exercise demonstrated how difficult it is to challenge deep-rooted stereotypes as no boys chose to include female prot-agonists in their stories and girls produced (all white) Barbie and Barbie-like superheroes who often relied on men to do the action (see Marsh and Millard 2000: 35–7). Nevertheless, such work did offer alternative versions in which children's normal expectations were disrupted and challenged and it provided a fruitful basis for further work. The activity enabled the children to trace how texts encourage readers to take up certain subject-positions and how this interpellation can be deconstructed. It provided an opportunity for the teacher to introduce the concept of literacy as performance in which certain subject positions can be practised, performed and solidified. However, critical literacy work such as this should not be introduced in an isolated and intermittent way. Children need to return to these activities over sustained periods of time if they are to build on their understanding. In addition, it is important to undertake the activities in ways which do not diminish the pleasures which children derive from such discourses. Finally, it is worth remembering that such work is not easy and is open to a range of contradictions, frustrations and surprises. The work of Bronwyn Davies illustrates this beautifully, as she outlines how a group of children resisted the feminist narrative of the picture book *The Paper-bag Princess* (Cole 1986), which portrays a princess who saves a Prince and fights a dragon, to reinstate traditional notions of what it means to be a princess and contest the choices that the heroine makes (Davies 1989). Thus, the 'power of the pre-existing structure of the traditional narrative to prevent a new form of narrative from being heard is ever-present' (Davies 1989: 69) and educators need to strive to provide consistent opportunities for children to interrogate these hegemonic narratives in ways which support their developing understanding.

Although research in this area is currently scarce (Comber 2003), there are other examples of popular culture being used to develop critical literacy. Dyson (1994, 1997, 2001) illustrates how 'author's theatre', in which children write stories that are then performed by classmates, offered opportunities for children to discuss and challenge traditional constructions of gender and 'race' in superhero narratives in ways which were not teacher-directed, but arose from the children's own concerns for equity. O'Brien (2001) asked 5- to 7-year-old children to analyse Mother's Day junk mail in order to deconstruct the images of women and motherhood presented by the texts and to explore the cultural construction of Mother's Day itself. However, critical literacy need not be limited to the analysis of texts themselves. Through a critical literacy framework, children can become engaged in the gender and literacy debate itself. In the course of exploring exactly what texts appeal to whom and why, and examining how far the schooled literacy curriculum reflects these interests, they may discover that things are more complex than they initially appear to be.

Conclusion

This chapter has argued for a slightly different approach than is often recommended in the drive to ensure that the primary literacy curriculum is appealing to both boys and girls. Isolated strategies and projects which focus on the needs of one gender at the expense of the other will not do. Instead, what is needed is careful attention to how well the current literacy curriculum reflects the needs and interests of *all* children in today's society, given the technological changes taking place and the wide range of cultural interests which inflect children's out-of-school literacy activities. Ensuring that a wide gulf does not exist between schooled literacy practices and children's out-of-school interests will not only motivate boys, it will ensure that girls are engaged in a wider range of literacy activities than may often be the case for them. In addition, offering critical literacy practices that enable children to analyse ways in which literacy is entrenched in discourses of power can provide opportunities for them to deconstruct traditional gendered positions and move beyond stereotypes in the search for narrative satisfaction. Ladson-Billings (1995) discusses the importance of developing a 'culturally-relevant pedagogy' which is rooted in the socio-cultural lives of children and is sensitive to their previous experiences and preferred ways of learning. In addition, we need to offer a culturally-relevant literacy curriculum which is embedded firmly in the world of childhood cultures if we are to inspire all children to become lifelong members of the 'literacy club' (Smith 1988).

Notes

1 For an overview of biological theories in relation to gender and literacy, see Maynard 2002: 23–6.
2 For a clear overview of the issues, see Francis (2000) and Skelton (2001a).
3 At the time of writing, comparative figures were not available for Northern Ireland and Scotland.
4 See Sukhnandan, Lee and Kellner (2000) on the National Literacy Trust website at: www.literacytrust.org.uk/database/boys/index.html and the DfEE Standards site at www.standards.dfes.gov.uk for examples of projects which aim to raise standards in boys' attainment.
5 These are significant developments that have major implications for literacy education in the twenty-first century, but this chapter cannot attend to the ways in which literacy is currently being reshaped through technology. For a detailed account of this, see Snyder (1998) and Cope and Kalantzis (2000).
6 See the National Literacy Trust website for information on the way in which primary literacy is approached across Northern Ireland, Scotland and Wales at www.literacytrust.org.uk/database/primary

References

Alloway, N. and Gilbert, P. (1997) Boys and literacy: lessons from Australia, *Gender and Education*, 9(1): 49–58.

Alvermann, D., Moon, J.S. and Hagood, M.C. (1999) *Popular Culture in the Classroom: Teaching and Researching Critical Media Literacy*. Newark, Delaware: IRA/ NRC.

Barrs, M. (1988) Maps of play, in M. Meek and C. Mills (eds) *Language and Literacy in the Primary School*. London: Falmer Press.

Bleach, K. (ed.) (1998) *Raising Boys' Achievement in Schools*. Stoke-on-Trent: Trentham.

Board of Education (1921) *The Teaching of English in England* (Newbolt report). London: HMSO.

Browne, N. (1999) *Young Children's Literacy Development and the Role of Televisual Texts*. London: Falmer Press.

Cohen, M. (1998) 'A habit of healthy idleness': boys' underachievement in historical perspective, in D. Epstein, J. Elwood, V. Hey and J. Maw (eds) *Failing Boys? Issues in Gender and Underachievement.* Buckingham: Open University Press.

Cohen, S. (1987) *Folk Devils and Moral Panics: The Creation of the Mods and Rockers,* 2nd edn. Oxford: Blackwell.

Cole, B. (1986) *Princess Smartypants.* London: Hamish Hamilton.

Comber, B. (2003) Critical literacy: what does it look like in early literacy? in N. Hall, J. Larson and J. Marsh (eds) *Handbook of Early Childhood Literacy.* London: Sage.

Comber, B. and Simpson, A. (eds) (2001) *Negotiating Critical Literacies in Classrooms.* Mahwah, NJ: Lawrence Erlbaum.

Cope, B. and Kalantzis, M. (eds) (2000) *Multiliteracies: Literacy Learning and the Design of Social Futures.* London: Routledge.

Davies, B. (1989) *Frogs and Snails and Feminist Tales.* London: Allen and Unwin.

Department for Education and Employment (DfEE) (1998) *The National Literacy Strategy: A Framework for Teaching.* London: HMSO.

Dyson, A.H. (1994) The Ninjas, the X-Men, and the Ladies: playing with power and identity in an urban primary school, *Teachers College Record,* 96(2): 219–39.

Dyson, A.H. (1996) Cultural constellations and childhood identities: on Greek gods, cartoon heroes, and the social lives of schoolchildren, *Harvard Educational Review,* 66(3): 471–95.

Dyson, A.H. (1997) *Writing Superheroes: Contemporary Childhood, Popular Culture, and Classroom Literacy.* New York: Teachers College Press.

Dyson, A.H. (2001) Relational sense and textual sense in a US urban classroom: the contested case of Emily, girlfriend of a ninja, in B. Comber and A. Simpson (eds) *Negotiating Critical Literacies in Classrooms.* Mahwah, NJ: Lawrence Erlbaum.

Francis, B. (1998) *Power Plays: Primary School Children's Constructions of Gender, Power and Adult Work.* Stoke-on-Trent: Trentham.

Francis, B. (2000) *Boys, Girls and Achievement: Addressing the Classroom Issues.* London: Routledge.

Freebody, P. and Luke, A. (1990) 'Literacies' programs: debates and demands in cultural context, *Prospect: The Journal of Adult Migrant Education Programs,* 5(3): 7–16.

Gillborn, D. and Mirza, H.S. (2000) *Educational Inequality: Mapping Race, Class and Gender.* London: HMSO.

Gorard, S. (2000) One of us cannot be wrong: the paradox of achievement gaps, *British Journal of Sociology of Education,* 21(3): 391–400.

Gorard, S., Rees, G. and Salisbury, J. (2001) Investigating the patterns of differential attainment of boys and girls at school, *British Educational Research Journal,* 27(2): 125–39.

Guthrie, J.T., Van meter, P., Dacey Mcanu, A. *et al.* (1996) Growth of literacy engagement: changes in motivation and strategies during concept-orientated reading instruction, *Reading Research Quarterly,* 31: 306–25.

Holland, P. (2003) *We don't Play with Guns Here*. Maidenhead: McGraw-Hill Education/Open University Press.

Kenway, J. and Bullen, E. (2001) *Consuming Children: Education – Entertainment – Advertising*. Buckingham: Open University Press.

Kinder, M. (1991) *Playing with Power in Movies: Television and Video Games from Muppet Babies to Teenage Mutant Ninja Turtles*. Berkeley, CA: University of California Press.

Kress, G. (2000) A curriculum for the future, *Cambridge Journal of Education*, 30(1): 133–45.

Ladson-Billings, G. (1995) Towards a theory of culturally relevant pedagogy, *American Educational Research Journal*, 32(3): 465–91.

Lave, J. and Wenger, E. (1991) *Situated Learning: Legitimate Peripheral Participation*. Cambridge: Cambridge University Press.

Livingstone, S. (2002) *Young People and New Media*. London: Sage.

Livingstone, S. and Bovill, M. (1999) *Young People, New Media*. London: London School of Economics.

Luke, A. (1994) *The Social Construction of Literacy in the Primary School*. Melbourne, Australia: Macmillan Education.

Luke, A. and Luke, C. (2001) Adolescence lost/childhood regained: on early intervention and the emergence of the techno-subject, *Journal of Early Childhood Literacy*, 1(1): 91–120.

Marsh, J. (1997) Batman and Batwoman go to school: a study of literacy and popular culture in socio-dramatic play of six- and seven-year-olds. Unpublished MEd dissertation, University of Sheffield.

Marsh, J. (2000) 'But I want to fly too!' Girls and superhero play in the infant classroom, *Gender and Education*, 12(2): 209–20.

Marsh, J. and Millard, E. (2000) *Literacy and Popular Culture: Using Children's Culture in the Classroom*. London: Paul Chapman.

Marsh, J. and Thompson, P. (2001) Parental involvement in literacy development: using media texts, *Journal of Research in Reading*, 24(3): 266–78.

Maynard, T. (2002) *Boys and Literacy: Exploring the Issues*. London: RoutledgeFalmer.

Millard, E. (1997) *Differently Literate: Boys, Girls and the Schooling of Literacy*. London: Falmer Press.

Millard, E. (2003) Gender and early childhood literacy, in N. Hall, J. Larson and J. Marsh (eds) *Handbook of Early Childhood Literacy*. London: Sage.

Millard, E. and Marsh, J. (2001) Sending Minnie the Minx home: comics and reading choices, *Cambridge Journal of Education*, 31(1): 25–38.

Moir, A. and Jessel, D. (1998) *Brainsex: The Real Difference Between Men and Women*. London: Mandarin.

Moss, G. (2000) Raising boys' attainment in reading: some principles for intervention, *Reading*, 34(3): 101–6.

Neuman, S. (1995) *Literacy in the Television Age: The Myth of the TV Effect*, 2nd edn. Norwood, NJ: Ablex.

O'Brien, J. (2001) Children reading critically: a local history, in B. Comber and A. Simpson (eds) (2001) *Negotiating Critical Literacies in Classrooms*. Mahwah, NJ: Lawrence Erlbaum.

Ofsted (1993) *Boys and English*. London: HMSO.

Orellana, M.J. (1995) Literacy as a gendered social practice: texts, talk, tasks and take-up: in two bilingual classrooms, *Reading Research Quarterly*, 30(4): 335–65.

Orellana, M.J. (1999) Good guys and bad girls, in M. Bucholtz, A.C. Liang and L.A Sutton (eds) *Reinventing Identities: The Gendered Self in Discourse*. New York, London: Oxford University Press.

Paechter, C.F. (2003) 'Masculinities and femininities as communities of practice', *Women's Studies International Forum*, 26(1): 69–77.

Qualifications and Curriculum Authority (QCA) (1999) *The National Curriculum*. London: HMSO.

Renold, E. (2001) Learning the 'hard' way: boys, hegemonic masculinity and the negotiation of learner identities in the primary school, *British Journal of Sociology of Education*, 22(3): 369–85.

Roskos, K. and Christie, J. (2001) Examining the play-literacy interface: a critical review and future directions, *Journal of Early Childhood Literacy*, 1(1): 59–89.

Skelton, C. (2001a) *Schooling the Boys: Masculinities and Primary Education*. Buckingham: Open University Press.

Skelton, C. (2001b) Typical boys? Theorizing masculinity in educational settings, in B. Francis and C. Skelton (eds) *Investigating Gender: Contemporary Perspectives in Education*. Buckingham: Open University Press.

Smith, F. (1988) *Joining the Literacy Club – Further Essays into Education*. London: Heinemann.

Snyder, I. (ed.) (1998) *Page to Screen: Taking Literacy Into the Electronic Era*. London: Routledge.

Sukhnandan, L., Lee, B. and Kellner, S. (2000) *An Investigation Into Gender Differences in Achievement, Phase 2: School and Classroom Strategies*. Slough: NFER.

Thorne, B. (1993) *Gender Play: Girls and Boys in School*. Buckingham: Open University Press.

Turner, J. (1995) The influence of classroom contexts on young children's motivation for literacy, *Reading Research Quarterly*, 30: 410–40.

Turner, J. and Paris, S.G. (1995) How literacy tasks influence children's motivation for literacy, *The Reading Teacher*, 48: 662–73.

Warrington, M. and Younger, M. (1997) Gender and achievement: the debate at GCSE, *Education Review*, 10(1): 21–7.

Wragg, T. (1997) 'Oh boy!', *The Times Educational Supplement*, 16 May.

5 Gender equity in primary science

Michael Reiss

Why this chapter?

Anyone interested in reading this book is likely already to be persuaded of the need to attend carefully both to issues of gender and to the primary phase of education (see, for example, Francis 2000; Martino and Meyenn 2001; Skelton 2001). But what's so important about science? In one sense, the answer is 'nothing' – we need equity, including gender equity, in all school subjects, pre-school and post-primary as well as at primary level. But in another sense, it is especially important to consider (gender) equity in science for two reasons.

First, in almost all countries – including England and Wales despite the recent concentration on literacy and numeracy – science occupies a privileged position in the curriculum. It demands particular resources (such as specialized equipment and distinctive training for teachers) and is held in high regard by parents, curriculum designers and policy makers.

Second, and at least as importantly, it is still very widely believed, albeit often somewhat unreflectively, that science is *the* way to truth. Put as baldly as that, the notion sounds absurd. After all, science has nothing to do with mathematical truths, moral truths, aesthetic judgements and religious values and little if anything to do with the establishment of historical and economic knowledge (such as the causes of the First World War or deflation). However, despite an increasing mistrust in many countries of 'experts', science is still seen as a most powerful source of valid knowledge of particularly wide currency. In the UK, for example, uncertainties about a whole range of issues from the origins of BSE, the possibility of human-caused global climate change, the safety of mobile phones, and whether or not we should hunt deer with hounds are typically addressed by engaging prestigious scientists (e.g. Fellows of the Royal Society) in coming to an answer.

So what is taught in school science, including primary school science, is likely – if we are not careful – to be taken as 'the way the world is'. If science tells us that too much fat is bad for the human diet, then chips are seen as bad for us; if it tells us that motile sperm race towards a waiting egg, then males are assumed to be active and females passive; if it tells us that genetically modified crops have higher yields, then the solution to famines may be held to be the abandonment of traditional agriculture and the growth of GM crops.

In the 1990s, primary science was widely seen as one of the success stories of the National Curriculum in England and Wales. However, success was generally measured either by pupil attainment on the Key Stage 2 tests for 11-year-olds or by teacher self-reported confidence (cf. Lunn 2002). A number of publications suggest that the introduction and establishment of the National Curriculum led to a loss of awareness of equal opportunities issues or to a highjacking of equal opportunities by a narrow focus on boys' underachievement (Myers 2000).

Prior to the advent of the National Curriculum, a number of teachers and researchers had attempted, mainly through feminist-inspired interventions, to reduce sex-specific behaviours in pupil actions in early years and primary science and technology (see chapters in Browne 1991). In Scotland, Helene Witcher (1985) had looked at strategies that nursery and infant teachers could adopt to counter the effects of sexism in the classroom. She found considerable variation among her sample of teachers in the extent to which her suggestion that they problematize and tackle sex-specific behaviour was taken on board. A nursery teacher, for example,

> had great reservations about the issue of intervention. Her whole training and experience had been based on the philosophy of 'free play' and the thought of hauling the boys out of the big climbing blocks to try something else and encouraging the girls there instead, caused her considerable concern.
>
> (Witcher 1985: 99–101)

With a similar philosophy, John Siraj-Blatchford and Jeremy Loud (1990) worked on an anti-sexist and anti-racist science project between a primary school and one of the secondary schools that it fed. A process science and problem-solving approach was adopted. The flavour of the intervention, and some of its consequences are best illustrated by an extended quote:

> Following a discussion of world energy demand and supply trends the pupils were invited to take part in a role play. The role of one of the groups was living in a poor country which had a lot of natural resources. They had to walk for up to six hours a day just to collect twigs for burning. Another group took on the role of old age pensioners in Britain, who found it hard to pay their energy bills. A group chose to represent the group of people who wanted fast cars that use a lot of petrol and another group ran a firm that used large amounts of

energy but did not want to spend money to 'Save It' with insulation. Another group pretended to live in East Asia and wanted to build factories to make washing machines and other things that would improve their standard of living. Others lived in a country that still had a lot of oil, although they did not have many factories and did not need to heat their homes. The pupils were given an information sheet summarizing some of the areas covered by the project and were invited to prepare an argument on behalf of their interest group. The ensuing discussion was excellent. The groups were finally instructed to compromise and come up with some policies acceptable to the majority. In every case the pupils chose price increases combined with state help for those in need. They all emphasized the need for everyone to save energy and two of the three groups even suggested that redistributive trade agreements were needed.

(Siraj-Blatchford and Loud 1990: 104–5)

One technique used to examine the extent to which pupils in science lessons see science as a gendered activity has been to ask them to draw a scientist. The drawings are then examined to see whether pupils (girls and boys examined separately) tend to draw scientists as male or female, white or black, in laboratories or in other settings, etc. It has been suggested that the images produced are becoming less stereotypical, show less gender bias and are more realistic (Matthews 1996). However, a subsequent study with a much larger sample size has concluded that between 1990 and 1996 primary pupil perceptions have not changed significantly (Newton and Newton 1998).

In the rest of this chapter I aim to do three things:

- examine the extent to which science is objective, neutral and value-free;
- discuss what a critical science education might be like that took seriously feminist scholarship and issues of ethnicity and social class;
- make some concrete suggestions for primary science teaching.

Is science objective, neutral and value-free?

The question of the nature of scientific knowledge, including the extent to which it is or is not value-free, is still a topic of heated debate among philosophers of science and science educators (see for example Chalmers 1999; Ziman 2000; Donnelly 2002). Even if we were to side-step this particular debate and accept a characterization of science as open-minded, universalist, disinterested and communal (Merton 1973), it would remain the case that all scientific knowledge is formulated within particular social contexts (e.g. Fuller

1997). At the very least, then, this means that the topics on which scientists work – and so the subject matter of science itself – to some extent reflect the interests, motivations and aspirations both of the scientists that carry out such work and of those who fund them. There is no doubt that the majority, almost certainly the great majority, of the funding provided for scientists, both currently and for some considerable time past, has been provided with the hope/ expectation that particular applied ends will be met. These might be the production of a new vaccine, the development of a new crop variety, the synthesis of a novel chemical dye, the construction of a better missile detection system, and so on.

The point is that values are inevitably and inexorably conflated with science in most cases. Both the scientists and those who fund them hope that production of a new vaccine will lead to more lives being saved (presumed to be a good thing), that the development of a new crop variety will lead to increased food yields (presumed to be a good thing), that the synthesis of a novel chemical dye will lead to greater cash flows, increased profits, improved customer satisfaction or increased employment (all presumed to be good things), that the construction of a better missile detection system will lead to increased military security (presumed to be a good thing) and so on. In each of these cases, the science is carried out for a purpose. Purposes can be judged normatively; that is they may be good or bad. Indeed, just beginning to spell out some of the intended or presumed goods (increased crop yields, increased military security, etc.) alerts us to the fact that perhaps there are other ways of meeting these ends or, indeed, that perhaps these ends are not unquestionably the goods that may have been assumed (Reiss 1999).

It can further be argued that the separation of science from values in general, and ethical considerations in particular, is a relatively recent, Western and secular phenomenon (cf. Haidar 1997; Cobern 1998). For example, Islamic science has been described as a science whose processes and methodologies incorporate the spirit of Islamic values (Sardar 1989). Early classifications of Islamic science included metaphysics, within which was knowledge of noncorporeal beings, leading finally to the knowledge of the Truth, that is, of God, one of whose names is the Truth (Nasr 1987). To this day Islamic science 'takes upon a more holistic human-centred approach that is grounded in values that promote social justice, public welfare and responsibility towards the environment' (Loo 1996: 285).

I would argue that much of school science, and not just in the UK but worldwide, is still too narrow in terms of what is covered and how it is treated in science lessons (Reiss 2002). Encouragingly, the recent history of many school science curricula has been a widening in their content and aims in a number of ways. However, this broadening of science education is piecemeal and more likely to be found at secondary than at primary level. Indeed, the advent in England and Wales of the National Curriculum has meant that since

1989, primary pupils, for all that they are now often taught more science than previously, are taught a narrow version of it. As I noted in my feedback to the Qualifications and Curriculum Authority (QCA), having agreed to comment on its draft scheme of work in science for Key Stages 1 and 2 (subsequently published as Qualifications and Curriculum Authority 1998), 'The science here is rather conventional in that, for example, there is very little about gender, multicultural issues and the history of science.' (Reiss 1998: 2).

What might a critical science education be like?

Gaell Hildebrand (2001) has argued in favour of what she terms 'critical activism'. She urges that there should be both participation in science (doing science) and participation in debates about science (challenging science). Elsewhere I have argued that science education should aim for social justice (Reiss 2003), where social justice focuses on the right treatment of others and the fair distribution of resources or opportunities. So what might be the characteristics of a critical science education? I suggest there are two essential ones – one to do with pupils and one to do with science.

There is a diversity of pupils

A critical science education would take account of pupil diversity. This point is not specific to science education but holds true for the education of all pupils. Pupils differ with regard to a very wide range of variables including socio-economic class, gender, ethnicity, preferred learning styles and the presence/absence of distinctive interests/disinterests and abilities/disabilities. Faced with such a litany, and a class of just around 30 pupils, it is hardly surprising that one of two tactics may suggest themselves. First, a busy teacher may rely, whether or not they admit it, on a handful of generalizations, such as 'boys are more likely to ask questions out loud than are girls' and 'Asian pupils are less boisterous than African Caribbean pupils'. Second, the same or another busy teacher may simply strive to 'treat all pupils as individuals'.

There is much to commend in both these approaches. There is a certain truth in many of the generalizations that teachers make about different pupil groups, even if teachers are more likely to hesitate nowadays to voice such stereotypes. And there is much to be said in treating all pupils as individuals. However, there are difficulties with both approaches. One obvious problem with the first approach is that even if some generalizations prove valid (at least in some lessons with certain teachers) when talking about the *average* behaviour of members of one group when compared with another (e.g. boys are more likely than girls to call out), there are almost always exceptions at the level of *individuals* (some girls call out more than the average boy and some boys never call out). Indeed, my prediction would be that quantitative analyses would usually show that only a minority of within-group variation can be accounted for statistically by such between-group differences.

A related danger in the first approach is that we see pupils as members of groups and assume that they will behave as such; a typical and frequent example is that many teachers tolerate different amounts of undesired calling out and movement around the class from different categories of pupils. This is perceived (with more than a certain logic) as unfair by some pupils. A further related danger is that pupils start to behave as expected. If I expect girls to be conscientious at physical science but not to show especial flair or insight at it, such an expectation (from a powerful being like a teacher) shapes and may well become the reality. In the particular context of racial inequality (but the argument holds generally) it has been pointed out that:

> Emphasising *difference* in attainment between groups can be part of a necessary analysis of inequalities in educational outcomes. However, care should be taken that such an approach does not lead to hierarchy of ethnic minorities based on assumptions of inherent ability.
>
> (Gillborn and Mirza 2000: 7)

There is, though, a danger in simply trying to treat each pupil as an individual and that is that a busy teacher with a large number of pupils may become swamped and end up treating pupils inequitably more or less in relation to pupil demand (Reiss 2000a). There is much to be said for pupils setting the agenda in lessons but there is much too to be said for teachers controlling the overall framework within which lessons take place. Pupils do not arrive at lessons the same as one another. Quite the reverse. They arrive with years of their lives already lived, shaped by themselves, their families and the wider influences of society. The role of a teacher concerned with equity is not meekly to acquiesce with this state of affairs but to be prepared, where necessary, to improve it.

If we take gender, ethnicity and social class as three of the major possible correlates of differences in educational outcome, we find that more research is done on – and far more attention paid in the popular media to – gender than ethnicity or social class. There may be several reasons for this. For one thing, it is far easier (i.e. quicker and more valid) to assign children to the categories of 'female' or 'male' – though even this categorization is not entirely unproblematic (Gilbert 2001) – than to assign them to various categories used for ethnicity and social class. In addition, categorizing people by gender is seen by many as 'safer' (*sensu* politically less problematic) than by ethnicity or social class.

And yet in England and Wales gender very probably explains (in a statistical sense) far less of the variation in education attainment than do ethnicity

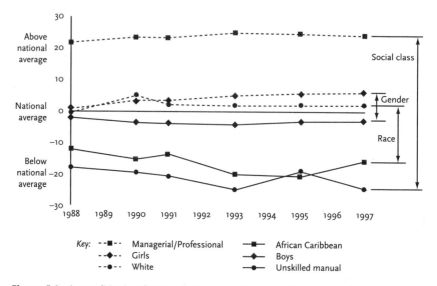

Figure 5.1 Inequalities in educational attainment by social class, race and gender as measured by the percentage of students gaining five or more GCSEs at grade C or above in England and Wales from 1988 to 1997 (from Gillborn and Mirza 2000).

Source: Youth Cohort Study (all pupils)

and social class. This is illustrated by Figure 5.1, which shows from 1988 to 1997, relative to the national average for each year, the performance at age 16 of:

- girls and boys
- white and African Caribbean pupils
- pupils from unskilled manual families and pupils from managerial/ professional families.

In each case the measure is the number of GCSEs at grade C and above. In 1997, the most recent year for which such data are available, the gap is 9 per cent for gender; exactly twice this, 18 per cent, for white versus African Caribbean pupils; and over five times this, 49 per cent, for pupils from unskilled manual families versus those from managerial/professional ones.

There is a diversity of sciences

The popular view of what science is and how it proceeds probably goes something like this:

> Science consists of a body of knowledge about the world. The facts that comprise this knowledge are derived from accurate observations

and careful experiments that can be checked by repeating them. As time goes on, scientific knowledge steadily progresses.

The advance of science then consists of scientists discovering eternal truths that exist independent of them and of the cultural context in which these discoveries are made. All areas of life are presumed amenable to scientific inquiry. Truth is supposed to emerge unambiguously from experiment like Pallas Athene, the goddess of wisdom, springing mature and unsullied from the head of Zeus.

A clear example of the shortcomings of this view of science is provided by Jane Goodall's seminal research on chimpanzee behaviour (Reiss 1993). When Jane Goodall first arrived to study the chimpanzees on the banks of Lake Tanganyika, the game warden who took her round made a mental note that she wouldn't last more than six weeks. She has stayed for more than forty years, producing the definitive accounts of chimpanzee social organization and behaviour in her fascinating and moving books (van Lawick-Goodall 1971; Goodall 1986).

An important point about Jane Goodall is that she had no formal training in ethology (the science of animal behaviour), having trained as a secretary after leaving school. As she herself wrote 'I was, of course, completely unqualified to undertake a scientific study of animal behaviour' (van Lawick-Goodall 1971: 20). However, she spent some time with the celebrated palaeontologist Louis Leakey and his wife, Mary, on one of their annual expeditions to Olduvai Gorge on the Serengeti plains. Louis Leakey became convinced that Goodall was the person for whom he had been looking for twenty years – someone who was so fascinated by animals and their behaviour that they would be happy to spend at least two years studying chimpanzees in the wild. Leakey was particularly interested in the chimpanzees on the shore of Lake Tanganyika as the remains of prehistoric people had often been found on lake shores, and he thought it possible that an understanding of chimpanzee behaviour today might shed light on the behaviour of our Stone Age ancestors.

Goodall couldn't believe that Leakey was giving her the chance to do what she most wanted to do – watch chimpanzees in their natural habitat. She felt that her lack of training would disqualify her. But, as she later wrote:

> Louis, however, knew exactly what he was doing. Not only did he feel that a university training was unnecessary, but even that in some ways it might have been disadvantageous. He wanted someone with a mind uncluttered and unbiased by theory who would make the study for no other reason than a real desire for knowledge; and, in addition, someone with a sympathetic understanding of animal behaviour.
>
> (van Lawick-Goodall 1971: 20)

Now the point, of course, is not that Jane Goodall could approach chimpanzees with a mind 'uncluttered and unbiased by theory' but that the clutter and theory in her mind was crucially distinct from that in someone who emerged from a university course in ethology. In the 1960s one of the great heresies of academic ethology was to be anthropomorphic – to treat non-humans as if they had human attributes and feelings. That is precisely what Jane Goodall did, and it allowed fundamentally new insights into chimpanzee behaviour. A flavour of Jane Goodall's approach can be obtained by reading the following quote:

> One day, when Flo was fishing for termites, it became obvious that Figan and Fifi, who had been eating termites at the same heap, were getting restless and wanted to go. But old Flo, who had already fished for two hours, and who was herself only getting about two termites every five minutes, showed no signs of stopping. Being an old female, it was possible that she might continue for another hour at least. Several times Figan had set off resolutely along the track leading to the stream, but on each occasion, after repeatedly looking back at Flo, he had given up and returned to wait for his mother.
>
> Flint, too young to mind where he was, pottered about on the heap, occasionally dabbling at a termite. Suddenly Figan got up again and this time approached Flint. Adopting the posture of a mother who signals her infant to climb on to her back, Figan bent one leg and reached back his hand to Flint, uttering a soft pleading whimper. Flint tottered up to him at once, and Figan, still whimpering, put his hand under Flint and gently pushed him on his back. Once Flint was safely aboard, Figan, with another quick glance at Flo, set off rapidly along the track. A moment later Flo discarded her tool and followed.
>
> (van Lawick-Goodall 1971: 114–15)

Other writers at the time did not give names to their animals; nor did they use language like 'getting restless', 'wanted to go', 'set off resolutely' and 'pottered about'; nor did they impute to their subjects the ability consciously to manipulate one another.

It is possible to suppose from the above that only certain areas of science, such as the study of behaviour, are affected by the presuppositions of the individuals who carry it out. Indeed, most practising scientists are happy with the notion that this is the case. However, many sociologists of science, and myself, want to go much further than this and argue that every science inevitably reflects the interests, the values, the unconscious suppositions and the beliefs of the society that gives rise to it (Longino 1990).

What is of significance for science education, then, is that there is no single, universal, acultural science. Rather, *every* sort of science is an ethnoscience. We should not assume that all scientific thinking operates within the same paradigm or scientific method. There is no single 'right' way of doing science any more than there is a single right way of writing a novel, proving Pythagoras' theorem, studying gender or undertaking any other creative and knowledge-generating activity. This is not, of course, to mean that all attempts to do science, write novels, prove Pythagoras' theorem or study gender are of equal validity. Every discipline has standards of truth verification. These may be imperfect but they cannot be abandoned – my paintings are simply not of the same quality as those of Raphael's and Mondrian's, however difficult it is to define quality in the visual arts.

Concrete suggestions for primary science teaching

Believe that you can make a difference

Theory is good but it is of little practical value unless it is used to change things. A number of studies have looked at classroom strategies for reducing stereo-typical gender constructions among girls and boys in primary schools. Francis *et al.* (2002) provide a thorough review of the literature for mixed-sex UK primary schools. They conclude that mixed-sex and single-sex groupings can each be effective, depending on the age of the pupils and other circumstances. Single-sex settings seem to be effective when the aim is to increase the self-confidence of girls, encourage their experimentation with non-gender-traditional activities, and help boys tackle aspects of undesirable masculine attitudes and behaviours. Mixed-sex groups may be more effective in encouraging cross-gender friendships, reducing gendered curriculum preferences (particularly with younger pupils), and tackling stereotypical attitudes and behaviours through discussion and awareness of the perspectives of the opposite sex (see also Matthews 2002). It seems as though both single- and mixed-sex grouping strategies can have similar desirable effects. To me this suggests that what may be of most importance is a commitment to the achievement of equity on the part of the teacher (preferably the whole school) rather than the particular classroom tactics adopted. Carrie Paechter (1998) provides a careful and historically-informed discussion of the arguments for and against sex-specific strategies in education, including the use of single-sex and mixed-sex classes for physical education (PE) and design and technology (D&T).

As noted earlier, a number of researchers have got pupils to draw what they think a scientist looks like. Lyn Harrison found that when she asked her Year 4 class 'What is science all about?' two of the conclusions her pupils came up with were:

- best scientists are old men with white coats and moustaches;
- they study a lot and are usually over 60.

(Harrison and Matthews 1998: 22)

In collaboration with Brian Matthews, Lyn Harrison began a study with her class to find out whether such stereotypes could be countered. The children were given worksheets on:

- Mae Jemison – first black female astronaut;
- Louis Latimer – black scientist who assisted in the development of the light bulb and invented improved filaments and bulbs;
- Jocelyn Bell Burnell – astronomer who worked at the Royal Observatory, developed theories on pulsars and quasars, but failed exams at school;
- Elizabeth Garrett Anderson – first woman in Britain to qualify as a doctor;
- Marion North – Victorian botanist who travelled the world and painted plants. Her pictures fill a house in Kew Gardens;
- Charles Drew – black scientist who pioneered blood transfusion.

Nearly three months after the teaching, each child was asked to draw two scientists who were working. The children were now more likely to draw female scientists, black scientists and scientists cooperating. For further examples of such case histories for use at primary level see Peacock (1991), Reiss (1993) and Thorp *et al.* (1994).

Keep in mind the possibility of a difference between equity and equality

Since the 1980s there has been a profusion of scholarship about gender issues in science education. At first such writings tried to address the perceived problem of too few women going into science, especially the physical sciences, by suggesting that science curricula should contain more girl-friendly topics, such as growing crystals (in chemistry) and the electronics of domestic machines (in physics). With the benefit of hindsight, it is now thought that such approaches, and many of the others undertaken in the 1980s, focused too narrowly on attempts to alter the option and career choices made by young women (see Byrne 1993; Henwood 1996; Barton 1998).

Research then shifted to the nature of pedagogy and to the effects of girls and boys on each other's learning and attitudes towards certain topics in science (e.g. Morgan 1989). It has increasingly been recognized how science texts may present different, biased messages about what it is to be female and what it is to be male and how teachers may differentially reward and react to students depending on their gender (e.g. Guzzetti and Williams 1996). While much of this work has simply emphasized the extent to which female pupils are (whether consciously or not) discriminated against, psychologists have explored the extent to which males and females have different ways of knowing.

Such work is controversial as one important strand of feminism, of course, has been to argue that there are no essential differences between men and women, only differences that result from our having been brought up in patriarchal societies. Nevertheless, the classic work by Gilligan (1982) has made it easier for educators to explore what might be the consequences of there being sex-specific differences in cognitive style (e.g. Paechter 1998).

John Head (1996) argues that there are four safe generalizations that can on average be made:

- Females tend to embed information in its context; males tend to extract it from its context.
- Females are more reflective; males more impulsive.
- When something goes wrong, females are more likely to blame themselves; males to locate the blame elsewhere.
- Females are more likely to cooperate; males to compete.

As stressed earlier in the discussion about any generalizations concerning groups of pupils, there are many exceptions to such statements. There are girls who have a penchant for analytical rather than synthetic thinking; there are boys who blame themselves. Nevertheless, any experienced teacher is likely to recognize the considerable truth in such generalizations. The question is, what should we do with them (Reiss 2000b)?

Take, for example, the first of Head's points, that females tend to embed information in its context while males tend to extract it from its context. Head argues that there are times in science when one needs to extract information from its context and there are times when one needs to embed it in its context. In other words, we may conclude that both extracting and embedding are skills that are of value in science. It may well be that an individual pupil naturally gravitates to one of these as a preferred style but each is of value and needs to be taught. Such an approach should enable all pupils to have their learning developed without any of them feeling that science is alien to them. Pupils could also be helped to recognize that people differ in their preferred learning styles, that sometimes it is fine to stick with learning in the style that suits you, and that sometimes there is value in learning in a different way. Pupils could also be taught that one of the reasons why it is often a good idea for people to work in groups is so that their skills and styles of working complement one another.

Strive for fair assessment

It is probably impossible to come up with a single assessment instrument that is universally fair to all pupils. For example, gender bias is accentuated by having science tests that consist only of answers requiring continuous prose (which generally favours girls) or contain only multiple choice items (which generally favours boys). The best practice is probably to adopt a mix of assessment procedures. Care also needs to be taken when setting and marking homework. While it is excellent practice to enable pupils to make use of their home environments, tasks that require access to books or home computers may severely disadvantage low income families.

A more subtle problem is that valid contributions may not always be recognized. In one notable instance researched by Patricia Murphy, pupils aged 8 to 15 years were given the task of designing boats to go around the world:

> The pupils' designs covered a wide range but there were striking differences between those of boys and girls. The majority of the boats designed by primary or lower secondary school boys were powerboats or battleships of some kind or another. The detail the boys included varied but generally there was elaborate weaponry and next to no living facilities. Other features included detailed mechanisms for movement, navigation and waste disposal. The girls' boats were generally cruisers with a total absence of weaponry and a great deal about living quarters and requirements, including food supplies and cleaning materials (notably absent from the boys' designs). Very few of the girls' designs included any mechanistic detail.
>
> (Murphy 1991: 120)

It was clear that if a teacher had in mind that what was crucial was the mechanical ability to go round the world, then the girls' designs would do less well. Related to this is the Pygmalion effect, that is, teachers tend to give work higher marks if it is from pupils whom they expect to get high marks. Experiments have shown that science scripts with boys' names on them are frequently marked significantly higher than identical scripts with girls' names on them (Spear 1984). (One hopes that this would no longer be the case but I am unaware of research on this.)

Help pupils to broaden their understanding of science and to critique it

Will Letts urges that 'In science class, not only can a variety of texts be examined and deconstructed, but the activities and experiments that constitute the "doing" of science can also be interrogated as part of the science lessons' (Letts 2001: 270).

I agree. To try and flesh this out, I end this chapter with some suggestions about how pupils might learn about the topic of 'materials' in primary science. Of course, this is meant to be seen as one way, not *the* way, of learning about the topic!

- Identify the different materials in the classroom. Devise a key to identify these different materials. (Employ the full range of senses, e.g.
  wood and metal sound different when struck. There is no single best
  way to make a key; dichotomous keys are useful but so are other
  types.)
- A blindfolded child standing barefoot on tiles of various materials can
  try to guess what they are and choose which one they prefer. Pupils
  can then think what sorts of tiles are used for bathroom and kitchen
  floors and why these may be different. (Done sensitively, this can be a
  positive experience for any blind or partially sighted children who
  will be used to this sort of activity in real life. Different cultures have
  different flooring materials. Some of the reasons for these differences
  will be due to differences in climate and the availability of materials;
  others will be due to aesthetic considerations and further cultural
  aspects, such as whether shoes are worn in kitchens and in
  bathrooms.)
- Research the range of materials used for making homes. Why are different materials used? (Availability, different materials have different
  properties, culture, etc.)
- Investigate the strengths of different types of fabric. How stretchy are
  they? The insulation of a beaker of warm water can be studied and
  related to clothing worn in cold weather. What other reasons determine the sorts of clothes we wear? (Include clothes worn by people
  with distinctive jobs, e.g. fire fighters, religious ministers. Pupils can
  be shown, if they don't already know, how to weave and knit. If they
  get really enthusiastic you can keep silk worms, grow cotton and flax
  and visit sheep at shearing time.)
- Make different types of paper including recycled paper. Why do
  people recycle paper? (This leads into environmental education, sus-
  tainability and ethics.)
- Use natural (e.g. from onions, grass and red cabbage) and artificial
  dyes to dye cloth. (Hours of fun. Also, think about colour from the
  plant's point of view. What's the point in red cabbage being red, grass
  green and bluebells blue? The 'right' answers aren't as important as
  pupils coming up with a variety of possible answers – hypotheses –
  and devising thought experiments, à la Einstein, that would allow
  them, if they had the necessary equipment and other resources, to test
  these answers.)
- Investigate the properties of clay (e.g. permeability and hardness)
  before and after firing. Make coil pots and fire them outside in the
  pupils' own sawdust-burning kiln. (A kiln can be made from ordinary
  bricks without mortar, covered by an iron lid. Every child should

make a pot while at primary school. Pottery preserved in archaeo-logical sites has possibly told us more about people in prehistoric times than anything else. Ceramics is both a craft and an art; in some cultures it is the preserve of women, in some of men, in others of both sexes.)

- Relate jewellery design and manufacture to the properties of different materials. (Some metals tarnish quickly, others don't. Some metals are very hard and have high melting points which makes them more difficult to work; others are soft and have melting points. Some metals are difficult to extract from ores in the ground; others can be extracted more easily or, in the case of gold, exist raw in a pure state. Visit a museum to see the historical uses of different materials for jewellery. Notice how in previous times and in many other cultures the decor-ation we see in current Western jewellery was also found on many household objects, in weaponry and other artefacts.)
- Devise and carry out an experiment to see whether sand, peat or gar-den soil provides the best germination and growing conditions for plants. (Extend into whether we should be using peat in this way or conserving peat bogs.)

Conclusion

Once it is kept in mind that good science is all about diversity and it is believed that no category of pupils should do less well at school science than any other category, a teacher of primary science can do a tremendous amount of social good. In addition, pupils will learn a richer form of science and will be more likely to enjoy it and do well at it. Feel free to email me at m.reiss@ioe.ac.uk and tell me how it goes.

References

Barton, A. C. (1998) *Feminist Science Education*. New York: Teachers College Press.

Browne, N. (ed.) (1991) *Science and Technology in the Early Years*. Milton Keynes: Open University Press.

Byrne, E. M. (1993) *Women and Science: The Snark Syndrome*. London: Falmer Press.

Chalmers, A. F. (1999) *What is this Thing called Science?* 3rd edn. Buckingham: Open University Press.

Cobern, W. W. (ed.) (1998) *Socio-cultural Perspectives on Science Education: An Inter-national Dialogue*. Dordrecht: Kluwer.

Donnelly, J. F. (2002) Instrumentality, hermeneutics and the place of science in the school curriculum, *Science and Education*, 11: 135–53.

Francis, B. (2000) *Boys, Girls and Achievement: Addressing the Classroom Issues.* London: RoutledgeFalmer.

Francis, B., Skelton, C. and Archer, L. (2002) A systematic review of classroom strategies for reducing stereotypical gender constructions among girls and boys in mixed-sex UK primary schools (EPPI-Centre Review), *Research Evidence in Education Library*, Issue 1. London: Evidence for Policy and Practice Information and Co-ordinating Centre, Institute of Education, University of London. Available at http://eppi.ioe.ac.uk/ (accessed 8 October 2002).

Fuller, S. (1997) *Science*. Buckingham: Open University Press.

Gilbert, J. (2001) Science and its 'Other': looking underneath 'woman' and 'science' for new directions in research and science education, *Gender and Education*, 13(3): 291–305.

Gillborn, D. and Mirza, H.S. (2000) *Educational Inequality: Mapping Race, Class and Gender – A Synthesis of Research Evidence, HMI 232.* London: Office for Standards in Education. Available at www.ofsted.gov.uk (accessed 8 October 2002).

Gilligan, C. (1982) *In a Different Voice: Psychological Theory and Women's Development.* Cambridge, MA: Harvard University Press.

Goodall, J. (1986) *The Chimpanzees of Gombe: Patterns of Behavior.* Cambridge, MA: Belknap Press of Harvard University Press.

Guzzetti, B. J. and Williams, W.O. (1996) Gender, text, and discussion: examining intellectual safety in the science classroom, *Journal of Research in Science Teaching*, 33: 5–20.

Haidar, A.H. (1997) Arab prospective science teachers' world view: presuppositions towards nature, *International Journal of Science Teaching*, 19: 1093–109.

Harrison, L. and Matthews, B. (1998) Are we treating science and scientists fairly? *Primary Science Review*, 51: 22–5.

Head, J. (1996) Gender identity and cognitive style, in P. F. Murphy and C. V. Gipps (eds) *Equity in the Classroom: Towards Effective Pedagogy for Girls and Boys.* London: Falmer Press and Paris: UNESCO.

Henwood, F. (1996) WISE choices? Understanding occupational decision-making in a climate of equal opportunities for women in science and technology, *Gender and Education*, 8(2): 199–214.

Hildebrand, G. M. (2001) Con/testing learning models. Paper presented to the Annual Meeting of the National Association for Research in Science Teaching, St Louis, 25–28 March.

Letts, W. (2001) When science is strangely alluring: interrogating the masculinist and heteronormative nature of primary school science, *Gender and Education*, 13(3): 261–74.

Longino, H.E. (1990) *Science as Social Knowledge: Values and Objectivity in Scientific Inquiry.* Princeton, NJ: Princeton University Press.

Loo, S.P. (1996) The four horsemen of Islamic science: a critical analysis, *International Journal of Science Education*, 18: 285–94.

Lunn, S. (2002) 'What we think we can safely say . . .': primary teachers' views of the nature of science, *British Educational Research Journal*, 28(5): 649–72.

Martino, W. and Meyenn, B. (eds) (2001) *What About the Boys? Issues of Masculinity in Schools*. Buckingham: Open University Press.

Matthews, B. (1996) Drawing scientists, *Gender and Education*, 8(2): 231–43.

Matthews, B. (2002) Why is emotional literacy important to science teachers? *School Science Review*, 84(306): 97–103.

Merton, R. (1973) *The Sociology of Science*. Chicago, IL: University of Chicago Press.

Morgan, V. (1989) Primary science – gender differences in pupils' responses, *Education 3–13*, 17(2): 33–7.

Murphy, P. (1991) Gender differences in pupils' reactions to practical work, in B.E. Woolnough (ed.) *Practical Science: The Rule and Reality of Practical Work in School Science*. Milton Keynes: Open University Press.

Myers, K. (ed.) (2000) *Whatever Happened to Equal Opportunities in Schools? Gender Equality Initiatives in Education*. Buckingham: Open University Press.

Nasr, S.H. (1987) *Science and Civilisation in Islam*, 2nd edn. Cambridge: Islamic Texts Society.

Newton, L.D. and Newton, D.P. (1998) Primary children's conceptions of science and the scientist: is the impact of a National Curriculum breaking down the stereotype? *International Journal of Science Education*, 20: 1137–49.

Paechter, C.F. (1998) *Educating the Other: Gender, Power and Schooling*. London: Falmer Press.

Peacock, A. (ed.) (1991) *Science in Primary Schools: The Multicultural Dimension*. Basingstoke: Macmillan Education.

Qualifications and Curriculum Authority (QCA) (1998) *Science: A Scheme of Work for Key Stages 1 and 2*. London: QCA.

Reiss, M.J. (1993) *Science Education for a Pluralist Society*. Milton Keynes: Open University Press.

Reiss, M.J. (1998) Unpublished fax to Rachel McNeela, QCA, 28 April.

Reiss, M.J. (1999) Teaching ethics in science, *Studies in Science Education*, 34: 115–40.

Reiss, M.J. (2000a) *Understanding Science Lessons: Five Years of Science Teaching*. Buckingham: Open University Press.

Reiss, M.J. (2000b) Science in society or society in science? in P. Warwick and R. Sparks Linfield (eds) *Science 3–13: The Past, the Present and Possible Futures*. London: RoutledgeFalmer.

Reiss, M.J. (2002) Reforming school science education in the light of pupil views and the boundaries of science, *School Science Review*, 84(307): 71–7.

Reiss, M.J. (2003) Science education for social justice, in C. Vincent (ed.) *Social Justice, Education and Identity*. London: RoutledgeFalmer.

Sardar, Z. (1989) *Explorations in Islamic Science*. London: Mansell.

Siraj-Blatchford, J. and Loud, J. (1990) A joint primary/secondary integrated science scheme, in E. Tutchell (ed.) *Dolls and Dungarees*. Milton Keynes: Open University Press.

Skelton, C. (2001) *Schooling the Boys: Masculinities and Primary Education*. Buckingham: Open University Press.

Spear, M.G. (1984) The biasing influence of pupil sex in a science marking exercise, *Research in Science and Technological Education*, 2: 55–60.

Thorp, S., Deshpande, P. and Edwards, C. (eds) (1994) *Race, Equality and Science Teaching*. Hatfield: ASE.

van Lawick-Goodall, J. (1971) *In the Shadow of Man*. Glasgow: Collins.

Witcher, H. (1985) Personal and professional: a feminist approach, in J. Whyte, R. Deem, L. Kant and M. Cruickshank (eds) *Girl Friendly Schooling*. London: Routledge.

Ziman, J. (2000) *Real Science: What it is, and What it Means*. Cambridge: Cambridge University Press.

6   Gender and special educational needs

Shereen Benjamin

Introduction

The education of children considered to have special educational needs (SEN) has received a good deal of attention since the early 1980s. In England, the introduction of the first Code of Practice for SEN in 1994, followed by its updated version in 2002, has required schools and teachers to think about, clarify and, in many cases, enhance the provision they offer to children who are not making typical progress (DfEE 1994; DfES 2001). Recent policy moves towards the inclusion of children who would until recently have been educated in special schools, together with the requirements of the Special Educational Needs and Disability Act 2002 (which requires schools to work towards becoming fully accessible), have ensured that SEN issues remain high on the agenda. But surprisingly little attention has been paid to the ways in which SEN issues are gendered.

A recent survey of SEN provision in Organisation for Economic Co-operation and Development (OECD) countries found that boys are consist-ently over-represented amongst those pupils considered to need specialist educational provision, both in special schools and in special classes in main-stream schools (OECD 2000). This chapter starts with a brief review of this, and other, statistical evidence. But to begin to unravel the stories behind those statistics, we need to look at the links between SEN, and masculinities and femininities – what it means to be a boy or a girl – in primary and special school classrooms. The bulk of the chapter is given over to an explor-ation of how masculinities and femininities interact with understandings of 'ability', as well as with understandings around ethnicity and social class, in the complex processes through which boys and girls come to be identified as having SEN. The chapter draws on research evidence in the form of inter-views and observations with children, parents/carers and teachers in four primary schools (three inner-city and one suburban) and an inner-city special school.

Gender and SEN: what do the statistics tell us?

To almost any SEN practitioner, the answer to this question is a very obvious one. Certainly, those of us who have worked in specialist schools and other settings for any length of time have become very used to seeing girls out-numbered by boys in most of our classes. The figures confirm this. In 2000, the OECD conducted a major survey into SEN provision in its member countries (OECD 2000). The findings on gender were fairly consistent across all the countries surveyed. Girls accounted for between 30 per cent and 40 per cent of special school pupils, with boys being a significant majority: in the UK 32.2 per cent of special school pupils were girls as against 67.8 per cent boys. The gen-der ratios in special classes in mainstream schools were very similar. When it came to the gender ratios of pupils with SEN in mainstream classes, the UK figure was identical at 32.2 per cent girls to 67.8 per cent boys, though the proportion in some countries evened out slightly, and in France, came close to an even balance at 48.4 per cent girls to 51.6 per cent boys.

When we examine the statistics further, other interesting variations come to light. In 1996, a team of researchers in England noted that the over-representation of boys in special schools and units

> is especially marked in schools for those with emotional and behavioural difficulties (6–8 times as many boys), language units (4 times) and autistic schools (2–4 times as many). Moreover, these gen-der disparities are strongly influenced by 'race': children of African Caribbean origin are over-represented in special schools and those of South Asian origin under-represented.
>
> (Daniels *et al.* 1996: 1)

In the case of schools for children considered to have emotional and behavioural difficulties (EBD), it is worth noting that there is considerable evidence that African Caribbean boys of both primary and secondary school age are at greater risk of exclusion (Parsons 1996; Hayden 1997; Wright *et al.* 2000; Blair 2001), and that many of these excluded children are considered to have SEN which are subsequently met in EBD schools or units. Tradition-ally, pupils of Asian origin have been less at risk of exclusion: there is evidence that this remains largely true for girls of Asian origin, whilst the proportion of boys of Asian origin excluded from school is growing (Mehra 1998). Meanwhile, Scottish Office figures confirm that working-class boys are found in greater numbers in the 'less acceptable' categories of moderate learning difficulties (MLD) and EBD, whilst the non-stigmatized category of specific learning difficulties is dominated by middle-class boys (Riddell 1996).

So the statistics indicate that there is definitely a 'story' to tell about gender and SEN: the processes of SEN assessment, designation and provision cannot be considered to be gender-neutral. They also tell us that the gender and SEN story is further nuanced by other indices of difference, including those of 'race'/ethnicity and social class. Whilst the statistics can and should alert us to the fact that there is a story here, we need to look beyond the figures in order to begin to understand why SEN provision is distributed unequally across the genders, and what the consequences of that unequal distribution might be.

In order to explain the over-representation of boys amongst children considered to have SEN, we need first to think about how we understand the phenomenon of educational needs. At one extreme, we could argue that SEN are entirely biologically- and physiologically-produced. We could then argue that boys are over-represented amongst those pupils considered to have SEN because they are 'naturally like that', due, perhaps, to some at present unknown aspect of male physiology. Or, at the other end of the continuum, we could argue that SEN are entirely socially-constructed, and that boys' over-representation is due therefore to social practices and societal inequalities. Somewhere between these two extremes is an understanding that SEN have a material, organic basis which can sometimes be easy to discern, but are sometimes far from obvious. This material origin produces a range of possibilities for an individual, which then interacts with social and relational practices.

This chapter will focus mainly on the 'high incidence' category of mild to moderate learning difficulties (MLD). This category is characterized by debates as to how far these perceived learning difficulties have a material, biological origin and as to what that biological origin might be. The category also presents something of a challenge to sociologists who might prefer explanations that are entirely social (Nash 2001). The understanding I am working with here is that material factors interact with social phenomena, and that, in the end, it is unproductive to try to tease out the 'real' from the socially-constructed, though it remains vital to interrogate the consequences of SEN designation. It is an understanding that foregrounds the study of school and pupil cultures in the context of society as a whole, that requires and enables us to take account of the production of unequal relations and practices, and that helps us to consider the consequences, in school and beyond, of SEN.

How does such an understanding work in practice, and how does it help us understand the gendering of SEN? In Norway, where 70 per cent of pupils considered to have SEN are boys, Skarbrevik (2002) argues that 'the higher incidence of boys in special education during the school years is caused by an interaction between genetic or biological factors and a pedagogy that does not match the educational needs of male students' (Skarbrevik 2002: 97). In other words, he argues that boys tend to be predisposed to have SEN, and that this combines with teachers' boy-unfriendly practice to produce an over-representation of boys amongst pupils considered to have SEN. But this is far from being a plausible explanation in a UK context. It does not give us any way of coming to understand the active participation of boys in the processes through which they come to be perceived as having SEN. Nor does it take account of gender as a lived social, and not just biological, practice. What is missing is an understanding of the interaction between discourses and discursive practices – the taken-for-granted meanings and actions – of SEN with those of masculinities. Connell (1995: 71) notes that:

> Rather than attempting to define masculinity as an object (a natural character type, a behavioural average, a norm) we need to focus on the processes through which men and women conduct gendered lives. 'Masculinity', to the extent the term can be briefly defined at all, is simultaneously a place in gender relations, the practices through which men and women engage that place in gender, and the effect of those practices in bodily experience, personality and culture.

Children with SEN conduct gendered lives, as do all children. The statistics tell us that there is a story to tell about the processes through which children considered to have SEN conduct particular versions of gendered lives. This story has two aspects. First, how does the gendering of school and pupil cultures produce a system through which boys are disproportionately considered to have SEN, and through which the extra resources associated with SEN are allocated disproportionately to them? Second how does the designation as having SEN constrain or create a specific range of possibilities within which children can conduct gendered lives?

Masculinities and SEN

Ryan spent most of his primary years in a mainstream school, transferring to the special sector at the beginning of Year 5 (9–10-year-olds). He brought with him an unhappy history of failing to make discernible academic progress, and of failing to make friends with other children as he went up the mainstream school. By the end of his first half term in a small all-age special school, he declared himself to be much happier, and began to make academic progress, albeit not at a typical rate. His mother described how she made sense of the improvements in Ryan's attitude towards schooling:

> We didn't want to put Ryan into a special school, but now that he's here, our family life, well, our family life has changed beyond recognition, he's like a changed boy . . . In [mainstream] school, all he could think about was playtime, it was a complete nightmare for him, you know, he couldn't make the football team, let's face it, he couldn't

begin to even kick the ball or even know which goalpost to aim for, and his playtimes were a complete nightmare, so he never wanted to go to school. It wasn't even that they bullied him, the teachers there were very good, they didn't allow bullying, it was just, I don't know, in the atmosphere somehow, between the children . . . He obviously wasn't a clever boy, not in the usual sense of the word, and the boys were either clever or good at football, it had to be one or the other, and poor Ryan, well, he just didn't fit in. There was another child in his class, she was a sweet little thing, Ryan used to like her, they sat on the same table, and they both went to [the Learning Support Unit] together, and she used to play with the little infants at playtime, but Ryan could hardly do that, could he, a boy his size? So it really dented his confidence, but now that he's here [in the special school] he's much better, he even tells me he joins in with football at dinner time sometimes.

(Interview, Greyhound School)

It is no coincidence that Ryan's mother attributes Ryan's more positive attitude largely to his inclusion in playground football. Sport in general, and football in particular, is one of the foremost sites for the production of masculinities in English primary schools. It is on the football field (or, in most urban schools, the allotted corner of the tarmac playground) that boys struggle over their hold on dominant versions of masculinity (Renold 1997; Gard 2001; Skelton 2001). The version of masculinity being struggled over is one of physical strength and skill, where that physical strength is associated with the considerable material rewards of top footballers, with the ability to win fights, and with heterosexual prowess and attractiveness to girls (Epstein and Johnson 1998; Benjamin 2001). As Thorne (1993) and others have noted, failure to excel in playground football is associated, for even very young boys, with 'gayness', and seen as the antithesis of successful masculinity. This failure is particularly marked for boys with SEN. Thorne observed that very successful boys – those who have many resources 'in the bank' on which to draw – can afford to be least invested in continual demonstrations of 'macho' masculinity, since their hold on success is secure. The opposite is true for many boys with SEN. Like Ryan, they cannot lay claim to many of the traditional markers of success. A group of boys in Year 6 (10–11-year-olds) at Ryan's special school described the importance of football:

The boys talked at length about the material rewards of 'winning'. Alex described the opulent lifestyle that he saw as the justifiable reward for success on the football pitch, contrasting this with the abject poverty of 'failure'. There was, for him, no intermediate position. For all three of the boys, the 'winner' indeed gained everything – money, acclaim and security – while the 'loser' was left with nothing . . . Inclusion was a priority mentioned by all the boys. Conflating football success, financial success and inclusion, Joe remarked that 'If you score the most goals, everyone will want you to be in their team, and you'll earn loads of money and have a big house and car'. Respect was also part of the overall picture. Ennis said that, 'When you're the best in the team no-one will laugh at you and call you names and say you're rubbish . . . Because they'll want to be your friends'.

(Benjamin 1997: 58)

The point here is that a constellation of practices around gender and SEN have made success in football, linked to very absolute notions of 'winning and losing', particularly desirable to these boys. They are boys for whom other markers of success have proved inaccessible: they have failed to make the normative academic progress required of primary school pupils, and their experience has all too often been of formal and informal exclusion from classroom and playground activities. Football is one of the few activities that they can make theirs, and that can allow them to dream of current and future success. The flip side of their investment in football is that the 'cultural package' that goes with it is also associated with aggression, homophobia and hetero/sexism (Epstein 1997; Kenway and Fitzclarence 1997). This can lead to a cycle in which boys' investment in football leads to or reinforces their disconnection from schoolwork, and channels them towards disruptive behaviour. Such attitudes and behaviour in turn reinforce their designation within SEN discourses, which may in turn have the unintended effect of re-inscribing them as academic 'failures'.

Connell outlines four versions of masculinity which he calls hegemonic, subordinate, complicit and marginalized (Connell 1995: 76–81). Of particular interest here are the first two of these. It is hegemonic masculinity that is most directly associated with male power: the men and boys who best embody hegemonic masculinity typically occupy positions of power, prestige and material wealth. Subordinate masculinities are associated with direct forms of oppression. In particular, homosexuality – which, Connell argues, is strongly related to femininity – is the 'dumping ground' of hegemonic masculinities, and the demonstration of distance from perceived gayness is crucial for men and boys who are struggling to access the power associated with hegemonic masculinities. As I will argue in more detail in the next section, SEN, associated with neediness, is also associated with vulnerability and femininity. As Ryan's mother remarked, he was not in a position to go and play with the infants in his previous school, unlike his sweet little girl classmate. To have done so would have been unthinkable, as it would have inscribed him as feminine, and positioned him firmly within the subordinate version of masculinity. The Year 6 boys at Ryan's school had developed a contamination chasing game, in which the chaser would be designated as 'gay', and in which he would pass the 'gayness' on through touching someone else, the object of the game being to avoid the chaser's touch. They also routinely engaged in collective appreciation of girls they deemed to be attractive, and in collective derogation of girls deemed unattractive, often using extremely hetero/sexist language, and readily engaging in fighting over the girls of their choice. I am not arguing here that *only* boys with SEN act in this way. But these boys' inability to access the formally-sanctioned, dominant sites of male power – their failure to make the linear progress associated with the incrementally-developing boy – together with their inscription into the 'neediness' connoted by SEN, made these informal 'macho' performances particularly imperative for them.

Femininities and SEN

Femininities produce a very different set of possibilities for girls with SEN. At present, a critical literature that specifically addresses 'femininities' has not been as fully developed as has the range of critical literature on masculinities, and this is particularly true of work in the field of education and schooling. The work that does exist points to the way in which femininity has been theorized as 'that which is different from masculinity which assumes femininity as a given' (Skeggs 1997: 20). Nonetheless, it is possible to draw out from the literature models of femininities that might help us understand something of the gendered lives of girls with SEN.

Whilst it would be inappropriate to argue for the existence of dominant femininities, there are clearly some femininities that are more associated with power than others. Recent work on children as consumers (Kenway and Bullen 2001) indicates the existence of feisty, in-your-face femininities, associated with heterosexual attractiveness and the desire to consume the 'right' goods and wear the 'right' brands: in schools, this type of femininity can encompass academic achievement, since better-than-average academic performance is also associated with choices and material success in adult life (NACETT 2000). Alongside this version is a more traditional version of femininity – the decades-old stereotypical 'dumb blonde' of popular culture – where heterosexual attractiveness connotes not so much a positive life choice, but the perpetual vulnerability of needing care and protection (Walkerdine 1997; Benjamin 2002). The 'dumb blonde' is an easily recognizable stereotype, and one that draws heavily on discourses of social class as well as 'race' to position some girls and women as inherently and essentially childlike, appealing (to men), and lacking in intellectual ability of all kinds.

'Cleverness', for girls, has tended to be seen as something struggled for: where the achievements of boys who do well tend to be attributed to 'natural' brilliance, the achievements of girls have been attributed to their capacity for hard work, borne out of a desire to please (Walkerdine 1988; Rossiter 1994), and out of physical inability to access, or disinclination towards, heterosexual attractiveness. Girls at the margins of SEN can blend into the normative range of the class by positioning themselves as hardworking and diligent, and their difficulties may escape 'official' detection. But girls whose difficulties are more severe may find their room for manoeuvre severely constrained by the expectation that they will remain rather endearingly vulnerable:

> I sit with the science group. Anna is struggling . . . She asks if I will help her, and to refuse seems inhumane. She doesn't seem to like writing. She wants me to point to each word as she copies it. I get the impression that she doesn't actually need this amount of help, but it's a way of securing and retaining my attention. Every time I turn to Joe and Kofi, who are sitting next to her, she stops work. They, also, are doing very little. I try to help Joe to write a draft of his conclusion. All he then has to do is copy it out, but he doesn't do this. Instead, he starts to tease Anna. He makes fun of her, talking in a voice that is clearly supposed to be an imitation of the younger-than-eight-sounding way in which she speaks. Kofi tells him to leave Anna alone . . . I try to reconnect him with his work, but he is not having this. He calls Anna 'Sabrina the teenage witch' and she retaliates by saying that she really *will* be a witch when she grows up, and will turn him into a frog. She turns to me and asks if this is indeed a possibility – can one realistically hope to become a witch? Her question is transparently coquettish.
>
> (Fieldnotes, Year 3, Bankside Primary)

Both Anna and Joe have been identified as having SEN, and described further as having MLD. In the above extract, Anna is positioning herself squarely within a discourse of rather charming, ultra-childlike vulnerability, securing the adult help that will enable her to complete her work but also re-inscribing herself as needy of help. There is a tendency for SEN discourses in school to draw upon what has been called the 'charity/tragedy model of disability' (Barton and Oliver 1997; Allan 1999; Thomas and Loxley 2001). The charity/tragedy model, which originated in the nineteenth century but continues to influence perceptions and practices today, positions people with disabilities as the helpless objects of pity, concern and charity, and is used to legitimate their control by non-disabled people. Likewise, SEN discourses can position particular children as the passive recipients of care and control (Tomlinson 1982), though this may not be the explicit intention of the educational professionals who work with them. As Riddell notes, 'there are clear connections between the child-centred approach in special educational needs and the individual tragedy discourse identified by disability theorists' (Riddell 1996: 4).

It is interesting to think about how class and 'race', as well as gender and

SEN, are played out in the Year 3 (7–8-year-olds) vignette. Anna had turned on me such a look of pathetic helplessness when I sat at her table that I could not do anything other than pay attention to what she was saying and doing. She was able to keep my attention focused on her through strategies that made her seem younger and less able to manage than was really the case: a conundrum of independence made to look like dependence, and activity made to look like passivity. Writ large in her production was the classed and 'raced' stereotype of the 'dumb blonde': a position made readily available to Anna who happens to be blonde, working class, and small for her age. Joe and Kofi aided and abetted her in this strategy. Kofi took up a 'gentlemanly' role in relation to Joe's teasing, positioning himself as Anna's protector. Joe's teasing worked to distance him from the model of needy, vulnerable child, enabling him to resist the position of 'helpee', and also drew attention to Anna's production of herself as needy and ultra-childlike. In parodying Anna's 'babyish' voice, he made the strategy look ridiculous, and also made me want to protect Anna from him, further inscribing Anna and myself within a helper/helped relationship. When my strategy for putting an end to the teasing was unsuccessful, Anna made use of a very different kind of feminine archetype – that of the witch – that Joe had introduced into the encounter. In momentarily abandoning the dumb blonde in favour of the mysterious and powerful figure of the witch, Anna threatened to strip Joe of his masculine power by turning him into a frog. But this repositioning was short-lived, and she threw herself straight back into neediness and vulnerability, by asking me, with what seemed like deliberate childlike 'charm', whether she could really be a witch.

Something paradoxical is going on. If girls can be much more readily recognized as vulnerable and needy, and SEN discourses draw on vulnerability and neediness, why is it that girls are less likely to be identified as having SEN? Perhaps the answer to this lies partly in the fact that SEN discourses draw partly on the (feminized) notions of care and concern for the helpless, but also on the masculine notions of imposing control through a technical, managerial apparatus. Girls' expertise seems to lie in securing informal help: which can mean they access the help they need without recourse to the official channels of SEN identification and assessment, but could also mean that their difficulties 'may remain undiagnosed and invisible' (Riddell 1996), and that their access to SEN resources is unduly limited. Once identified as having SEN, however, girls find themselves all-too easily inscribed within traditional discourses of vapid and vulnerable femininities.

Addressing disparities in gender and SEN

In their study of differential SEN provision in mainstream primary schools, Daniels *et al.* note that

> Boys' learning seems to be more teacher-dependent than girls', and
> boys have various anti-learning behaviours. Girls, on the other hand,
> have a capacity collectively to 'keep out' of SEN provision by generally
> supporting each other's learning, not demanding too much of the
> teacher's time, and giving each other appropriate help.
>
> (Daniels *et al.* 1996: 3)

Daniels and colleagues go on to recommend that mainstream schools should address the disparity in SEN provision through objective assessment criteria, resulting in equal provision for equal levels of educational need. This is fine, as far as it goes. But it does raise questions about how to prioritize educational needs that cannot be measured in the same currencies. How, for example, would we quantify the needs of a child with global learning difficulties, whose proficiency at reading is roughly that expected of a child four years younger, in comparison to a child with, say, an autistic spectrum disorder, who is able to decipher print but has not yet developed the skills of making sense of what they read? Perhaps it is more useful to keep in mind the necessity of equal provision across both genders, and to develop assessment and allocation systems accordingly, but in the context of attention to the gendered nature of school, classroom and playground cultures.

This is a long-term agenda, and, whilst the development of appropriate tools and strategies for the management of SEN is important, so, too, is an understanding of the implications of masculinities and femininities in the construction of SEN. Raphael Reed (1998: 72) critiques the tendency of school effectiveness and school improvement literature to demonize the 'under-achieving boy', and argues that, instead, what is needed is a reformulation of social justice ideals that will include 'a critical focus on gendered actions and school cultures alongside a continuing debate on the nature of the curriculum'. This critical focus has to take into account the reality that SEN are produced in relation to a school system in which testing, and the achievement of externally-determined 'expected levels' (DfEE 1999), have already, to some extent, positioned children with SEN as academic failures.

This kind of critical focus can be hard to operationalize in the current climate of accountability through test results and league tables, but it is not impossible. Hilltop Junior School in the Midlands, and George Holt Primary in London (not their real names) are high-achieving schools that prioritize the inclusion of children with SEN. George Holt is specifically resourced by its local education authority to provide places for up to twelve children who have been identified as having EBD and who have been excluded from other primary schools[1]. The headteachers of both schools are passionate about a range of social justice issues, and maintain a belief in the possibility of addressing social inequalities through schooling. Both headteachers are committed to the inclusion of children for whom schooling has been a struggle, and they both share the view that this can be done without compromising 'standards': indeed, both schools are characterized by an orientation towards 'high standards', broadly conceived beyond the requirements of test results and performance management:

> Jack and Daisy are sitting on the same table, not next to each other, but near. Meg [the teacher] tells the class they can start. I'm not at all surprised when Jack's first response is to walk over to the waste-paper bin and spend ages sharpening his pencil. Daisy is alternately staring into space and swinging on her chair. The other children on the table – two girls and a boy – don't appear to be bothered by this, but get started on their own work. I begin to wonder whether Meg will have to intervene. One of the girls on the table nudges the boy, and indicates towards Jack. The boy gets up, goes over to where Jack is sharpening and re-sharpening his pencil, and offers to lend him one of his. Jack accepts, and returns to the table, where the boy shows him what to do. The two girls, who have been working together, lean over to help Daisy.
>
> (Fieldnotes, Year 5, Hilltop)

This incident, which I witnessed during my first classroom observation, turned out to be typical. Daisy and Jack are children who might, until recently, have found themselves in schools for children with MLD. They stand out fairly sharply in this mainstream classroom, as children for whom the ordinary work of the class is a struggle, and they are not always able to make sense of what is going on in the classroom. The class's literacy and numeracy targets, which are written on the board at the front of the classroom, are not accessible to Daisy and Jack, immediately positioning them as vulnerable. In many ways this is an unanswerable conundrum in primary schools, since there are activities and concepts that cannot be made meaningful to everyone. At Hilltop, this is a problem that is addressed head-on through flexible grouping policies that sometimes set children according to academic proficiency for discrete activities, and sometimes require them to work in mixed-proficiency groups. In the incident described above, and in many others I saw at Hilltop, both girls *and* boys appeared to be acting in the ways noted by Daniels and his colleagues: the giving and receiving of help seemed to be taken for granted.

Hilltop emphasizes education as a collective project, and a team enterprise, as does George Holt. Whilst neither school can completely resist 'the allure of competitive success in education which derives from [a] masculine world-view' (Potts 1997: 185), they are able to mediate this through a very active construction of themselves as learning communities. George Holt has three 'golden rules': high standards, teamwork and celebrating success. Because these three rules operate very much as an integrated whole, they go some way towards re-configuring what counts as success: they carry with them the notion that individual success counts for much more when it is shared by the community, and that if an individual within the community 'team' is prevented from being successful, then the community is the poorer. I video-taped some Year 6 lessons at George Holt, and was struck, watching the videos, by the amount of 'helping' – the pursuit of shared, collaborative success – that went on, almost unseen, and taken for granted.

> Ken tells the children to get into groups of four. There is instant noise and movement, as children negotiate their groupings. I zoom in on Stephen, who remains sitting, cross-legged, looking up and around him with a look of utter bewilderment on his face. I am somewhat surprised when Jermaine goes over to him, invites him to stand up, then puts an arm around Stephen's shoulder and negotiates for them both to join two girls. I wouldn't have been surprised if one of the high-status boys, or a girl, had looked after Stephen in this way. But I would have thought that Jermaine, who always seems to have an insecure grip on both academic and micro-cultural success, and who often acts 'macho', would have been resistant to grouping himself with a boy with SEN and two girls.
>
> (Fieldnotes, Year 6, George Holt)

George Holt Primary and Hilltop Junior both have robust SEN policies and procedures, with assessment criteria that are rigorously applied. This goes some way to ensuring gender parity in the allocation of SEN provision. Crucially, though, both schools address, on an ongoing basis, what Corbett (1999) has called 'deep culture', and this is what seems to make the difference in both schools. What they are doing is freeing up room for manoeuvre by both girls and boys: when 'help' is recast as shared pursuit of success, boys can take up helping and helped roles without consequent loss of masculine status, and girls who are struggling can access help without needing to position themselves as overly vulnerable or ultra-childlike. This is not to claim that either school has found the perfect solution. But both schools show us that, by paying attention to the gendering of SEN provision and to the gendered lives of children considered to have SEN, we can address disparities in provision and generate conditions of greater equality for children in primary schools.

Conclusion

Issues of gender are at the core of policy, practice and provision in relation to SEN. Whilst the statistical evidence shows very clearly that this is the case, little attention has been specifically focused on the intersection between SEN and gender beyond the popular notion of boys' 'underachievement'. This chapter has focused on the classroom experiences of girls and boys: it has explored both the ways in which assessment and common-sense understandings contribute to boys' over-representation amongst children considered to have SEN, and the differential implications and consequences of this over-representation. In drawing attention to masculinities and femininities as organizing categories of analysis, I have shown how common-sense understandings and their gendered implications for SEN policy, practice and provision are played out in primary and special school classrooms.

Studies of gender and SEN in the primary and special schools detailed in this chapter indicate that the reasons for, and implications of, gendered inequality are not amenable to easy resolution through simple, single solution 'quick fixes'. In two of the case-study schools, the inequalities and disparities generated for and by SEN provision were tackled head-on, through strategies that permeated the cultures of the two schools. Both schools were committed to high standards, within an environment that encompassed – but was not determined by – standard measures of academic achievement. Neither school reduced the complexities of creating a learning community to the managerial level of targets set and met: rather, they both paid attention to the ways in which girls and boys lead gendered lives, and to the ways in which those gendered lives are nuanced by issues of perceived academic ability as well as by other indices of 'difference'. The experiences of the two schools suggest that change can be made at local (school and classroom) level when staff develop an understanding of how gender and SEN shape children's classroom lives, and when they are committed to opening up room for manoeuvre for girls and boys across the perceived ability spectrum.

Note

1   The data from George Holt Primary School was gathered as part of the Inclusion in Schools Project, funded by the Open University. I am grateful to project co-directors Janet Collins, Kathy Hall, Melanie Nind and Kieron Sheehy for permission to use this data here.

References

Allan, J. (1999) *Actively Seeking Inclusion: Pupils With Special Needs in Mainstream Schools*. London: Falmer Press.

Barton, L. and Oliver, M. (eds) (1997) *Disability Studies: Past, Present and Future*. Leeds: Disability Press.

Benjamin, S. (1997) *Fantasy Football League: Boys in a Special (SEN) School Constructing and Reconstructing Masculinities*. London: Institute of Education.

Benjamin, S. (2001) Challenging Masculinities: disability and achievement in testing times, *Gender and Education*, 13(1): 39–55.

Benjamin, S. (2002) *The Micropolitics of Inclusive Education: An Ethnography*. Buckingham: Open University Press.

Blair, M. (2001) *Why Pick on Me? School Exclusion and Black Youth*. Stoke-on-Trent: Trentham.

Connell, R. W. (1995) *Masculinities*. Cambridge: Polity Press.

Corbett, J. (1999) Inclusivity and school culture: the case of special education, in J. Prosser (ed.) *School Culture*. London: Paul Chapman.

Daniels, H., Hey, V., Leonard, D. and Smith, M. (1996) *Gender and Special Needs Provision in Mainstream Schooling*. Swindon: Economic and Social Research Council.

Department for Education and Employment (DfEE) (1994) *Code of Practice on the Identification and Assessment of Special Educational Needs*. London: DfEE.

Department for Education and Employment (DfEE) (1999) *National Learning Targets for England for 2002*. Sudbury, Department for Education and Employment: HMSO.

Department for Education and Skills (DfES) (2001) *Inclusive Education: Children with special educational needs*. Statutory Guidance to Local Education Authorities, Health and Social Services in England. London: DfES.

Epstein, D. (1997) Boyz' Own Stories: masculinities and sexualities in schools, *Gender and Education*, 9(1): 105–15.

Epstein, D. and Johnson, R. (1998) *Schooling Sexualities*. Buckingham: Open University Press.

Gard, M. (2001) 'I like smashing people and I like getting smashed myself': addressing issues of masculinity in physical education and sport, in W. Martino and B. Meyenn (eds) *What About the Boys? Issues of Masculinity in Schools*. Buckingham: Open University Press.

Hayden, C. (1997) *Children Excluded from Primary School*. Buckingham: Open University Press.

Kenway, J. and Bullen, E. (2001) *Consuming Children: Education, Entertainment, Advertising*. Milton Keynes: Open University Press.

Kenway, J. and Fitzclarence, L. (1997) Masculinity, violence and schooling: challenging 'poisonous pedagogies', *Gender and Education*, 9(1): 117–33.

Mehra, H. (1998) The permanent exclusion of Asian pupils in secondary schools in central Birmingham, *Multi-Cultural Teaching*, 17(1): 42–8.

NACETT (2000) *Aiming Higher: NACETT's Report on the National Learning Targets for England and Advice on Targets Beyond 2002*. Sudbury: National Advisory Council for Education and Training Targets.

Nash, R. (2001) Class, 'ability' and attainment: a problem for the sociology of education, *British Journal of Sociology of Education*, 22(2): 189–203.

OECD (2000) *Special Needs Education: Statistics and Indicators*. Paris: Organisation for Economic Co-operation and Development, Centre for Educational Research and Innovation.

Parsons, C. (1996) Permanent exclusions from schools in the 1990s: trends, causes and responses, *Children and Society*, 10(3): 255–68.

Potts, P. (1997) Gender and membership of the mainstream, *International Journal of Inclusive Education*, 1(2): 175–87.

Raphael Reed, L. (1998) 'Zero Tolerance': gender performance and school failure, in D. Epstein, J. Elwood, V. Hey and J. Maw (eds) *Failing Boys? Issues in Gender and Underachievement*. Buckingham: Open University Press.

Renold, E. (1997) 'All they've got on their brains is football': sport, masculinity and the gendered practices of playground relations, *Sport, Education and Society* 2(1): 5–23.

Riddell, S. (1996) Gender and special educational needs, in G. Lloyd (ed.) *'Knitting Progress Unsatisfactory': Gender and Special Issues in Education*. Edinburgh: Moray House Institute of Education.

Rossiter, A. B. (1994) Chips, Coke and rock-'n'-roll: children's mediation of an invitation to a first dance party, *Feminist Review*, (46): 1–20.

Skarbrevik, K. J. (2002) Gender differences among students found eligible for special education, *European Journal of Special Needs Education*, 17(2): 97–107.

Skeggs, B. (1997) *Formations of Class and Gender*. London: Sage.

Skelton, C. (2001) *Schooling the Boys: Masculinities and Primary Education*. Buckingham: Open University Press.

Thomas, G. and Loxley, A. (2001) *Deconstructing Special Education and Constructing Inclusion*. Buckingham: Open University Press.

Thorne, B. (1993) *Gender Play: Girls and Boys in School*. New Brunswick: Rutgers University Press.

Tomlinson, S. (1982) *A Sociology of Special Education*. London: Routledge and Kegan Paul.

Walkerdine, V. (1988) *The Mastery of Reason*. Cambridge: Routledge and Kegan Paul.

Walkerdine, V. (1997) *Daddy's Girl: Young Girls and Popular Culture*. Basingstoke: Macmillan.

Wright, C., Weekes, D. and McGlaughlin, A. (2000) *'Race', Class and Gender in Exclusion from School*. London: Falmer.

7 Gendered and gendering spaces
Playgrounds in the early years

Paul Connolly

Introduction

The importance of self-directed play to young children's development is now widely accepted among early years practitioners (Moyles 1989, 1994; Blenkin and Kelly 1996b; Smidt 2002). Children are generally regarded as actively involved in their own development and to learn best when they are given the space to explore themselves and their social and physical environment at their own pace. Play represents one of the principal means through which this can be done and provides the opportunity for young children to develop a wide range of physical, social, cognitive and emotional skills (Dau 1999). Given the importance of play and the need for young children to be in control of their own learning, it is not surprising to find that there is considerable resistance to any attempt by adults to direct or control young children's play and, by extension, the playgrounds and other social spaces within which it takes place. Depending upon the particular developmental perspective ascribed to, the role of the adult is restricted either to one of facilitator (i.e. ensuring that young children have access to a range of experiences) or encourager (i.e. letting children take the lead but then providing them with the necessary and appropriate support to learn and achieve what they want to) (Marsh 1994; Smidt 2002).

When including gender into the analysis, however, the picture becomes more complex. As MacNaughton (1999) has argued, play and playgrounds are also dangerous spaces. They tend to reflect positions of power and are characterized by relations of domination and subordination. There are the more overt examples of male dominance of the playground, the exclusion of boys or girls from certain activities and the incidents of teasing and sexual harassment. However, equally importantly, research has also repeatedly drawn attention to the routine gender segregation that takes place within play and the restrictions imposed upon boys and girls by the binary and oppositional identities of masculinity and femininity that are constructed and reinforced through play (Best

1983; Thorne 1993; Kelly 1994; Connolly 1998; Skelton 2001). Play and playgrounds, therefore, not only represent dangerous spaces but can also significantly restrict and curtail girls' and boys' access to the full range of experiences and challenges available and thus, by extension, can often limit their development.

As MacNaughton (2000) has highlighted, a possible tension exists therefore between the need to recognize and protect young children's self-directed play and also the responsibility to actively intervene and challenge the types of gender relations that can often severely limit that play. It is this tension that provides the focus for this chapter. The chapter will begin by looking in a little more detail at the importance of play before setting out the particular dangers that are associated with it in relation to gender. This will be done by drawing upon examples taken from observations of 5–6-year-old children's behaviour in three different playgrounds. As will be seen, these case studies reflect a theoretical approach that emphasizes the socially constructed nature of gender and the active role that children play in constructing, maintaining and policing their gender identities. In this sense the approach taken can be located broadly within the phenomenological tradition in social research and is heavily influenced by feminist and poststructuralist work (see, for example, Davies 1989; Walkerdine and Lucey 1989; Walkerdine 1990; Thorne 1993; MacNaughton 2000).

More specifically, the theoretical approach taken departs significantly from traditional 'sex role socialization' models of gender identities in two respects. First, rather than depicting children as passive receptacles of the socialization of others, it recognizes the central role they play in the negotiation of their own sense of identity. Second, given the agency of children and thus the diverse ways in which they come to interpret and appropriate ways of being 'a boy' or 'a girl', this approach also challenges the tendency of traditional sex-role socialization theories to construct just two, universal categories of masculinity and femininity (Davies 1979; Connell *et al.* 1982; Skelton 2001). Rather, and as will be seen, children tend to construct their gender identities in diverse ways, reflecting their particular experiences and social worlds and how these are structured through class, 'race' and ethnicity (Walkerdine and Lucey 1989; Connolly 1998).

This theoretical approach to the understanding of children's gendered worlds has specific implications for how teachers and early years practitioners may most appropriately and effectively begin to address the dangers that exist in the playground with respect to gender and thus promote equality of opportunity. These will be considered in the final part of the chapter. It will be argued that far from representing a break or conflict with current developmental perspectives with their focus on child-centred play, such strategies derive naturally from the 'encourager' role advocated for adults.

The importance of play and playgrounds

The pioneering work of the developmental psychologist Jean Piaget (1962, 1965), which began in the 1920s and spanned over fifty years, has had a significant role in highlighting the importance of play to young children's development. While much of the detail of his work has been heavily criticized for underestimating the social and cognitive abilities of young children and for maintaining an overly rigid conception of children passing through discrete stages of development (Vander Zanden 1993; Smith *et al.* 1998), his general emphasis on the active role that children play in their own learning remains highly influential. In essence, Piaget argued that children developed mental structures – or what he termed *schemas* – for making sense of their world. These schemas are continually being revised, expanded and made more complex as children attempt to make sense of an ever-increasing range of experiences. The child does this through the twin and complementary processes that Piaget termed *assimilation* and *accommodation*. For each new experience that the child encounters, they either understand it and fit it into their existing schemas (assimilation) or they adapt and/or extend their schemas to make sense of it (accommodation).

The central importance of Piaget's work derives from the way it challenged previous constructions of children as passive receptacles there simply to be taught by adults and, instead, proposed an understanding of children as actively involved in their own development; of progressively constructing knowledge and developing skills for themselves. This approach has, in turn, a number of key implications for the education of young children. For Piaget, the role of adults is not to impart information but to facilitate children's learning. Rather than the teacher taking the lead, it should be the child who directs and sets the pace for their own learning. According to Piaget, children will only effectively learn and develop by slowly building upon their own existing repertoire of knowledge and skills. Children therefore need to be allowed to examine and explore what they feel important as judged from their existing standpoint and the role of adults should thus be confined to that of facilitator, ensuring that children are able to encounter and experience a diverse range of materials and situations that can encourage their learning (Smith *et al.* 1998; Smidt 2002).

While highly important and influential, a number of feminist writers have drawn attention to the way that Piaget's work, as applied in practice, has often tended to sustain and at times actually reinforce young children's gender identities. There are three particular ways that this has been done. First, because the notion of children's self-directed play has now become the taken-for-granted orthodoxy in early years practice, it has tended to significantly discourage attempts by anyone who wishes to intervene in children's play. For those who would like to adopt a more proactive approach to challenging existing gender stereotypes in play, for example, they can often be left feeling that this is 'bad practice' and at odds with what is in the best interests of the child (MacNaughton 2000). Second, the scientific study of young children's development in the work of Piaget and others has tended to reify and 'naturalize' children's behaviour. As mentioned earlier, there certainly exists much debate about the precise nature and details of Piaget's work. However, all of these debates still tend to construct a view of how children learn and, more importantly, *what* they learn as natural and inevitable. This, in turn, denies any critical consideration of the development of children's gender identities and certainly removes any need to attempt to intervene in their play, other than possibly ensuring that both boys and girls have equal access to the same range of toys and materials. This naturalization of children's play means that when girls and boys consequently choose to play in different ways then this is viewed uncritically and regarded, instead, as a 'normal' and inevitable part of children's development.

Third, and finally, this model of children's self-directed learning tends to privilege the needs and interests of boys and, conversely, tends to deny and subjugate those of girls. At the heart of the model is the view of the child as a 'little scientist' – naturally inquisitive about their immediate social environment and forever exploring and experimenting with it. This construction of the child as active, assertive and confident reflects the stereotypical traits traditionally associated with males and masculinity. Moreover, it also directly contradicts those associated with females and femininity of being dependent, passive and subservient. As such, it creates an environment in which boys' inquisitive and demanding behaviour tends to be accepted and rewarded whilst that same behaviour from girls is more likely to be regarded as transgressive and thus discouraged and punished (Belotti 1975; Walkerdine 1990; Francis 1998).

Overall it can be seen that a danger exists, therefore, in relying simply upon the work of Piaget and the restricted role that he has created for adults as one of mere facilitator. Indeed from the discussion above it would appear that the desire to challenge existing gendered behaviour among young children is simply incompatible with child development theory and practice. This, however, is not the case and there exists the basis for a more proactive role for adults to take in children's learning and play in the work of other developmental psychologists, particularly that of Vygotsky (1978) and Bruner (1963). While their work was more generalized in nature and not concerned with gender, it has stressed the need for teachers and practitioners to take a more interventionist approach in encouraging children to extend their knowledge and skills. More specifically, Vygotsky suggested that children can learn most effectively when they are introduced to a new experience that is beyond their existing understanding but not so far removed as to be unintelligible to them.

This potential space for encouraging children's development – between their current developmental level and what they are capable of achieving with help – has been called the *zone of proximal development* by Vygotsky.

The significance of this concept lies in the fact that while it encourages adults to take a more interventionist role in children's learning, it stresses the need for any intervention to be built upon the child's existing repertoire of knowledge and skills. In this sense, the emphasis is still upon the child taking the lead and setting the pace for their own development. The role of the adult is then one of encourager where they plan their interventions carefully, based upon the child's own interests and activities. One of the principle means of doing this is by *scaffolding*, as Bruner termed it, whereby the adult provides the means by which the child can achieve goals that they have set for themselves but which they would be unable to achieve on their own. Examples of scaffolding would include modelling a particular action or breaking down a more complex procedure into manageable stages for the child to complete in turn. As will be argued later, this overall approach can be used more specifically to inform the development of strategies aimed at encouraging young children to develop a more rounded and critical understanding of gender as it impacts upon their own lives and those of others.

Overall, whatever particular approach is advocated in relation to work with children (whether that of facilitator and/or encourager), it is clear to see how children's play has come to occupy a central role within early years practice. Play distinguishes itself from other forms of behaviour by the fact that it is an activity that the child has chosen to do. This type of self-directed behaviour therefore enables children to set the direction and pace for their own learning and development and allows for the acquisition of a wide range of knowledge and skills. As a growing body of research has shown (see, for example, Moyles 1989, 1994; Blenkin and Kelly 1996b; Smidt 2002), by playing with various toys and materials young children begin to understand and appreciate key mathematical concepts such as number, size and shape and also the physical properties of particular materials including their texture, strength and weight. Moreover, the use of construction toys to represent things like houses, cars and people encourages young children to develop what has been termed 'symbolic thought' – the crucial foundation of more complex forms of understanding and intelligence. In addition, young children's tendency to engage in varied and elaborate role play not only encourages further the development of this form of symbolic thought but it also provides the means by which children can re-enact and explore the social worlds they see around them and develop a wide range of social and communication skills.

Given this emphasis on the importance of play, it is surprising to note that the existing literature on children's play and early years education has spent relatively little time focusing explicitly on play within the playground (see, for example, Moyles 1989, 1994; Abbott 1994; Dau 1999). This is not to suggest, however, that the playground has been completely neglected. A small but growing body of work is emerging that stresses the significance of the playground within the social worlds of young children (Blatchford 1989; Blatchford and Sharp 1994). Such work has drawn attention to the fact that the playground represents the space within which children have most freedom from adult interference and control. It therefore not only provides a further space that can facilitate the types of activity and learning outlined above but it also represents an important opportunity for encouraging children's physical development, particularly their gross motor control. Moreover, as Sluckin (1981) has argued, the peer interaction that characterizes playground behaviour represents a relatively unique space for young children to develop a range of social skills including: turn-taking and cooperative play; conflict resolution; and the complex web of rules and behaviour that surrounds the making and breaking of friendships.

A number of studies, most notably those of Opie and Opie (1969; Opie 1993) and later Sluckin (1981), have done much to document the rich and vibrant worlds of the playground and the complex and sophisticated activities and games that the children play in it. All of this has led to the emergence of what Blatchford (1989) has termed a 'romantic view' of the playground that emphasizes its positive role and stresses that it should as far as possible remain the children's domain, free from adult interference. As Opie and Opie (1969: 16) have argued, for example, 'in the long run nothing extinguishes self-organised play more effectively than does activity to promote it'.

The dangers of play and playgrounds

The importance of play to young children's development and the prominent position it has taken in early years practice can, however, detract us from the fact that it is also an inherently dangerous activity (MacNaughton 1999). In terms of gender, it can not only lead to some children experiencing aggressive and harassing behaviour but it also tends to be routinely characterized by segregation with powerful processes operating that significantly restrict the development of both boys and girls. These are points that will now be illustrated further through the use of three short case studies involving the playground activities and behaviour of 5–6-year-old children observed in three different schools.[1]

East Avenue Primary School

East Avenue Primary School[2] is located in a multi-ethnic, inner-city housing estate in England. Approximately half of the children are white and a quarter South Asian and Black respectively. The housing estate is a relatively bleak place, comprising a number of tower blocks and maisonettes with few green spaces or play areas for children. The majority of adults are either economically inactive or unemployed and the estate has increasingly gained a reputation for being the place where 'problem families' are housed by the city council. The playground at the school comprised a concrete area and a small field with bushes and a few small trees around the perimeter. The concrete area had relatively few markings (consisting mainly of a couple of numbered snakes and hopscotch squares) and these were now fading. When the weather was dry, the children were allowed on the field as well and some would be seen playing in and around the perimeter areas, making use of the bushes and trees to hide from each other and create more enclosed and private spaces.

As in any playground, the children's games and activities were diverse and varied. However, just two factors will be drawn out for the purposes of the current discussion. The first relates to the dominance of boys' games of football in the playground. This is certainly not unique to East Avenue Primary School and, actually, appears to be a very common feature of life in the playground (Blatchford *et al.* 1990). At this school, however, especially when the weather had been wet and the children were not allowed to play on the grass, it tended to dominate the central space of the playground, forcing those who did not play to the peripheries. It was also a particularly gendered activity, being played exclusively by boys with girls not only being prevented from playing but also sometimes fearful of going near (see also Barnett 1988; Boulton 1992). The interest that senior teaching staff (including the headteacher) showed in football and, in particular, the school football teams (all comprised of boys) tended to increase the visibility and status of the game in the playground (see also Skelton 2001). Indeed the headteacher was observed on several occasions joining the older boys in the playground during lunchtime to play football.

The boys who played football regularly had gained much status and prestige among their peers. The public nature of the games – located as they were in the centre of the playground and thus having a captive audience – certainly increased the visibility and presence of the boys. The physical nature of the games and the skills they required also ensured that it provided an effective means for them to construct and maintain their masculine identities (see also Skelton 2000). Given the (masculine) status that was associated with football, it was not surprising to find that the boys heavily controlled who could and could not play. More specifically, to be seen playing football with children who were regarded as weaker and/or less skilled would certainly undermine the masculine identities that the boys had so carefully constructed. For these boys, this meant that not only were girls routinely excluded from football games but also South Asian boys who had generally been constructed through racist discourses as inferior and effeminate. Only one South Asian boy, Prajay, was occasionally allowed to play, mainly because he was in the same class as the boys who controlled the football games. The importance of football to these boys' constructions of status and identity and their consequent tendency to exclude those boys felt to be inferior (in this case South Asian boys) is illustrated clearly in the following discussion. Here I had begun by asking the boys who played football with them[3]:

> PC: So I'm just trying to figure out who plays [football] – so Prajay plays does he?
> Paul: Yeah
> PC: [. . .] What about, er, Ajay and Malde [*both in another, parallel class*]
> Daniel: Urrr no!
> Paul: Nah!
> Daniel: They're rubbish!
> Jordan: They're always playing crap games!
> PC: Why are they rubbish though Daniel?
> Daniel: Because they're Paaa-kis!/
> Stephen: /No, no no! Because they can't run fast! [. . .]
> Paul: Because they're small! [*laughs*]
> Stephen: No! [. . .] Cos, cos they're Pakis and Pakis can't run fast!
> PC: Why? Why aren't they the same as everybody else?
> Daniel: Don't know!
> Stephen: Cos . . .
> PC: Well they are aren't they?
> Stephen: [*Shouting frustratedly*] Cos they're slow and everything!
> Jordan: An' they want to be on your side cos you're fast ain't it Stephen?
> PC: [. . .] But you let Prajay play – is he slow?
> Paul: No!
> Stephen: He's quite fast!
> PC: Yeah but he's Indian?
> Stephen: Yeah, so, he ain't got a dot on his head!
> Jordan: His mum has!
> PC: Yeah but Ajay hasn't got a dot on his head!
> Stephen: Yes he has!
> Daniel: No he hasn't!
> Stephen: He's got a black one so there!

Alongside the distinctly gendered and racialized nature of football in the playground at East Avenue Primary School, the other factor that will be briefly drawn out here is the popularity of games of kiss-chase between the boys and girls. Such games played a central role in publicly signifying boyfriend/girlfriend relationships and were the topic of much discussion and gossip between the children. For the most part, these chasing and catching games involved children who were clearly enjoying the activity and who gained a significant amount of status from taking part (see also Hatcher 1995; Epstein 1997). However, games of kiss-chase would also on occasion encourage more negative and/or aggressive behaviour. During one incident, for example, a game of kiss-chase had begun where a boy was chasing a girl around the field. Initially, the chasing was characterized by much laughing and excitement as the girl successfully out-ran the boy and skilfully dodged and dived in differing directions to avoid his outstretched arms. Eventually he grabbed hold of her jumper, pulled her towards him and then clasped his arms around her. For a short time the girl simply stood there catching her breath and smiling. Viewed from across the playground, however, it became clear that she eventually became frustrated by the fact that the boy did not seem to want to release her and she began to struggle. At this point he swung her around and tipped her over onto the grass where he manoeuvred himself so that he lay on top of her, pinning her arms to the ground. The boy then appeared to simulate sex by thrusting his pelvis up and down and the girl quickly became increasingly distressed. The boy saw me walking towards them and jumped up and ran off.

On another occasion, a group of nine girls were huddled together playing a game called 'Orange Balls'. This game basically consisted of one girl being 'on' who would then stand away from the others who would, out of earshot of this girl, choose a boy's name. Having done this they would then form a ring around the girl and dance in a circle singing a rhyme. The rhyme would involve the girls singing the name of the boy chosen and how he loves her. Great delight would then be taken by the girls in observing the response of the girl who was in the centre. On this occasion, the girls (who were mainly White but included two Black girls) had chosen the name of a South Asian boy. When they sang his name, the girl who was 'on' pulled a face and went 'Urrghhh! No!' The girls then chased her around the playground teasing her for having Jayesh as a boyfriend. Within the context of the broader discourses on 'race' within the playground and the construction of South Asian children generally as different and inferior, such teasing was clearly racist in its tone. A couple of the girls also ran over to Jayesh and teased him, in fits of laughter, that the girl fancied him.

North Parade Primary School

North Parade Primary School is located in a socially-deprived Protestant working-class area in Northern Ireland. It, too, is an area that suffers from high levels of unemployment and is also relatively isolated and bleak, with a number of boarded-up houses and significant amounts of graffiti and litter. It is also an area where loyalist paramilitaries are organized and influential – evident through some of the graffiti and painted wall murals supporting particular paramilitary groups. The playground at the school was much smaller than that at East Avenue. The concrete area was about half the size and there was no field attached for the children to play on. The playground itself had few markings painted on it and those that were there were faded. Because of the restricted size of the playground, football was banned. Occasionally, the teachers and/or lunchtime supervisors would bring out a box of toys for the children to play with (that usually consisted of stilts, large plastic hoops and skipping ropes). However, usually the only toys that were evident in the playground were a few skipping ropes that a small number of girls would use at the side of the playground.

On the whole, the children were left to play by themselves with the teachers and/or dinner lunchtime supervisors intervening mainly to break up fights or respond to complaints or problems that individual children would approach them with. The only exception to this was the tendency for the adult staff, who were all female, to join in and organize skipping games with the girls. A larger skipping rope would be used with the adult rotating one end, a girl the other, and other girls either queuing up to take turns to skip or crowding round to watch and/or join in the rhyme that was being sung. Such skipping games proved to be very popular and would often attract the involvement of more than two-thirds of the girls in the playground.

In contrast, the boys were generally left to their own devices. Common games played by the boys were those involving racing and chasing games, often with a fantasy element based upon monsters or cartoon or television characters. However, in addition, carefully choreographed displays of violence and aggression were also very common, often reflecting local paramilitary activities. On one occasion, for example, three boys were seen to be chasing a fourth. When they had caught him, two of the boys held each of his arms and pulled them, tightly, round his back so that his chest protruded forward. The third boy then stood in front of him and proceeded to pretend to punch him, violently, in the stomach. On each punch, the boy who was being held jerked his body forward and let out a deep groaning sound. The two boys behind him would then sharply pull his arms back, thus thrusting his stomach out again, and the boy in front of him would proceed to punch him again. On another occasion, four boys were seen to be playing a shooting game where they would pretend to have handguns and be shooting at each other. Again, however, the actions of the boys were heavily choreographed and stylized with the boys standing with their legs astride, their arms outstretched with their hands clasped together pointing the gun. Each shot they made was accompanied by a deep shooting sound and the gun sharply recoiling back and upwards.

Alongside such stylized displays of violence, overtly aggressive behaviour and fighting would also occur at times. On one occasion, for example, two boys were chasing a third boy, grabbing him by the jumper and swinging him around. The aggressive nature of the two boys' behaviour as they violently pulled at him and caused him to stumble over twice clearly indicated that this was not 'play'. The third boy became increasingly distressed as the other two boys pulled off his jumper and then teased him with it. He sat on the ground and began to cry. The other two boys then looked around nervously, saw that one of the lunchtime supervisors had noticed the incident, threw the jumper at the boy and ran off laughing. The third boy remained sitting on the floor, clutched the jumper to his chest and then slumped forward on top of it, rolling himself up into a ball. He maintained this position for about a minute before slowly pulling himself to his feet and walking away.

South Park Primary School

In contrast to the other two schools, South Park Primary School is located in a relatively affluent, Protestant middle-class area in Northern Ireland. The school itself is less than ten years old and has been purpose built with the headteacher and staff having a significant degree of input into the design of the building and the playground. The playground itself is relatively large and forms an 'L' shape around two sides of the main school building. Alongside a large concreted area, there is a smaller field that the children can also play on when the weather is dry. The concreted area has extensive markings painted on it including numbered snakes, hopscotch squares, roads, a school bus, an airplane and a large snakes and ladders board. During breaktimes there would also usually be some additional toys made available to the children including skipping ropes, large plastic 'noughts and crosses' and a couple of large foam dice. Interestingly, again, football and other ball games were not allowed in the playground.

Overall, partly because of the greater resources available and the absence of any ball games, the children tended to play in smaller groups in comparison with those in the other two schools. Moreover, while most of these groups were same-sex, a noticeable minority were mixed with boys and girls playing together. As in the other two schools, games of kiss-chase were also popular in the playground at South Park Primary School and also tended to provide a key focus for children's discussions, gossips and teasing about boyfriends and girl-friends. One noticeable factor worth drawing out in relation to this play-ground, however, was the strict gender segregation that occurred in relation to the skipping area. This area was located around the side of the building and purposely created by the teachers to avoid any accidents that may otherwise occur with children being hit by skipping ropes. In theory, while it was an area open to both boys and girls, in practice it was dominated by girls. Of the 20 to 30 children that would usually be playing skipping games individually or in small groups in this area, only one or two would be boys. It was an area that was clearly seen by the girls as their own. One day, for example, I was standing on the edge of the skipping area watching what was going on and a girl came up to me. I commented how 'there are not many boys around here are there?' and she agreed replying 'no.' When I asked her why not she answered: 'because it's a section for girls'.

Being clearly identified as a girls' section, however, meant that it attracted the attention of some of the boys who would set themselves the task of attempting to break into the area to disrupt the girls games. As one of the lunchtime supervisors commented to me: 'You've got to keep an eye on them here skipping. The boys won't let them [skip] if you give them half a chance.' On several occasions, small groups of two or three boys would be seen hiding round the corner of the building occasionally peeping round to view the skipping area. Following much activity that included intense whispering and pointing they would run, in a line and crouched down as if engaged in a military operation, into the skipping area. Sometimes they would be content just to run through, around and out again and other times they would push a girl or purposely grab hold of her skipping rope.

During one occasion, however, two boys focused their attention on the only boy who was in the area playing on his own with a skipping rope. After carefully planning their attack on the edge of the area they ran in and stood immediately behind the boy. The boy continued to skip and one of the other two put his leg out and kicked him up the behind. The boy stopped skipping, turned around and shouted 'Stop it!' He then tried to continue to skip and the same boy kicked him again up the behind. After again being told to 'Stop it!' the boy turned to his friend and they both laughed. The other boy then grabbed his skipping rope and pulled at it. The boy just stood there holding onto his rope. After a while the two boys ran off.

Young children 'doing' gender

There are five key issues that I want to draw out emerging from the brief case studies above. The first, and most obvious, is the dangerousness of children's play and behaviour in the playground. This is clearly evident by reference to the incidents of male violence and aggression discussed above and also the sexual harassment of girls and boys. However, the dangers are also much more than this. They are connected to the tendency for gender segregation in all three playgrounds and the existence of dominant forms of masculinity and femininity associated with each. In this sense the development of both boys and girls are severely proscribed and restricted with the children finding it very difficult to engage in activities associated explicitly with the other sex. Girls at East Avenue, for example, were simply excluded from football games while boys at both North Parade and South Park were similarly actively discouraged from playing skipping. Moreover, and as Francis (1998) has shown, these two dominant forms of gender identity are essentially oppositional and tend to reproduce relations of power as the constructions of femininity position girls in subservient roles to the dominant (and dominating) ones constructed through masculinity.

Second, it is evident that young children are actively involved in the construction and maintenance of their gender identities. Very much in line with the Piagetian view of children's learning processes outlined earlier, these young children are not only recognizing and picking up a wide range of gendered ways of thinking and behaving but they are also actively appropriating them, forever rehearsing and exploring them and, in the process, continually developing and adapting them to fit into their own social worlds. These are, therefore, not passive young children simply being trained into stereotypically masculine and feminine roles as many of the traditional sex-role socialization theories would suggest (see, for example, Davies 1979; Connell *et al.* 1982; Skelton and Hall 2001). Rather, they are active, critical children carefully moulding and re-fashioning existing gender signs and symbols to suit their own purposes. As seen through the case studies, the children are centrally involved in what Davies (1989) has called 'gender category maintenance work' and Thorne (1993) 'borderwork', whereby they are carefully and continuously attempting to police and reinforce the boundaries that demarcate masculine and feminine behaviour.

Third, given the active role that young children play in constructing their own gender identities and adapting them to suit the particular social contexts within which they are located, it is clear that differing forms of masculinity and femininity will emerge as hegemonic in differing schools. For example, the dominant forms of masculinity at East Avenue tended to reflect the nature of the local area and were therefore constructed around physicality (often displayed through football), racism and sexuality. In contrast, while those forms of masculinity that came to predominate at North Parade were also founded upon physicality, they were manifest in different ways, reflecting the particularly violent and paramilitary nature of the local area. For the boys at South Park, however, physicality did not have the same significance. Rather, their specific constructions of masculinity tended to be based more upon competition around knowledge and expertise in particular games, reflecting the more affluent, resourceful and middle-class locality. Overall, therefore, the three case studies illustrate the limited and simplistic picture of traditional sex-role socialization theories that tend to be predicated on just two, fixed and universal identities of masculinity and femininity (Davies 1979; Connell *et al.* 1982; Skelton 2001).

Fourth, it is also clear that there is not just considerable variation between schools in terms of the particular forms of masculinity and femininity that come to predominate but there is also significant variation within each school. In this sense, whatever constructions of masculinity and femininity achieve hegemonic status in a particular school, there will remain many examples of children who actively attempt to undermine or resist these dominant gender dichotomies (Thorne 1993; Francis 1998). In studies of masculinities, for example, Thorne (1993) points towards the 'big man bias' where the characteristics of the powerful, elite males are simply applied to the population of men as a whole. However, and as she identified in relation to her own research of gender relations in a primary school:

> When I mould my data into shapes provided by the literature characterising boys' social relations (in this case, the claim that boys are organised into large, hierarchical groups), I have to ignore or distort the experiences of more than half the boys in [the] classroom.
>
> (Thorne 1993: 98)

This is true in relation to the three case studies discussed above. The majority of boys at East Avenue, for example, did not regularly play football but were also relegated to the peripheries of the playground. A significant minority of girls at North Parade and also South Park were similarly not interested in playing skipping games. While it is important, at least analytically, to identify the forms of masculinity and femininity that tend to dominate in particular schools, there is a real danger therefore in simply imposing these identities onto all boys and girls. Consider the following observations from Opie (1993) based upon her own extensive studies of children's play in the playground. She demonstrates no sense of the glaring contradiction between stressing innate differences between boys and girls while also prefacing this with an acceptance that not all boys and girls fit the gender roles she so forcefully outlines:

> The innate differences between the sexes are easily perceptible in the playground, always allowing for the presence of a few girls who are keen footballers and marbles players, and who are known (and accepted) as 'tomboys', and a few timid little boys who stay under the protection of the older girls. Boys, in general, are more egotistical, enterprising, competitive, aggressive, and daring than girls. They are comedians, exhibitionists . . . Girls . . . are different. They enjoy talking as a purely social activity, and take far more interest in people than do the boys. They are hospitable and helpful . . . Girls refuse to play some games because they are 'rough – only boys play them'; they are thinking of the damage there might be not only to their persons but also to their clothes.
>
> (Opie 1993: 7–8)

Fifth and finally, the case studies demonstrate the role and influence that the school itself can have on children's activities and relationships in the playground. As the example of South Park has shown, a certain degree of diversity can be introduced through the provision of additional play resources, whether they be more physical and permanent in relation to the design and layout of the playground itself or in terms of the types of toys and games that are made available to children during each playtime. Moreover, adult intervention can also be seen to have significant effects on the children's play. Most obviously, banning football can in one simple act significantly change the social dynamics within the playground. The involvement of adults in games, for example the skipping games at North Parade, can also have a significant impact. In this latter case it actually tended to increase gender segregation. However, other research has shown how adult involvement in playground games can lead to greater mixing between boys and girls (Thorne 1993; Connolly 1998).

Helping young children 'un-do' (or at least 're-do') gender

There are three key implications arising from the above discussion with regard to practice. The first relates to the need for schools to re-assess the physical environment of the playground, the toys and materials that are made available during playtimes and to think creatively about how the playground can be used positively to increase the range and depth of experiences available for young children. Unfortunately, as Kelly (1994: 63) has observed: 'Most school playgrounds are bleak sites – empty spaces between buildings and perimeter walls which do not invite or encourage creative play and which lower the spirits until filled with the noise and bustle of children released from the class-room.' It is certainly interesting to note the strong and consistent advice for early years teachers and professionals that they should ensure their classrooms are filled with rich and diverse play and learning opportunities (see, for example, Moyles 1989, 1994; Blenkin and Kelly 1996b; Dau 1999; Smidt 2002) and contrast this with the lack of concern given to playgrounds in these same texts. Given that a little under a third of the school day typically consists of dinnertime and playtime (Tizard *et al.* 1988: 151), this omission would cer-tainly seem to represent an important opportunity lost in terms of positively encouraging young children's development. Moreover, in the absence of posi-tive intervention, these types of 'miserable, bleak and desolate landscapes', as Lucas (1994: 80) has described them, will always have the tendency to encour-age gender segregation and the rehearsals and displays of hyper masculinities and femininities given that large numbers of children are being forced together in small spaces with little else to do.

It is important to stress that such interventions in the design and organ-ization of playground activities need not undermine the central principle of children's self-directed play. As advocated by Sheat and Beer (1994), any plans

for the playground should be made in consultation with the children themselves. Moreover, as with all early years practice, any facilities developed
should be based upon careful observation of the children (Smidt 2002) to
ensure that they genuinely meet their existing needs and interests and thus
help them to further extend their play opportunities in directions of their own
choosing. Also, none of this is to suggest that children's play should be organized and structured by adults. On the contrary, it is about providing greater
freedom and choice for children to decide what they would like to do. Ultimately, such suggestions can be viewed simply as good early years practice,
regardless of the gender dimension. However, as found in the case study of
South Park Primary School, the more that the playground can be broken up
and transformed into one that offers a rich and diverse range of play opportunities for children, the more likely it is that the salience of gender and the
segregation that accompanies it may lessen.

The reduction of gender segregated play, however, is unlikely to be
achieved simply through the provision of a greater range of facilities in the
playground. This leads onto the second implication for practice that is concerned with ensuring equality of access to the facilities that are available.
Given the power of gender and the accompanying discourses on masculinity
and femininity, it is likely that many of the toys and materials that could be
provided in the playground will soon become gendered (if they are not already
so) and labelled as boys' or girls' toys. Once this is reinforced by a group of boys
or girls appropriating and playing with the particular toy or material, then it
will be very difficult, not to mention extremely risky, for children of the
opposite sex to attempt to join in with that play. It is therefore important that
staff in the playground develop an awareness of which children are engaging
in what activities and whether patterns of gender segregation appear to be
developing. In such circumstances it is important for staff to intervene and/or
develop appropriate strategies to encourage greater and more equitable access
to the facilities available.

The third and final implication arises out of a recognition of the power of
gender to influence and shape young children's identities in ways where it
becomes naturalized and taken for granted. The three case studies described
earlier certainly provide some evidence of the importance and centrality of
particular forms of masculinity and femininity in the lives and self-
perceptions of the young children. As MacNaughton (1998) has found, simply
ensuring equality of access to various activities and facilities, important
though this is, is unlikely to fundamentally challenge existing gender identities and relations. Rather, as a growing number of feminist researchers advo-
cate, what is required is a more proactive strategy whereby teachers and other
early years professionals actively encourage young children to question their
taken-for-granted assumptions on gender and deconstruct their existing
frameworks (Davies 1989; MacNaughton 1998; Francis 1998, 2000).

For such interventions to be successful, however, they need to be grounded in and built upon the young children's interests and activities. Relations within the playground will clearly provide an ideal opportunity for this as the children continually struggle to create and maintain gender categories and boundaries. Not only can existing preconceptions and behaviour be challenged in practice by encouraging boys and girls to play games that have become associated with the other sex, but playground activities and behaviour can also provide a rich source of material for discussion and reflection in the classroom. In this sense the teacher can actively challenge the children's existing gender constructions by promoting, as Francis (1998) advocates, a 'discourse of innate equality' between boys and girls. As illustrated in the discussion about the exclusion of South Asian boys from football reported early with a group of boys from East Avenue Primary School, young children are capable of being challenged in this way and being encouraged to see the contradictions of their existing attitudes and behaviour.

The key point in relation to any attempt to help encourage young children to deconstruct their existing gender attitudes is to ensure that it is based upon their own knowledge and experience. Rather than attempting to engage in some form of abstract discussion concerning gender equality, young children need to be encouraged to reflect upon and deconstruct events and incidents that they have personally been involved in or at least have direct knowledge of. In many ways, such attempts can be seen as being located within the 'encourager' role for adults working with young children based upon the work of Vygotsky and Bruner as discussed earlier. Such discussions and attempts to encourage children to reflect upon and deconstruct their existing gender attitudes and behaviour can be seen as taking place within the zone of proximal development – providing children with the appropriate scaffolding (in this case carefully directed discussion) whereby they can develop their skills of critical reflection and slowly come to develop their thinking beyond the crude and rigid gender thinking that tends to characterize children's thought in the early years (Damon 1977; Lloyd and Duveen 1992; Francis 1998).

Conclusions

Overall, given the limited space available, it has not been possible to elaborate further on the three key implications outlined above. It is therefore recognized that they remain at a relatively high level of abstraction and much work is needed to consider how these can effectively translate into practice (see, for example, Yelland 1998; Skelton and Hall 2001). The key aim of this current chapter has been more limited, however, and has been underpinned by two objectives. The first has been to illustrate, in relation to gender, the ways in which play and the playground in particular can represent dangerous spaces for young children. With this in mind, it has been argued that a need exists, therefore, for those working with young children to develop proactive strategies of intervention to effectively address these. Following on from this, the second objective has been to argue that such forms of playground intervention should not be regarded as undermining or standing in opposition to approaches that stress the importance of self-directed play to young children's learning and development. Indeed it has been argued that, if planned carefully and with the children's existing knowledge and behaviour in mind, interventions of this type should be regarded as examples of good early years practice. In essence they would help to ensure that all children are provided with the opportunity to encounter as wide and diverse a range of experiences as possible and that they are also given the appropriate scaffolding and support to begin to develop their skills of critical reflection and to move beyond the simplistic and rigid constructions of gender categories that they tend to be working with at this age.

Notes

1   The observations were made in relation to two separate ethnographic studies, one involving a multi-ethnic, inner-city primary school in England (East Avenue Primary School) where the fieldwork was conducted between 1992 and 1993 (see Connolly 1998). The second study is based in two controlled primary schools in Northern Ireland, one in a socially deprived working-class area (North Parade Primary School) and the other in an affluent, middle-class area (South Park Primary School). The vast majority of the children in both schools were from Protestant backgrounds and the fieldwork was conducted between 2001 and 2002 (see Connolly forthcoming). For both studies, alongside extensive observations of the children in the playground and the classroom, relatively unstructured small group interviews were conducted with them. More details of the methodological approach adopted is provided elsewhere (Connolly 1997).

2   The names of the schools and children are all pseudonyms to protect anonymity.

3   A key to the transcripts can be found below.

Key to transcripts

/   Interruption in speech.

[. . .] Extracts edited out of transcript.

. . . A natural pause in the conversation.

[*Italic text*] Descriptive text added to clarify the nature of the discussion.
[normal text] Text added to help clarify the point the child is making.

References

Abbott, L. (1994) 'Play is fun but it's hard work too!': the search for quality play in the early years, in L. Abbott and R. Rodger (eds) *Quality Education in the Early Years*. Buckingham: Open University Press.

Barnett, Y. (1988) 'Miss, girls don't like playing big games; they only like playing little games': gender differences in the use of playground space, *Primary Teaching Studies*, 4(1): 42–52.

Belotti, E. (1975) *Little Girls*. London: Writers and Readers Publishing Co-operative.

Best, R. (1983) *We've All Got Scars: What Boys and Girls Learn in Elementary School*. Bloomington, Ind.: Indiana University Press.

Blatchford, P. (1989) *Playtime in the Primary School: Problems and Improvements*. Windsor: NFER-Nelson.

Blatchford, P., Creeser, R. and Mooney, A. (1990) Playground games and playtime: the children's view, *Educational Research*, 32(3): 163–74.

Blatchford, P. and Sharp, S. (eds) (1994) *Breaktime and the School: Understanding and Changing Playground Behaviour*. London: Routledge.

Blenkin, G. and Kelly, A. (1996a) Education as development, in G. Blenkin and A. Kelly (eds) *Early Childhood Education: A Developmental Curriculum*, 2nd edn. London: Paul Chapman.

Blenkin, G. and Kelly, A. (eds) (1996b) *Early Childhood Education: A Developmental Curriculum*, 2nd edn. London: Paul Chapman.

Boulton, M. (1992) Participating in playground activities, *Educational Research*, 34(4): 167–82.

Bruner, J. (1963) *The Process of Education*. New York: Vintage Books.

Connell, R., Ashenden, D., Kessler, S. and Dowsett, G. (1982) *Making the Difference: School, Families and Social Divisions*. London: George Allen and Unwin.

Connolly, P. (1997) In search of authenticity: researching young children's perspectives, in A. Pollard, D. Thiessen and A. Filer (eds) *Children and Their Curriculum: The Perspectives of Primary and Elementary School Children*. London: Falmer Press.

Connolly, P. (1998) *Racism, Gender Identities and Young Children*. London: Routledge.

Connolly, P. (forthcoming) *Boys and Schooling in the Early Years*. London: RoutledgeFalmer.

Damon, W. (1977) *The Social World of the Child*. San Francisco, CA: Jossey-Bass.

Dau, E. (ed.) (1999) *Child's Play: Revisiting Play in Early Childhood Settings*. Sydney: Maclennan and Petty.

Davies, B. (1979) Education for sexism: moving beyond sex role socialisation and reproduction theories, *Educational Philosophy and Theory*, 21(1): 1–19.

Davies, B. (1989) *Frogs and Snails and Feminist Tales*. London: Allen and Unwin.

Epstein, D. (1997) Cultures of schooling/cultures of sexuality, *International Journal of Inclusive Education*, 1(1): 37–53.

Francis, B. (1998) *Power Plays: Primary School Children's Constructions of Gender, Power and Adult Work*. Stoke-on-Trent: Trentham Books.

Francis, B. (2000) *Boys, Girls and Achievement: Addressing the Classroom Issues*. London: Routledge.

Hatcher, R. (1995) Boyfriends, girlfriends: gender and 'race' in children's cultures, *International Play Journal*, 3: 187–97.

Jordan, E. (1995) Fighting boys and fantasy play: the construction of masculinity in the early years of school, *Gender and Education*, 7(1): 69–86.

Kelly, E. (1994) Racism and sexism in the playground, in P. Blatchford and S. Sharp (eds) *Breaktime and the School: Understanding and Changing Playground Behaviour*. London: Routledge.

Lloyd, B. and Duveen, G. (1992) *Gender Identities and Education*. London: Harvester Wheatsheaf.

Lucas, B. (1994) The power of school grounds: the philosophy and practice of Learning Through Landscapes, in P. Blatchford and S. Sharp (eds) *Breaktime and the School: Understanding and Changing Playground Behaviour*. London: Routledge.

MacNaughton, G. (1998) Improving our gender equity 'tools': a case for discourse analysis, in N. Yelland (ed.) *Gender in Early Childhood*. London: Routledge.

MacNaughton, G. (1999) Even pink tents have glass ceilings: crossing the gender boundaries in pretend play, in E. Dau (ed.) *Child's Play: Revisiting Play in Early Childhood Settings*. Sydney: Maclennan and Petty.

MacNaughton, G. (2000) *Rethinking Gender in Early Childhood Education*. St Leonard's, NSW: Allen and Unwin.

Marsh, C. (1994) People matter: the role of adults in providing a quality learning environment for the early years, in L. Abbott and R. Rodger (eds) *Quality Education in the Early Years*. Buckingham: Open University Press.

Moyles, J. (1989) *Just Playing? The Role and Status of Play in Early Childhood Education*. Milton Keynes: Open University Press.

Moyles, J. (1994) *The Excellence of Play*. Buckingham: Open University Press.

Opie, I. (1993) *The People in the Playground*. Oxford: Oxford University Press.

Opie, I. and Opie, P. (1969) *Children's Games in Street and Playground*. Oxford: Oxford University Press.

Piaget, J. (1962) *Play, Dreams and Imitation in Childhood*. London: Routledge and Kegan Paul.

Piaget, J. (1965) *The Moral Judgement of the Child*. Harmondsworth: Penguin.

Sheat, L. and Beer, A. (1994) Giving pupils an effective voice in the design and use of their school grounds, in P. Blatchford and S. Sharp (eds) *Breaktime and the School: Understanding and Changing Playground Behaviour*. London: Routledge.

Skelton, C. (2000) 'A passion for football': dominant masculinities and primary schooling, *Sport, Education and Society*, 5(1): 5–18.

Skelton, C. (2001) *Schooling the Boys: Masculinities and Primary Education*. Buckingham: Open University Press.

Skelton, C. and Hall, E. (2001) *The Development of Gender Roles in Young Children: A Review of Policy and Literature*. Manchester: Equal Opportunities Commission.

Shuckin, A. (1981) *Growing Up in the Playground*. London: Routledge and Kegan Paul.

Smidt, S. (2002) *A Guide to Early Years Practice*, 2nd edn. London: RoutledgeFalmer.

Smith, P., Cowie, H. and Blades, M. (1998) *Understanding Children's Development*, 3rd edn. Oxford: Blackwell.

Smith, P., Morita, Y., Junger-Tas, J., Olweus, D., Catalano, R. and Slee, P. (1999) *The Nature of School Bullying: A Cross-national Perspective*. London: Routledge.

Thorne, B. (1993) *Gender Play: Boys and Girls in School*. Buckingham: Open University Press.

Tizard, B., Blatchford, P., Burke, J., Farquhar, C. and Plewis, I. (1988) *Young Children at School in the Inner City*. Hove: Lawrence Erlbaum Associates.

Vander Zanden, J. (1993) *Human Development*, 5th edn. New York: McGraw-Hill.

Vygotsky, L. (1978) *Mind in Society: The Development of Higher Psychological Processes*. Cambridge, MA: Harvard University Press.

Walkerdine, V. and Lucey, H. (1989) *Democracy in the Kitchen: Regulating Mothers and Socialising Daughters*. London: Virago.

Walkerdine, V. (1990) *Schoolgirl Fictions*. London: Virago.

Wolke, D., Woods, S., Stanford, K. and Schulz, H. (2001) Bullying and victimization of primary school children in England and Germany: prevalence and school factors, *British Journal of Psychology*, 92: 673–96.

Yelland, N. (ed.) (1998) *Gender in Early Childhood*. London: Routledge.

8 Working with primary school children to deconstruct gender[1]

Bronwyn Davies

How do we become gendered beings? How are 'male' and 'female' constituted as opposite categories of being, with 'male' superior to and more powerful than 'female'? What part do schools play in this? Is it possible to deconstruct and move beyond these hierarchical oppositions? Can this be done in the school context? What part does poststructuralist theory play in enabling us to examine such questions?

In *Frogs and Snails and Feminist Tales: Preschool Children and Gender* (Davies [1989] 2002) I undertook a feminist poststructuralist analysis[2] of the ways in which gender is constituted amongst preschool children through the discourses with which we speak and write ourselves into existence. I looked in particular at storylines through which gender is constructed. *Shards of Glass. Children Reading and Writing Beyond Gendered Identities* (Davies [1993] 2002) presents an extension of that earlier study in that it further explores the processes through which our maleness and our femaleness are established and maintained during childhood. Working with 10- and 11-year-old children from mixed social and ethnic backgrounds it also explores the radical possibility of giving children reading and writing strategies to disrupt the dominant storylines through which their gender is held in place.

Unlike strategies for change based on sex role socialization theory, my work does not seek to explore how we might act upon girls to shape them differently, to make them more autonomous, to give them self-esteem, or to make them want to do maths and science (Kenway and Willis 1990). Poststructuralist theory opens up the possibility of a quite different set of strategies for working with both boys and girls based on a radically different conceptualization of the process of becoming (gendered) persons. Within the frame of this different understanding it makes more sense to introduce children to the discursive strategies that enable them to see for themselves the storylines through which gendered persons are constituted, to see the cultural and historical production of gendered persons that they are each caught up in. In this different approach, children can be introduced to the possibility, not of learning the culture, or new aspects of it, as passive recipients, but as producers of culture, as writers and readers who make themselves and are made within the discourses available to them. It allows them to see the intersection between themselves as fictions (albeit intensely experienced fictions) and the fictions of their culture – which are constantly being (re)spoken, (re)written and (re)lived.

The initial strategy that I adopted with Chas Banks, who worked with me on the project, was to have the children study a wide variety of texts to see the detail of the ways in which gender is constituted through text. First they looked at photos of male and female children, seeing how body language and placement of people in particular physical positionings in relation to each other and to objects within the picture were constitutive of the idea of male and female as opposite. These observations were linked to discussions about their own experience of themselves as embodied males and females and to the ways they experience that embodiment and also to the ways they sign their locatedness in one category or the other. Central to this discussion was the concept of positioning, which was used as a way of making problematic the taken-for-granted concepts of the individual as architect of their own subjectivity (Davies and Harré 2000).

The children then brought photos of themselves as small children to the study groups so they could read those photos as gendered texts, finding the ways in which they were being culturally located as male or female. These photos were discussed, stories told and written about them and photocopies of the photos used to make a collage of photo and story about themselves as gendered beings. Following a discussion of Chappell's photography workshops with adolescent girls (Chappell 1984) they then discussed the idea of telling their own lives in the present through photos they might take themselves and stories that could be told about these photos. They were given disposable cameras and instructed on some aspects of photography, including the idea of looking for 'naturally occurring scenes' rather than asking people to pose for them. The aim of this project was to create images and to tell stories in relation to those images about their relationships with the people that mattered to them.

They were also introduced to written text and to the idea of reading those texts in the way they had read the photographs – looking at the text itself to see the way in which character, emotion, and desire are created. Central to these discussions was the concept of *positioning* of the reader within the text. They examined the ways in which they entered into the text, positioning themselves with particular characters and reading the story from that character's own position within the story. They also talked about films they had seen and books they had read where they had been aware of how they had positioned themselves in the context of the story. They talked about how that positioning influenced their patterns of desire in relation to both lived and fictional stories.

They then read stories together, this time using the concepts of *storyline* and *desire* as central to the analysis of story. In reading *Snow White*, for example, they were shown how to discard, for the moment, the detail of the story and to see that the storyline is made up of specific well-known images or patterns within the culture. The storyline of a vulnerable young woman falling victim to a powerful adult, being cast adrift from the domestic scene and only able to be returned to the safety of a new domestic scene through the agency of a heroic male was thus made both visible and analysable in terms of its constitutive force. It becomes evident, for example, that the attraction of the heroic male to the heroine, his desire to save her, depends on her absolute virtue and on her passivity. And in Snow White's case, this is a passivity approximating death. The relevant desire for any reader positioning herself as the character Snow White would therefore be to be sufficiently virtuous and passive that she might be saved by a prince who would give her security in an otherwise dangerous world.

The children discussed these stories in terms of their own readings of them and their own bodily and emotional responses to each story as they had listened to it. They also looked more closely at the detail in the text to see how these interactions between reader and text are created. They looked for the *silences* in the text, the *cultural givens* – the things that the author did not think s/he had to say since they can be taken for granted.

Their own relations with each other and their experience of being gendered were made relevant to these discussions. The political implications of the boys' positioning of themselves with the powerful male in the text were discussed along with the emotions and patterns of desire made relevant by that powerful positioning. They examined the ways in which stories become their own lived stories through a process in which they take up as their own the obviousnesses, the patterns of interpretation, and the patterns of desire. Central to these discussions was the recognition that there is no one story to be heard in any one text, and that there is not even any one set of obviousnesses to be assumed in any specific text. Their different readings and the relation of these to their own lived experiences and to the gendered struggles they engaged in with each other around these readings were fundamental to the discussion.

These readings of traditional stories were followed by readings of feminist stories such as Cole's *Princess Smartypants* (1986) and Corbalis's *The Wrestling Princess* (1987). The ways in which the female hero in these stories resists the dominant discourse were explored in detail as were the implications in their own lives of such possibilities. The conversations around these texts included the boys' anger at being cast out of the heroic role and the girls' pleasure in the new possibilities that were being opened up. It also included the boys' open attacks on the girls (as well as their attacks on the heroic female characters in the text) that usually took the form of sexualizing them, making them vulnerable to sexual attack, presumably in an attempt to re-position them in the traditional romantic storyline where they not only know their place but desire that place.

In relation to the discussions of both feminist and traditional stories, the study groups also talked about their own futures and the ways they imagined these falling out. The apparent inevitabilities of marriage, heterosexuality, powerful work for men and childcare for women were examined in detail, both in terms of the ways in which the children already felt bound by traditional expectations and desires and in terms of the ways these traditional patterns were already changing in the world around them.

Following on from these discussions the study groups took on the task of writing their own group story that resisted the dominant discourse. This, they discovered, was extraordinarily difficult to do. They repeatedly drew on traditional patterns and images, not knowing how to abandon them or how to find alternatives. Their embeddedness in binary forms of thought, particularly in relation to women (if they are not pretty and desirable they must be ugly) had to be constantly struggled with. Resisting the dominant discourse seemed to them to involve simple reversals, the use of whatever is opposite. The meaning of what a discourse of resistance might be had therefore to be established as something much more subtle and complex than this. Also, the work that some of the boys engaged in to maintain their ascendancy created tensions needing constantly to be dealt with. The main task in this group story writing was not so much to create a perfect finished product but to give the children an opportunity to examine the process, to experience the task itself and to make that experience observable, analysable and thus something that could be changed. The project ended with each of the participants producing their own fictional deconstructive story.

Deconstructive reading

Generally discourses and their attendant storylines are taken up as one's own in a way that is not visible, since discourse is understood as the transparent medium through which we see real worlds. Just as we disattend the pane of glass in order to look at the view out of the window, so we generally disattend discourse. (It is not until the glass fractures or breaks, for example, that we focus differently.) Precisely because discourse is understood as transparent, then, any text that mobilizes that discourse is taken to describe a real and *recognizable* world. One understands oneself, in reading, to be *re-cognizing* that which the author of the text cognized. A reading that is thus achieved is experienced as a true, even authoritative reading of the text. This aspect of understanding text has been made a central feature of much of the current reading practice taught in schools, most notably reader response theory. Reader response theory may lead readers to read characters as if they were real (in the same sense that they, the readers are real) and to place a great deal of confidence in their own ability to read the 'truth' of those characters. In drawing on their own experience they may make a personal investment in their reading and not do the critical work of seeing how they managed to produce such a reading. This can lead to heated arguments among students as to who is right about the character in the text. By inserting themselves into the text and by drawing from their own experience of life without necessarily understanding how they have done so, they may import unreflective sexism and oppressive and limited forms of thought into the text. Because their own readings are granted legitimacy in classrooms that use reader response theory, the critical reflection on their readings may be less salient than their own authoritative readings of texts, readings that may confirm the legitimacy of the oppressive world they live in (Gilbert 1993).

Using their own history of living in the world and the interpretive work necessary for survival in that world, and presuming that the obviousnesses of the everyday world apply in the worlds in texts that authors write about, the children bring a wealth of general, cultural and specific personal knowledge to bear on the task of interpreting text and of making a coherent reading of that text. Just as they have learned not to attend to the interpretive work they do to make the everyday world coherent (which is constituted as real rather than a fiction), so with text. The fictional world of the text is made real in the same way.

It is not enough to simply expose children to feminist texts, nor is it enough to ask them to interpret those texts on the basis of their experience, if we want them to be able to 'read against the grain' or to grasp feminist storylines and use them to deconstruct and call in question the sexist texts that make up so much of the everyday world. They need as well to discover themselves in the act of sense making, of importing their own knowledges into the text (and of importing ideas and images from text into their lived storylines) in order to examine the complex relations between lived experience and text. They need to discover the ways in which their category memberships (as male or female, as white or black) lead them to interpret differently and to be positioned differently in the text. They need to discover the way in which the cultural patterns constantly repeated in stories are taken up as their own, becoming the thread with which life is woven and desire is shaped. They need to see the author as a person with intentions and ways of understanding that are expressed through shared cultural symbols, assumptions, connections, images, metaphors and storylines. They need to see that while on the one hand, authors cannot guarantee meanings because of the active way in which their texts are read, their intentions may nevertheless be discernible and might be called into question. In other words the authority of the author needs to be disrupted, the author being reconstituted as one like any other who draws on what is known to fashion something that is both able to be imagined and yet new. They need to find the silences and gaps in texts, to question what it is the author understood as obvious and not in need of saying, and to understand the power of those silences to reinforce the obviousness of what does not need to be said. And finally they need to find authors and texts who break the silences, who begin to say the un-sayable, and to become writers themselves, creating texts that disrupt certainties and open up new possibilities.

Central to the work Chas Banks did with the study groups were the ideas that:

- any authoritative message that they find in texts is both culturally and historically specific;
- lived storylines are fictional and the gendered nature of these is examinable;
- discourses of resistance are legitimate disruptions to unwanted and oppressive impositions.

Some examples of the children's work

Although there were often tensions and difficulties to be dealt with through-out the project – power struggles of various kinds, between boys and girls and between Chas and the students – there were also times when the children became very excited about what they had begun to understand:

Charlotte: It is amazing. All the things you ever thought you ever think about.
Jennifer: Yeah
Charlotte: I mean you get taught this and this and this but you never get taught all the different perspectives and all the different ways of look-ing at it, like discourses, all the different things it could mean.

In what follows I will take some examples of the struggles towards understand-ing that the children collectively engaged in. In the study group session that ended with this excited talk, Chas and the children had made their own life stories and the stories they encountered in text and on screen relevant in their talk as they made their way together through this complex new way of inter-acting with text. Chas had used the concept of positioning to talk about the way each person locates themselves in a story when they read it. Her purpose had been to explore the link between positioning, gender, power, storyline and desire:

1 Chas: OK, so you understand this idea that when we read a story it's something that we do very actively. And we position ourselves and insert ourselves into the story as one of the characters. Now usually

what happens is boys position themselves with the male characters and girls position themselves as the female characters. It's very very rare that you'll get a swapping over.

2 Stacey: I read a book just recently and there was this girl called Lara in it

3 James: Lara Higgin?

4 Stacey: No and she sometimes, she was out in the bush and all this and she had her favourite dog and I just positioned myself, me as herself as her and for days on end I kept on thinking I was her and I was always going to be like her.

5 Chas: That's very interesting. Yes. That's very interesting indeed. So in fairy tales boys are always positioned as the heroic rescuers/[3]

6 Jennifer: Muscular/

7 Chas: And girls generally are positioned as the ones to be rescued, the victims/

8 James: Damsels/

9 Chas: of the treacherous parents, aren't they, in fairy tales?

10 Zak: The dragons/

11 Stacey: The ones that can't defend themselves but have to be defended by others.

12 Chas: Right, so in fairy tales you're positioned powerfully if you're a boy . . . and if you're a girl you're positioned powerlessly as the victim usually, can you see that?

13 Several at once: Yeah

14 Jennifer: Like what you said before, like the older is always the more powerful and the younger is powerless so you're sort of saying that if you were a girl sometimes you are really quite powerless

15 Chas: That's right

16 Charlotte: Sometimes I wouldn't like to be the one that's the victim, like just sometimes I think about watching Ninja movies, I'd like to kill for the CIA or something like that and/

17 Zak: Yeah, your mind plays tricks on you, if you see a really gross movie

18 James: See a movie like *Nightmare on Elm Street*

19 Zak: And you don't like the thought of going to bed on that/

20 James: But I'm not/

21 Chas: It does too, your mind does play/

22 Zak: You feel like you're gonna/

23 Stacey: Yeah me too

24 Chas: OK, so the important thing is that we position ourselves . . . according to gender, don't we, that's the first thing we must remember, OK so what it means is that boys when they read this story, this is the thing I want to get across to you, when boys read this story, their hearing of the story is very different to when girls read it because they position themselves differently. OK, and the messages that they

get from the story are going to be very different. The messages that girls get/

25 Stacey: It's like when you're first read that story to you and the child is old enough, well nearly old enough to know what it needs they say 'oh well I have to be the princess or the queen' and the boys think 'oh I have to be the prince and live up to what the prince means' and that's how we've got our sort of/

26 Jennifer: Yeah, another influence

27 Chas: That's right, that's what I'm trying to get across to you

28 Stacey: It's another influence

29 Chas: Yeah, it's another influence, exactly . . . We take those stories and we put them into our head and they become our stories.

30 Stacey: Or actually our lives.

31 Chas: Yes

32 Stacey: Influence what we do

33 Chas: Yes, that's right/

34 Jennifer: And what we say

35 Chas: Right, and because of the gender differentiation, that's one of the ways that we maintain that gender difference is through stories. OK, great so fairy tales in a way offer sort of guidance don't they to the way we should live our lives

36 Stacey: That's just one of the whole discourses of being a man and a woman

Chas linked active reading with the idea of positioning or inserting oneself into the story and reading the story from the point of the character of the same sex (1). Stacey instantly recalled reading a book in which she positioned herself as a girl called Lara, not only reading the story from her point of view, but imagining being in the world both now and in the future as Lara (2, 4). Chas explained the way in which the subject positions in stories are so often the male hero who has power, and the female victim who is powerless (5, 7, 9, 12). Throughout her explanation the children offered words and phrases such as 'muscular' and 'damsels' showing they knew what she was talking about and thus contributing to the explanation (6, 8, 10, 11). Stacey then made a link between the imbalance of power in gender relations and the earlier discussion on adult-child relations (14). Charlotte then returned to the point Chas made at the outset about readers imaginatively positioning themselves as the same sex character. She offered an example of positioning herself as the male aggressor (16). The others picked up, not on the cross-gender aspect of Charlotte's point, but on the uncharacteristic emotions that one can experience watching a violent movie (18–23). Probably without conscious intention the link that they made negated and undermined Charlotte's imagining of herself stepping out of her gendered positioning since they construed it as her mind 'playing tricks' on her. Chas re-stated her original point (24). The children then made a number of significant connections with the influence on young children's thinking about how to be male and female from the stories they are read (25–9), and how these stories become lived stories (30–4). Chas picked up and reiterated their point (35) and Stacey linked the discussion to the concept of discourse (36).

This was a significant discussion for these children. They had started to see discourse as visible and as powerfully constitutive of their lives, not as an inevitable and natural process (though this was a hard assumption to disrupt, as becomes evident in the transcript that follows), but as a process that can be opened up for critique and transformation. Their active involvement in the conversation, drawing on their own immediate experience and building on the words and meanings they already have access to means that they were able to position Chas not as authoritative adult/teacher who closes down discussion, but as someone from whom they can gain new and important concepts and with whom they can open up discussion on ways of using those concepts to make sense of their own lived experience.

Following these discussions, the group read together two children's stories, *Snow White* and *Princess Smartypants*. These were chosen, rather than stories more appropriate to their age group, for the practical reason that their length made it possible to both read and discuss them in one session, and because they readily lend themselves to deconstructive readings. What was of particular interest in the discussions around these stories was the movement in and out of the text, revealing both the extent to which the children emotionally positioned themselves with the same sex characters, such that criticisms of those characters were received as criticisms of themselves, and *at the same time* their use of the concepts to which they had been gaining access to see the storyline as oppressive and the images and assumptions, the gaps and silences, as highly problematic. In the discussion about *Princess Smartypants* (a princess who does not want to get married and who succeeds in outsmarting all her suitors) the warfare between the male and female characters and children goes on at the same time, and is interwoven with, the deconstructive work they are learning to do. It is interesting to observe the way James positions himself and is positioned. He tries to line himself up outside the gender lines, and to engage in deconstructive critique, but it is difficult for the girls to read him as 'on their side'. James appears to appreciate the story from Smartypants' point of view, defending her action in terms of the oppressive nature of parental authority and gender relations. Zak and Philo more predictably carry the flag for Prince Swashbuckle. In doing so they not only find themselves negating the validity of Smartypants' resistance, but denying the oppressiveness of gender relations while at the same time engaging in oppressive talk in relation to the character of Smartypants (and thus also of the girls).

1 Philo: That was a hopeless story

2 Chas: Alright. Why was it hopeless, tell me why you thought it was hopeless

3 James: It was exactly the opposite

4 Philo: I don't know, you just thought, you just knew what was going to happen

5 James: That's probably because you had a look at it

6 Stacey: That one was a good story because it showed that/

7 James: She was resisting

8 Stacey: She yeah she's resisting the female discourse/

9 James: Yes/

10 Stacey: She was doing what she pleased and not/

11 Philo: (she was) riding motor bikes

12 James: Not what her parents wanted her to do/

13 Stacey: Not just/

14 James: Get a handsome/

15 Stacey: She was just riding motor bikes, roller skating, not doing things that Princesses do/

16 Jennifer: I like roller skating

17 Stacey: would do

18 James: I can't

19 Stacey: And raise pets and/

20 James: I don't have any things/

21 Stacey: And and she still has some of those really magic in fairy tales like a magic ring and a magic kiss and all those things like that but she's but she's not a tom boy but she's resisting the female discourse

22 Chas: Right, the dominant female discourse. What sort of person do you think she was?

23 Jennifer: Not a snob

24 Chas: She wasn't a snob

25 Charlotte: Independent (*very softly*)

26 Zak: She was a snob

27 Chas: She was a snob?

28 James: Snob's totally different/

29 Chas: Tell me Zak why you thought she was

30 Jennifer: Zak doesn't know what a snob is

31 Philo: He should he's looking at one/ (softly referring to Jennifer)

32 Zak: Well she um wanted them to think of her

33 Charlotte: He keeps looking at Jennifer

34 James: That's not snobbish

35 Chas: No can you let him finish and then we'll/

36 Zak: She wanted him to feed her pets and she wanted them to um to do things that um/

37 Philo: Were virtually impossible

38 Zak: Yeah

39 James: That's not snobbish, that's the male discourse. They have they do things that are literally/

40 Zak: Yeah but none of them accomplished it except one

41 Charlotte: She was independent

42 Chas: Ah ha. What do you think Philo. What sort of person do you think she was? You don't have to like her. I mean you know there's no, I want you to honestly say what you think. What sort of person do you/

43 Philo: I think she'd be best for a doormat

44 Chas: Why do you think that?

45 Philo: Oh because you know if she set all the Princes on one task and go and do it then it, um like they'd have to travel away and all that and that'd be heaps heaps better like most fairy tales but that one was just totally different and *stupid*

46 Charlotte: That means you're being sexist though 'cause/

47 Jennifer: You just said you like the story

48 Charlotte: Yeah you said that/

49 Philo: No

[interruption]

50 Stacey: What happens is that you think that what happens is the female should be the helpless one and the male should be the ones to prove her wrong but she ended up winning in the end. Not the male. That's why/

51 Zak: Philo just doesn't like the story

52 Charlotte: Well that means you're being sexist, saying that about the doormat/

53 Zak: We've all got different opinions/

54 Charlotte: Um then that means that you think that she should just *have* to do exactly what her mother says and have to follow that um discourse that her parents have set that she has to go out and marry a man and live happily ever after

55 Zak: Well we've all got different opinions

56 Charlotte: Yeah I know, and I put that opinion about his opinion, I can still say that

57 Chas: Ah ha. What sort of opinion do you think that Smartypants had of herself?

58 James and Stacey: She thought she was good

59 Chas: She thought she was pretty good

60 Philo: She thought she was the best because no one could carry out what she could do

61 James: No one could carry out her deeds

62 Jennifer: But she could carry out what she'd set down. So it must mean
you know for once that she's not going to be the helpless one
63 Charlotte: It doesn't mean that she was/
64 James: Yeah it is going to be the men that are the helpless one, the
women with strength
65 Jennifer: Yeah it's about time something happened like that

Philo rejects the story on the grounds that it was a simple reversal of roles and therefore too predictable (1–4). When Stacey and James start elaborating the virtues of Smartypants as one who resisted the 'female discourse' (6–10) he only briefly contributes to the description of who she is (11). Stacey notes with enthusiasm the use of elements of the old stories, such as the magic kiss, combined with a discourse of resistance (21). A series of attacks and counter attacks then breaks out with claims that Smartypants is a snob from Zak (26), with claims from Jennifer that Zak doesn't know what a snob is (30) and Philo claiming that Jennifer is a snob (31)[4]. Zak and Philo say that Smartypants' tasks were impossible and James points out that it is part of the male discourse to have to carry out impossible tasks, so has nothing to do with Smartypants being a snob. Charlotte tries twice to get a different line of discussion going around Smartypants' independence but this is not taken up (25, 41). Chas asks Philo to elaborate his attitude to Smartypants and he states that the best thing for her was to be a 'doormat' (43) presumably her heroic actions warranting putting her down completely. There is confusion at this point over Philo's attitude to the story and over where he stands, but it is pointed out to him by the girls that his attitude is sexist, his rejection of the story being because of his investment in adult authority and in the imposition of their oppressive discourses on womanhood (46, 50). Zak comes in saying one can like or dislike stories without these political implications but his argument doesn't convince anyone (51–6). (From the point of view of reader response theory however, his view would have been confirmed and his reading regarded as unproblematic.)

Chas then turns the talk to Smartypants' view of herself and they say that she not only thought she was good, she *was* good: she could carry out all the tasks she set and for once there was a woman who wasn't going to be helpless (57–64). 'It's about time something happened like that' says Jennifer, her imagination caught by the strength and competence of Smartypants, her magic and her ability to resist oppressive social structures (65).

What emerges in these conversations is the impressive power of traditional storylines to assert oppressive gender relations as natural and correct. As readers position themselves as characters in the text, finding themselves being able to *read* the characters from their own experience (the girls wanting to be beautiful and perfect, the boys wanting to be strong and heroic), they understand the text as telling a fiction; but it is a fiction of what they experience as the real world. In imaginatively bringing the characters to life they draw the detail, the threads, the emotions of their own experience to bear on the words on the page and so make the characters live. The text then seems real, the repeated storylines, the storylines of life – the way life is. The battle between the characters in the stories and the characters reading the story are almost impossible to disentangle from each other.

It might be argued on the basis of the sexism of the boys that the girls would be better off without them when doing this kind of work. Yet the girls in the single-sex study group did not achieve the kinds of insights displayed here. They imported oppressive male perspectives into their discussions without having to have the boys present to do so. In the mixed-sex groups the sexism is more visible and therefore able to be analysed and rejected. This is not to say that there are not occasions in which girls can profit from being together without boys, but that even where they are present in a sexist way, this is not necessarily an argument for separating them off. The more important consideration is the development of the analytic/deconstructive skill in both sexes with which they can begin to see and to shift oppressive patterns in the texts of their everyday lives and in the written texts they encounter and produce.

The ability to read against the grain requires knowledge of 'real world' critiques of the apparent inevitability of the gender order. It also requires imaginative constructions of desirable alternatives, and the conceptual tools to make the text visible as something constructed from a particular vantage point and with constitutive force and with political implications. Fundamental to the deconstruction of the written and lived texts that constitute a sexist world is the ability to imaginatively create alternatives, to imaginatively know ways of being which might replace the existing ones. Writing plays an important part in the imaginative construction of those different ways of being.

Writing beyond the male-female binary

The children in the study groups were invited, towards the end of their meetings with Chas, to write their own stories. They had already told autobiographical stories in relation to their photographs, read traditional and feminist stories and learned to deconstruct them, and discussed at length their own experience of being gendered and the relation of the process of gendering to storyline and to power and powerlessness. Having struggled with the task of writing their own group stories, with Chas pointing out to them some of the ways in which they were falling into tellings which reconstituted a sexist world, some of the children, at Chas's invitation, set out to write a story of their own.

The example of the children's writing I will show you here is Charlotte's story. Charlotte situates her story in another time and another culture. Her story nevertheless takes up oppressive elements of present day culture: the obligation of each person to become identifiably male or female, and parental authority to insist on this. Cleverly she weaves a tale in which the female child resists this imposition first by listening to her parents and attempting to do what they ask. Only when she finds this beyond her does she find a way to escape the problem by transforming herself. She does so using both recognizable threads of traditional femininity, along with the name her parents have given her.

Malu Kungka

A long time ago in the Dreamtime there was a young girl called Malu Kungka, 'malu' meaning 'kangaroo' and 'kungka' meaning 'girl'. She was from an Aboriginal tribe called 'Walungi' and she was a very strong and independent girl. Sometimes her father would even take her hunting. She didn't resemble a girl at all or even a child for that matter. She was always wandering off into the scrub looking for an adventure while all the other children would play in the tribal ground where they had set up camp and would play all day with each other.

Many years passed and Malu Kungka was still carrying on her tradition of wandering off and exploring new places and things.

One night Malu Kungka's parents were talking about Malu Kungka, they decided that her father would not take her hunting with him any more because she was growing up and she must be like the other children and learn how to be a woman, for it was not long before she would be an adolescent and she still hadn't a care in the world except for the animals and trees and all those sorts of things. The next day Malu Kungka's parents told her what they thought, though they regretted it because now she was sad and puzzled.

That day she did not eat as she usually did, she sat down in the red dust and drew pictures of things whilst pondering over what her parents had said.

She was confused, 'What do I have to do to prove I am a woman, I am a woman aren't I?' she thought Now she was more confused than ever, she did not know much of these things for she never thought of them as important, therefore she never thought of them at all.

The next day she set about finding a way of proving that she was a woman. The first thing she did was to watch all the other Kungkas practising what they had learnt from their parents. She observed that they would sit in groups and weave baskets, sing songs and make carriers out of bits of hollowed out trees and big pieces of bark. She tried doing all these things, unfortunately in vain for she could not do any of these things. Still she practised each of these things every day, for she was determined to get it right.

The initiation would be held at the next full moon and the moon was already three quarters full, she had only one week in which to become a woman. Finally she realized she could not become a woman that way and she would have to find a spiritual way of becoming a woman and the only way of doing that would be to ask for the help of Malu Biamee because the kangaroo was her symbol and 'Malu Biamee' meant 'Kangaroo God'. Now she would have to hold a special ceremony. So the night of the initiation when the moon was high she gathered ten of the wisest and oldest women of the tribe and pleaded with them to help, finally they agreed.

They collected the things essential for a ceremony of this type and set off following Malu Kungka to a special place that she had often seen the kangaroos meet at. The moon was shining as bright as day when they began to paint, they used special ground rocks and the melted fat of a kangaroo, they painted various kangaroo symbols all over their bodies. Then they put a hollowed out kangaroo's body on the back of Malu Kungka and then they started dancing a special dance with songs to go with it. When that was over they all placed different offerings in the centre of the circle.

The next day Malu Kungka's parents did not find their daughter in her usual place for Malu Biamee had taken pity on her and given her to her one love . . . Nature, where she would be happy for the rest of her life. Malu Biamee had turned her into her true self . . . a Malu!!!

The story begins with a direct challenge to a number of binaries. Malu Kungka's name is part animal and she does not look as if she is either a child or female. She spends time hunting with her father or adventuring in the scrub on her own, in marked contrast to other children. Her parents decide she must become like the others. She ponders and questions this decision, then makes every attempt to do what her parents want. But she cannot. She decides to find a 'spiritual way of becoming a woman'. With the aid of the spiritual power of the older women she is transformed, as in any traditional romance story, into her 'true self' and 'given to her one love'. Further, in becoming a kangaroo, she simply takes up the name her parents gave her. It is a radical solution, precisely because it is woven out of threads that her parents cannot legitimately object to, yet at the same time refusing the path they have pushed her towards. The alternative path is one that disrupts the boundary between nature and culture, one of the significant metaphors that holds the male/female binary in place. Malu Kungka shifts to the female side in order to escape the restrictions of the binary itself – a version of Cixous's 'writing the feminine'.

Conclusion

The children in the study groups revealed the destructive ways in which boys return repeatedly to practices that sexualize and oppress girls. And the girls too revealed the ways they have taken up oppressive ways of reading themselves into the world. These patterns of power and powerlessness must be made visible. In order to do that, both teachers and children need the conceptual tools that will enable them to 'catch themselves in the act' of taking up oppressive or oppressed ways of being. The children also show that they know there is something wrong with these oppressive relations and they show an interest in deconstructing and moving beyond them. It is not that they are ignorant of the social changes that have been taking place over the last decade or so, it is that they are enmeshed in old discursive practices that take some subtle, patient and long-term work to move beyond.

Gender has rarely been taught explicitly. It is implicit in acts of learning to talk, learning to read, learning to be a 'good child' or a competent person. Because of its embeddedness in approved dominant discourses its creation and maintenance are invisible and also somewhat intractable. Poststructuralist theory opens up the possibility of making it visible. But making it visible to the children in the study groups was accompanied by repeated (re)turnings to the dominant discourses through which they knew themselves, through which they achieved the (pleasurable) sense of themselves as competent members of the social world. The struggle for transformative, collective stories was begun in this project, but could be no more than a contested beginning, given the limitations on the time we spent with the children, but also the hegemony of the competing discourses through which the children were ongoingly subjected.

At the same time, children have a boundless, exploratory energy and a passion for understanding, not necessarily of the contents of any lesson, but of life itself. They want to talk about their experience of the social world and their embeddedness in it, their emotional bodily relations to it, and their pleasurable experience of competencies in relation to it. Their endless energy in talking about and exploring their experiences and their desire for agency are central to the opening up of a different kind of agency – one in which they are able to see and articulate and critique the very fabric in which they are embedded. Their creative energy opens up the possibility of working with them towards the production of collectively transformative stories in which sexism and other forms of narrow-mindedness can be worked beyond.

Notes

1 This chapter is an edited version of the two final chapters of B. Davies ([1993] 2002) *Shards of Glass. Children Reading and Writing Beyond Gendered Identities.*

2 I will show what I mean by a feminist poststructuralist analysis later in this chapter. A very good introduction to this approach to research can be found in Chris Weedon's (1987) *Poststructuralist Theory and Feminist Practice* or indeed in my book *Frogs and Snails and Feminist Tales* (Davies [1989] 2002).

3   /symbol indicates interruption in speech.
4   It may be that this is a sexually loaded attack if 'snob' is being used in the same way here as it was in other conversations where it appeared to signify an upper class girl who does not take up her femininity properly and so needs to be sexually attacked.

References

Chappell, A. (1984) Family fortunes: a practical photography project, in A. McRobbie and M. Nava (eds) *Gender and Generation*. London: Macmillan.

Cole, B. (1986) *Princess Smartypants*. London: Hamish Hamilton.

Corbalis, J. (1987) *The Wrestling Princess and Other Stories*. London: Knight Books.

Davies, B. ([1989] 2002) *Frogs and Snails and Feminist Tales. Preschool Children and Gender*, 2nd edn. New Jersey: Hampton Press.

Davies, B. ([1993] 2002) *Shards of Glass. Children Reading and Writing Beyond Gendered Identities*, 2nd edn. New Jersey: Hampton Press.

Davies, B. and Harré, R. (2000) Positioning: conversation and the production of selves, in B. Davies (2000) *A Body of Writing*. Walnut Creek, CA: AltaMira Press.

Gilbert, P. (1993) *Gender Stories and the Language Classroom*. Geelong: Deakin University Press.

Kenway, J. and Willis, S. (eds) (1990) *Hearts and Minds. Self Esteem and the Schooling of Girls*. London: Falmer Press.

Weedon, C. (1987) *Poststructuralist Theory and Feminist Practice*. Oxford: Blackwell.

9 'Troubling, troubled and troublesome?'

Working with boys in the primary classroom

Diane Reay

Introduction

There is a long history of concern in relation to boys' behaviour in primary classrooms. My own career has been inextricably entangled with, and defined by, that concern. My 10-year stint from 1975 until 1985 as Head of an off-site centre for children with emotional and behavioural difficulties unsurprisingly was primarily about working with disaffected boys. The Inner London Education Authority (ILEA) 1988 survey of the characteristics of pupils attending special units found that they were overwhelmingly male (ILEA Research and Statistics Department 1988). I had to fight to get girls referred and even then there were only ever one or two out of a total of twelve at any one time. Hey *et al.* (1998) write about boys' domination of special needs provision in the UK and when I became Head of Special Needs in 1985 most of my time was yet again devoted to working with boys. After becoming a Gender Equality Advisory Teacher in Ealing, London, even more of my energies went into boys. Despite my own desire to work on gender projects that involved girls, the pressing concerns of the primary school teachers I was working with, dictated that the vast majority of the projects that I initiated focused on boys. As I wrote in the article describing my work on gender in Ealing:

> In the last two years over a dozen teachers, all female, have approached me to discuss boys in their class who were presenting problems by demanding an excessively high proportion of teacher time and attention; in terms of discipline in both the classroom and the playground; and through lower levels of engagement with the English curriculum resulting in lower levels of achievement than the girls.
>
> (Reay 1993: 13)

The inevitable consequence was that gender work became work with boys. So, in the mid-1990s, after 17 years as a primary practitioner whose main tasks had been variously motivating, 'rescuing' and 'reforming' boys, I was amused by the allegedly new discovery of boys' underachievement and disaffection. Where had everyone been for the past two decades? Certainly not in any of the inner London schools that I had been working in. This concern about boys' disaffection has continued into the millennium. But unlike the period when I was trying to do something about the boys, when there was very little literature to inform practice, (the exceptions being Spender 1983; Clarricoates 1978 and Askew and Ross 1988), there is now a wealth of material (Epstein *et al.* 1998; Francis 1998; Skelton 2001a,b; Frosh, Phoenix and Pattman 2002).

In this article I want to revisit some of that work and my subsequent academic research on gender in schools in the context of this more recent literature and contemporary debates about boys' underachievement and disaffection. Epstein *et al.* (1998) argue that lessons can be learnt from feminist interventions in schools in the 1970s and 1980s but that cognisance needs to be taken of the new and less favourable conditions such work would have to operate under in the new millennium. I want to explore whether my own work with boys in the 1970s and 1980s still has any salience and relevance in the 2000s. Do any of the insights and lessons I learnt from working with boys bear scrutiny in the new century? Or have conditions in primary classrooms changed so much such work can only really be seen as a relic of the long gone 'equal opportunities era' when, as Estelle Morris, the 2001 Labour Education Secretary claimed, too much emphasis was placed on the 'equal' and not enough on the 'opportunities'. Already 'at LEA level, equal opportunity practice is generally low key with few specific or specialist posts for gender and little evidence that gender equality constitutes a priority' (Arnot *et al.* 1996: 99). Yet, the pressing concern about boys has not gone away. In 2000 Gillian Plummer (2000: vii) claimed that 'the greatest national concern at the present time is the underachievement of boys' and since then the discourse of 'the failing boy' and the fear of male working-class disaffection has become more, not less, pervasive. My first close encounter with disruptive boys came on my first teaching practice in a primary school located on a sprawling council estate in Gateshead in 1970, but similar encounters came thick and fast once I moved to take up a post as a primary class teacher in Holloway, Islington. So the first key point to make is that it is primarily, although not exclusively, a class phenomenon. The research by Frosh *et al.* (2002) is very useful here, demonstrating how challenging the teacher is an integral component of popularity among male peer groups across social class, although the middle-class boys, and particularly those attending private schools, also recognize the need to work hard academically. The second key point to make about boys and disaffection is that it has a very long history, stretching back to the institution of compulsory state education for all in the 1870s. This 'new' phenomenon is very old indeed.

The more things change the more some things remain the same

It is the history of boys' underachievement and disaffection that I briefly want to turn to in order to locate current concerns within historical context. Too often the contemporary preoccupation with 'failing boys' ignores, or oversimplifies, what has gone before. As Michele Cohen (1998) points out, 'the problem of the boys' was being recognized as long ago as 1868. She quotes one of the witnesses at the School Inquiry Commission: 'Girls come to you to learn; boys have to be driven'. However, sixty years later the same gender disparity in attitudes to learning was being noted: 'Many girls will work at a subject they dislike. No healthy boy ever does!' (Brereton 1930: 95). So the concern about boys is centuries rather than years old and has traditionally been seen through the lens of gender binaries.

Similarly, gender work in the 1970s and 1980s was represented as operating within narrow gender binaries. Too often since it has been depicted in terms 'of a stifling dualism produced by frameworks which saw only girls' disadvantage and boys' advantage' (Jackson 1998: 84). The fiction created about those two decades is that feminist activism in schools resulted in more favourable treatment for girls; an unremitting focus on developing girls' confidence and assertiveness. Well I, together with feminist colleagues, did set up projects to develop girls' confidence and assertiveness (for instance, the Anti-Sexist Working Party in 1989, see Reay *et al.* 1989), but the reality was much more about fitting such work around more pressing demands to focus on boys. It was always, then as now, much messier than simply viewing girls as disadvantaged and boys as advantaged. And even when we did take such a view the exigencies of working in inner London schools meant dealing with the boys frequently took precedence. For example, the Anti-Sexist Working Party also doubled as a feminist reading group and we had all read and discussed Dale Spender's (1983) and Kathleen Clarricoates' (1978) work yet invariably we all gave boys more attention in the classroom and often chose boy, rather than girl, friendly subjects for class projects. Survival came before idealism. Teaching as a vocation may be about passion, principle and commitment but on a day-to-day basis it is governed by pragmatism and compromise. Such pragmatism and compromise were evident in the boys' project I ran for four years in the late 1980s. Writing about the aims underpinning the project, I tried to untangle the contradictory objectives I was trying to meet:

On one level, the rationale for the project was defined as meeting the boys' own interests – their personal self-development. On another level, the project was about meeting management needs which entailed the smooth running of the school. Admittedly there was a substantial area of overlap between the two objectives but there were also areas of conflict. Management goals do not easily coalesce with children's rights. Initially I found my role an uneasy one, primarily because of the policing component implicit in producing compliant, responsible adherents of the school discipline policy. Discussion with staff allayed many of my initial fears. Emphasis was to be placed on what the boys wanted from the group . . . with the boys and myself left to negotiate the aims and content.

(Reay 1990b: 270)

This project, like many others I have been involved in, had to reconcile a number of competing tensions between child-centred approaches, respect for children's rights and management priorities. My work with the boys became a continual uneasy balance between challenging and accommodating the male peer group hierarchies – too much challenge and I would have alienated the boys, too much complicity and I would have failed to provide them with any resources to help them move forward. So my experience as a feminist practitioner has been characterized by uncertainties about, and struggles to find, the best ways to proceed, uneasy compromises and changes in direction – a far cry from how feminist and equal opportunities work of the 1970s and 1980s has been depicted since.

Classed and racialized masculinities

However, the educational context of boys' disaffection is very different now to what it was in the late 1980s. The tensions I referred to earlier have both increased and intensified. There has been a widening of social class inequalities, an increasing privatization of education, the implementation of the National Curriculum and an intensification of both selection and testing (Reay 2003). As David Jackson (1998: 79) points out, these processes have resulted in many boys feeling 'brushed aside by dominant definitions of school knowledge – their home and community languages, their often raw but direct insights and their everyday, street knowledges have all been experienced as invalid' as a limited, exclusive definition of school knowledge has gained dominance.

So in order to understand boys' disaffection with schooling we need to focus on classed and racialized masculinities and the ways in which they are differentiated. Bob Connell (2000: 164) writes that 'the making of masculinities in schools is far from the simple learning of norms . . . It is a process with multiple pathways, shaped by class and ethnicity, producing diverse outcomes'. Competitive grading, testing and streaming have instituted a steep academic hierarchy which have emphasized differences between masculinities and have widened the gap between 'failing and disruptive boys' (particularly white working-class and African Caribbean boys) and successful boys (predominantly white and middle class). Paul Connolly (1997) captures the racialization of disaffection in his account of the overdisciplining of Black boys in primary schools; a process which sets up a vicious cycle of stereotyping. Connolly describes how the overdisciplining of 'the bad boys', four African Caribbean boys in the primary school he studied, generated a peer group context in which they were more likely to be physically and verbally abused. Connolly (1997: 114) concludes that as a consequence they were more likely to be drawn into fights and to develop 'hardened' identities which then meant they were more likely to be noticed by teachers and disciplined for being aggressive.

The current educational climate has exacerbated an entrenched culture of winners and losers broadly along social class and ethnic lines, and, in doing so, increased the already existing working-class and racialized alienation from schooling. Willis (1977) captured the powerful, and often explosive, combination of anger, fatalism, alienation and resistance that characterized white working-class male relationships to schooling in the 1970s but in the 2000s the conditions that generated such disaffection are even more pervasive. And, in primary classrooms across the UK, the resulting social exclusion and academic rejection such conditions generate entice failing boys 'into a compensatory culture of aggressive laddism' (Jackson 1998: 80). Lucey and Walkerdine attribute this 'aggressive laddism' and the anti-reading and anti-school position that underpins it to 'a defence against fear. They act against study for fear of the loss of masculinity'; a masculinity that, they go on to argue, 'is already seriously under threat in terms of the disappearance of the jobs which require it' (Lucey and Walkerdine 2000: 49). However, it is important to recognize that there are other losers from boys' disruptive behaviour – girls and teachers – and we need to explore how they are affected by boys' disaffection.

At the receiving end?: the impact of boys' behaviour on girls and women teachers

Girls have often been used by teachers as allies in controlling deviant boys. Epstein *et al.* (1998: 9) write about the utilization of girls 'to police, teach, control and civilise boys'. One of the main reasons for the promotion of co-education over the past century has been the expectation that girls would provide incentive and emulation for boys to work harder (Grant and Hodgson

1913; Dale 1974; Cohen 1998). However, as the growing flight of female students from mixed sex state secondary schools testifies, boys can be a problem for the females who have to co-exist with them in co-educational settings.

Women teachers, classroom assistants and female pupils can be dominated and oppressed by certain boys in primary classrooms. A classic study by Valerie Walkerdine (1981) describes the humiliation of a female nursery teacher by a 4-year-old boy. Almost all women teachers can recite low level incidents of rudeness and abuse by a small number of boys who have been in their charge. I am no exception:

> As a teacher, both at an off-site unit and in primary classrooms, I have frequently felt oppressed by the boys in my charge. I have been verbally abused and on a number of occasions, physically assaulted. At the time I rationalised that I was not a 'good enough' teacher. Since then I have often seen women teachers in similar situations, challenged and upset by the aggression of a few boys in their class, and realised the problem was not one of ineptitude but of sexism. Boys also challenge male teachers, and sometimes draw on gender stereotypes by implying that the teacher is not 'a real man'. However, disruptive boys seldom rely to the same extent on devaluing male teachers because of their sex.
>
> (Reay 1993: 16)

With hindsight the attribution of boys' disruptive behaviour to their sexism seems too simplistic. For one it fails to make explicit the mediations of class and ethnicity. But the quote does recognize both the male power and agency central to what Connell (2000) terms 'protest masculinities'; those masculinities formed in opposition rather than conformity to the pressures of schooling and academic learning. According to Connell, 'taking up the offer of protest masculinity is key to understanding disciplinary problems in schools and boys' involvement in violence and sexual harassment' (2000: 163). He argues that certain boys engage in these practices in order 'to acquire or defend prestige, to mark difference and to gain pleasure. Rule breaking becomes central to the making of masculinity when boys lack other resources for gaining these ends' (p. 163). As an academic researcher I have since observed many classrooms where girls were routinely subordinated as inferior by the male peer group. For example, in one inner London Year 4 (8–9-year-olds) primary classroom

> the working class, white and mixed race boys were more preoccupied with football than the academic curriculum. When they were not playing football in the playground they would often be surreptitiously exchanging football cards in the classroom. Alongside regular

jockeying for position within the male peer group which occasionally escalated into full blown fights, there was routine, casual labelling of specific girls as stupid and dumb. The three Bengali boys at the bottom of this particular male peer group hierarchy compensated by demonising, in particular, the three middle class girls.

(Reay 2001: 157)

In this classroom, as in many others I have worked and researched in, it is girls who are at the bottom of male peer group hierarchies! It is easy to forget when responding to the pressure to change boys' behaviour, and the media hype that 'the future is female', that it is still necessary to engage in work that focuses on girls' learning as well. What boys and girls need are gender equality programmes which privilege both sexes rather than a focus on the needs of one at the expense of the other (Skelton 2001b).

Practicalities: what can teachers do?

So how can teachers work productively on changing male peer group hierarchies rather than either challenging or accommodating them? And how do they improve the classroom environment for the girls and the majority of boys who, as Connell (2000: 162) points out, 'learn to negotiate school discipline with only a little friction'? It is important to remember that in spite of popular scare stories about underachieving and uncontrollable boys, the majority of boys in primary school relate perfectly well to their female teachers and girls. I still believe that paradoxically bringing the concerns of the pupil peer group into the classroom is important in reducing and addressing disaffection. There is an even greater temptation now with the National Curriculum and the relentless testing and auditing to leave those concerns at the classroom door but I strongly believe that they will flood in anyway, impacting on behaviour and learning, creating at best divisions amongst children, at worst major disruption. This is particularly so in relation to bullying. Salisbury and Jackson (1996) argue that bullying behaviour can be an expression of constructed masculinity. Which is why physical bullying is so pervasive among boys. They found that their work with secondary school boys was extremely productive and responded to with great fervour and relief by the boys. I had a very similar response to the projects on bullying that I initiated with primary school boys. A great deal of my work with boys in the 1980s focused on bullying because that was an issue that all the boys' groups identified as a major problem for them. Writing about the boys' group I ran in 1988/9 I stated:

The sessions we had on bullying were among the most productive of the year. First there was genuine relief amongst the boys that the subject was being tackled directly. Everyone, including myself recalled an incident in which they had been bullied, while just over a third of the boys admitted to having bullied on at least one occasion. It was obviously a very emotive issue and one, that for the year six boys was inextricably bound up with their fantasies and fears about moving on to secondary school. We spent two sessions attempting to work through such fears and fantasies, focusing on how to use humour, peer group support and adult authority to prevent bullying.

(Reay 1990b: 276–7)

Of course now there would not be the space for such sessions among the contemporary preoccupation with Standardized Assessment Tasks (SATs) but perhaps what I did with the Year 5 (9–10-year-old) boys would be more of a possibility. I integrated a focus on bullying into their maths and information communication technology (ICT) curriculum. We designed a questionnaire for a whole school survey on bullying, worked out a representative sample and then the boys carried it out. An integral part of their task was to impart the strategies for dealing with bullying we had discussed and agreed in the group sessions to any younger child who disclosed that they had been bullied. As only two children in the sample claimed never to have been bullied, the boys had lots of opportunities to rehearse preventative strategies. Since this work on bullying, my own more recent research and that of others (Reay and Wiliam 1999; Frosh *et al.* 2002) has revealed that working hard at school can lead to boys being bullied. Frosh *et al.* (2002) found a polarization of popularity and schoolwork in which popular masculinities are pervasively constructed as antithetical to being seen to work hard academically, leading to hardworking 'clever' boys being demonized within the male peer group. In my research with Dylan Wiliam, we make a direct link between bullying and the growing regime of testing in primary classrooms. We describe the consequences of regular SATs practice for the position of high attaining boys within the male peer group:

In earlier interview sessions, carried out over the autumn term, children often compared themselves academically to Stuart, citing him as the cleverest child in the class. Such comments were presented simply as statements of fact and there was no malice or ill-feeling expressed. However, towards the end of the Easter term with a programme of daily maths tests and regular science and English SATs practice, Stuart's situation among the peer group, particularly with the other boys, was becoming increasingly vulnerable. On one occasion, after the teacher had pointed out that Stuart was the only child to get 20 out of 20 for the maths test and that everybody else must try to do better, Terry leaned over and thumped him hard in the back. Twice Stuart came back from playtime with scratches either to his cheek or the back of his neck. He was not sure 'exactly who was responsible' but complained that the other boys had started to 'gang up' on him. The language other children used to describe him shifted discernibly. Before he had simply been recognised as clever; now he was increasingly labelled as 'a swot' by both girls and boys. There are frequent entries in the fieldnotes which testify to a growing climate of hostility towards Stuart. But Stuart had not started to show off. Rather, the classroom practices in 6S over the spring term had dramatically increased processes of differentiation which in turn had led to a growing polarisation among the peer group.

(Reay and Wiliam 1999: 352)

It seems that work on bullying is even more important in the current climate of testing and regular assessment. Recent research has uncovered disturbingly high levels of bullying in primary schools. Whitney and Smith (1993) revealed that over 25 per cent of primary school pupils were being bullied in Sheffield, while according to MacLeod and Morris (1996) 50 per cent of primary pupils in London and the South-East reported being bullied in school during the previous year.

A further continuing concern for primary school teachers is boys' literacy practices. In my own work with boys I tried to combine 'doing' with writing activities through book making projects involving both mixed and boys only groups. Setting the groups the task of producing book proposals that appeal to the widest possible class readership both challenges and modifies existing stereotypes, and if supported by whole class surveys, generates useful information for the teacher as well as the children (Reay 1993). The subsequent process of designing layout, working out the graphics, producing publicity and marketing materials, as well as writing the text, meets the requirements of English, maths, art and ICT curricula at the same time as helping to change preconceived ideas about gendered preferences.

In addition to concerted work on bullying and literacy a lot of my time in the sessions was spent helping the boys to question conventional gendered characterizations. Any work with boys needs to recognize gender as relational (Francis 1998; Skelton 2001a) and focus on the images of femininity as well as those of masculinity that boys bring with them, and construct in the context of schooling. Relatedly, I would argue that such work also needs to recognize the relationships between gender, class and ethnicity. The other curriculum interventions I developed were rooted in this belief that gender cannot be explored in isolation from other powerful aspects of identity. The anti-racist work on Black history was enjoyed by all the boys and even prompted the most writing phobic boys in the group to commit pen to paper. One of my main worries about the National Curriculum is that it has marginalized any notion of 'really useful knowledge' (Johnson 1979) for the working classes but anti-racist work that looks at the lives of 'ordinary but heroic' black people like Rosa Parks is clearly both useful and inspiring. So was the work on the franchise and working-class histories I covered. At the time I wrote that the primary aged boys I was working with suffered the fate of all low status groups in society, be they black, female or working class: 'They had had no access to a meaningful history which explained why they and others like them came to be situated in a particular social location' (Reay 1990b: 279). Today the literacy and numeracy hours and the obsession with 'the basics' have left even less space for curriculum initiatives that I still see as vital in predominantly working-class schools like those I was working in.

Devolving power to pupils and instituting more collaborative, reflexive and democratic ways of working are also simultaneously ways of tackling disaffection. It is good to see the 'new-found' enthusiasm for formative assessment (Black *et al.* 2002) as that underpinned learning in the boys' groups that I was teaching in the 1980s. The self and peer evaluation with its focus on pupil discussion and responsibility for learning that has become fashionable in the late 1990s was a pivotal part of the boys' groups I ran in the late 1980s:

> From the beginning I instituted a process of self-evaluation where boys evaluated their ability to work co-operatively on a scale of one to ten. They then made a group assessment which involved evaluating the input of other members of their group in addition to their own contribution. I fed back my own observations and we negotiated a final score. Initially, their contributions were brief to the point of curtness but by the summer term they seemed to have a much better grasp of what self and group evaluation entailed, giving far more detailed comments.
>
> (Reay 1990b: 273)

Black *et al.* (2002) argue that both self and peer assessment are valuable but that peer assessment is especially valuable because pupils accept from one another criticisms of their work – and I would add behaviour – which they would not take seriously from their teacher. As is implicit in the quote above, peer assessment also allows the teacher space to observe and reflect on what is happening and to frame useful interventions.

Implicit in all the above is the view that the issue of tackling boys' disaffection and disruption in primary classrooms needs to be intrinsically, irrevocably linked to a project of social class, gender and racial justice in education. This does not mean suspending the National Curriculum and instituting a series of boys only discussion groups. As a primary school teacher in the 1980s I had to get the curriculum covered and there is even more pressure on teachers now. Rather, the curriculum and attainment targets need to be creatively rethought. A good starting point is to find out 'the gender state-of-play' in your classroom and cover mathematics, ICT and English curricula at the same time by getting the children to research what ideas pupils hold about men and women and how they differ by sex (see Francis 1998). When I attempted something similar I was pleasantly surprised:

> I came to the boys group with a set of preconceived ideas about boys not being able to express their feelings and expecting female servicing. I was not entirely wrong but like all stereotypes my preconceptions were far too simplistic. It transpired that I was drawing on more traditional notions of masculinity in the spheres of domestic labour and tears than were the boys.
>
> (Reay 1990b: 274)

However, as Christine Skelton (2001b) points out, work on the images of masculinity and femininity children bring with them into school and act out in the classroom and playground needs to be accompanied by parallel work on the dominant images of masculinity and femininity schools reflect to their pupils. Reflecting on and questioning dominant gender categories is something the staff need to do as much as the boys and girls in their classes.

The bigger picture: contextualizing boys' disaffection

Despite the disproportionate amount of my time and energy going into work with boys, my commitment throughout the late 1970s and 1980s was not to 'redeem' boys but to ensure working-class educational success. It is difficult in retrospect to evaluate the extent to which I managed to achieve that, if at all, although the EPPI review (Francis *et al.* 2002) of gender work in primary schools indicates a degree of success, albeit with the limitations and unforeseen consequences I discuss in my reporting of that work (Reay 1990a,b; 1991; 1993). I am certain, however, that such work would be even more difficult to undertake now than it was at the time and it was very difficult then. In Shaun's story (Reay 2002) I write about a white, working-class boy, who, in spite of a contradictory, ambivalent relationship to schooling (that, I would argue, characterizes almost all, and especially white, working-class relationships to education) desperately wants to achieve educationally. The article raises questions about the possibilities of bringing together white, working-class masculinities with educational success in inner-city working-class schooling. Lucey and Walkerdine (2000: 43) argue that 'to be both academically successful and acceptably male requires a considerable amount of careful negotiation on the part of working class boys'. I argue that to combine the two generates heavy psychic costs, involving boys and young men not only in an enormous amount of academic labour but also an intolerable burden of psychic reparative work. Shaun's situation reveals the tenuousness of working-class, and in particular male, working-class relationships to schooling. In the article I describe how he is caught between two untenable positions, continually engaged in a balancing act that requires superhuman effort; on the one hand ensuring his masculinity is kept intact and on the other endeavouring to maintain his academic success. Inner-city schools and their wider contexts are often spaces in which success is in short supply and, as a consequence, it is frequently resented and undermined in those who have it. Below we see both the enormous effort Shaun puts into reconciling two contradictory aspects of self, and also the ways in which they are beginning to come apart:

> It's getting harder because like some boys, yeah, like a couple of my friends, yeah, they go 'Oh, you are teacher's pet and all that'. Right? What? Am I teacher's pet because I do my work and tell you lot to shut up when you are talking and miss is trying to talk? And they go, yeah so you're still a teacher's pet. Well, if you don't like it go away, innit.
> (Reay 2002: 228)

Shaun's ambitions are created under and against conditions of adversity. Reputation in his school comes not through academic achievement but is the outcome of a jockeying for position among a male peer group culture, in which boys are 'routinely reproducing versions of themselves and their peers as valued because of their hardness, appearance, or capacity to subvert schooling' (Phoenix and Frosh 2001). As O'Donnell and Sharpe (2000) point out, many inner-city schools are engaged in a losing battle to counterbalance the collective influence of the male peer group. Shaun's narrative suggests that the problem of 'failing boys' cannot be solved alone through school based initiatives. How can Shaun both set himself apart from and remain part of the wider working-class male collectivity? That is the task he has set himself and the dilemma it raises lies at the very heart of class differentials in attainment within education. I conclude that until social processes of male gender socialization move away from the imperative of privileging the masculine and allow boys to stay in touch with their feminine qualities the problem of 'failing boys' will remain despite the best efforts of teachers and researchers. As Quicke (1999) points out, the ways in which boys, and particularly working-class boys, distance themselves from femininity particularly restricts their abilities and performance in literacy and language based subjects.

Frosh and his colleagues (2002) offer further helpful insights into male peer group cultures in school in their delineation of popular and unpopular masculinities and the classroom behaviours that underpin them. They found that 'an important part of being "cool" and popular entailed the resisting and challenging of adult authority in the classroom' (Frosh *et al.* 2002: 200).

Popular boys were expected to 'backchat' teachers, while boys who were seen as too conscientious were made fun of. Although they were researching boys in the first two years of secondary schooling, the genesis of this 'laddish' behaviour is also evident in primary classrooms. As Christine Skelton (2001b) demonstrates through her case study of Shane, primary school boys who consistently challenge the teacher's authority earn themselves not only significant amounts of teacher attention but also the attention and tacit approval of their male peers. Here we can see a frightening correlation between popularity among the male peer group and getting into trouble in primary classrooms.

So have I moved from a counsel of hope to a counsel of despair? I am definitely not arguing that work on gender equality is no longer vital or that it is pointless to try and tackle male disaffection in primary classrooms. Rather, there need to be ways of working to improve things that avoid pathologizing female teachers on the one hand and male working-class pupils on the other, but recognize the many ways in which boys and men continue to retain social advantages at the expense of girls and women, and that acknowledge that some constructions of masculinities can be damaging to both boys and girls. Tackling masculinities and the way they are constructed in the context of schooling is the most important step. Popular masculinities in primary schools are too often protest masculinities. At times the research and literature in the area appears overwhelming, giving the impression that the male peer group is so dominant there is little teachers can do. However, as I've tried to show in the section on practicalities, teachers can make a significant difference and not just in terms of curriculum offer which is the area I have concentrated on, but also in terms of ethos and culture. Boys (and girls) respond best to teachers who can keep order and have fun with pupils. All children have a keen sense of unfairness: for example, they resent being punished collectively when only one or two boys have misbehaved. Frosh *et al.* (2002) found in their interviews with boys that many reported that their teachers treated boys unfairly with some also saying that teachers particularly picked on black boys. They conclude that

> While this does not necessarily indicate that most teachers are unfair in these ways – particularly since, from their own accounts boys can make life difficult for teachers – the pervasiveness of this narrative from boys is important to considerations of boys' educational attainment.
>
> (Frosh *et al.* 2002: 224)

Conclusion

I am certainly not advocating my ways of working as the answer. For one, I fell into the trap that yawns open for all women primary school teachers

(Steedman 1988). Ironically, while attempting to challenge and transform the gender stereotypes that the boys had invested in, I was entangled in one of my own. I became the nurturer, the surrogate mother and treated my work as a vocation rather than a profession – children regularly came round at weekends to stay. I even fostered one child for 6 months while the family were having extreme difficulties. In retrospect my work was not sustainable, certainly not over the period of a working life and very definitely not in the current educational climate. However, there are many other options lying between being the mother on one extreme and giving up on boys on the other. I have tried to give some indication of which strategies worked best in the educational contexts that I was working in during the 1970s and 1980s. I have also tried to map out how 'the problem' of boys has changed since the late 1980s and suggested, through recounting some of Shaun's story, that only partial solutions can ever lie with teachers and schools. Wider constructions of both masculinities and femininities need to change and while teachers have a part to play, it is ultimately a challenge that the whole of society needs to face up to.

References

Arnot, M., David, M. and Weiner, G. (1996) *Educational Reforms and Gender Equality in Schools*, Research Discussion Series no. 17. Manchester: Equal Opportunities Commission.

Askew, S. and Ross, C. (1988) *Boys Don't Cry: Boys and Sexism in Education*. Milton Keynes: Open University Press.

Black, P., Harrison, C., Lee, C., Marshall, B. and Wiliam, D. (2002) *Working Inside the Black Box: Assessment for Learning in the Classroom*. London: King's College Publications.

Brereton, C. (1930) *Modern Language Teaching in Day and Evening Schools*. London: University of London.

Clarricoates, K. (1978) Dinosaurs in the classroom: a re-examination of some aspects of the 'hidden curriculum' in primary schools, *Women's Studies International Quarterly*, 1: 353–64.

Cohen, M. (1998) 'A habit of healthy idleness': boys' underachievement in historical perspective, in D. Epstein, J. Elwood, V. Hey and J. Maw (eds) *Failing Boys: Issues in Gender and Achievement*. Buckingham: Open University Press.

Connell, R. W. (2000) *The Men and the Boys*. Cambridge: Polity Press.

Connolly, P. (1997) *Racism, Gender Identities and Young Children*. London: Routledge.

Dale, R. (1974) *Mixed or Single-Sex School*, vol. 3. London: Routledge and Kegan Paul.

Epstein, D., Elwood, J., Hey, V. and Maw, J. (eds) (1998) *Failing Boys: Issues in Gender and Achievement*. Buckingham: Open University Press.

Francis, B. (1998) *Power Plays: Primary School Children's Constructions of Gender, Power and Adult Work*. Stoke-on-Trent: Trentham Books.

Francis, B., Skelton, C. and Archer, L. (2002) A systematic review of classroom strategies for reducing stereotypical gender constructions among girls and boys in mixed-sex UK primary schools (EPPI-Centre Review). In: *Research Evidence in Education Library*. Issue 1. London: EPPI-Centre, Social Science Research Unit, Institute of Education.

Frosh, S., Phoenix, A. and Pattman, R. (2002) *Young Masculinities*. London: Palgrave.

Hey, V., Leonard, D., Daniels, H. and Smith, M. (1998) Boys' underachievement, special needs practices and questions of equity, in D. Epstein, J. Elwood, V. Hey and J. Maw (eds) *Failing Boys: Issues in Gender and Achievement*. Buckingham: Open University Press.

Jackson, D. (1998) Breaking out of the binary trap: boys' underachievement, schooling and gender relations, in D. Epstein, J. Elwood, V. Hey and J. Maw (eds) *Failing Boys: Issues in Gender and Achievement*. Buckingham: Open University Press.

Johnson, R. (1979) Really useful knowledge: radical education and working-class culture 1790–1948, in J. Clarke, C. Critcher and R. Johnson (eds) *Working Class Culture: Studies in History and Theory*. New York: St Martin's Press.

Grant, C. and Hodgson, N. (1913) *The Case for Co-Education*. London: Grant Richards.

Lucey, H. and Walkerdine, V. (2000) Boys' underachievement: social class and changing masculinities, in T. Cox (ed.) *Combating Educational Disadvantage*. London: Falmer Press.

MacLeod, M. and Morris, S. (1996) *Why Me? Children Talking to Childline About Bullying*. London: Childline.

O'Donnell, M. and Sharpe, S. (2000) *Uncertain Masculinities: Youth, Ethnicity and Class in Contemporary Britain*. London: Routledge.

Phoenix, A. and Frosh, S. (2001) Positioned by 'hegemonic' masculinities: a study of London boys' narratives of identity, *Australian Psychologist*, 36(1): 27–35.

Plummer, G. (2000) *Failing Working Class Girls*. Stoke-on-Trent: Trentham Books.

Quicke, J. (1999) *A Curriculum for Life*. Buckingham: Open University Press.

Reay, D. (1990a) Girls' groups as a component of anti-sexist practice – one primary school's experience, *Gender and Education*, 12(1): 37–48.

Reay, D. (1990b) Working with boys, *Gender and Education*, 12(3): 269–82.

Reay, D. (1991) Intersections of gender, race and class in the primary school, *British Journal of Sociology of Education*, 12(2): 163–82.

Reay, D. (1993) 'Miss, he says he doesn't like you': working with boys in the infant classroom, in H. Claire, J. Maybin and J. Swann (eds) *Equality Matters: Case Studies from the Primary School*. Clevedon: Multilingual Matters.

Reay, D. (2001) 'Spice girls', 'nice girls', 'girlies' and 'tomboys': gender discourses, girls' cultures and femininities in the primary classroom, *Gender and Education*, 13(2): 153–66.

Reay, D. (2002) Shaun's story: troubling discourses of white working class masculinities, *Gender and Education*, 14(3): 221–34.

Reay, D. (2003) Reproduction, reproduction, reproduction: troubling dominant discourses on education and social class in the UK, in J. Freeman-Moir and A. Scott (eds) *Yesterday's Dreams: International and Critical Perspectives on Education and Social Class.* New Zealand: University of Canterbury Press.

Reay, D. and Wiliam, D. (1999) 'I'll be a nothing': structure, agency and the construction of identity through assessment, *British Educational Research Journal,* 25(3): 343–54.

Reay, D., Granados Johnson, J., Helliwell, J. *et al.* (1989) Equality in the early years, in M. Cole (ed.) *Educating for Equality: From Theory to Practice.* London: Routledge.

Salisbury, J. and Jackson, D. (1996) *Challenging Macho Values: Practical Ways of Working with Adolescent Boys.* London: Falmer Press.

Skelton, C. (2001a) Typical boys? Theorising masculinity in educational settings, in B. Francis and C. Skelton (eds) *Investigating Gender: Contemporary Perspectives in Education.* Buckingham: Open University Press.

Skelton, C. (2001b) *Schooling the Boys: Masculinities and Primary Education.* Buckingham: Open University Press.

Spender, D. (1983) *Invisible Women.* London: Writers and Readers Press.

Steedman, C. (1988) The mother made conscious: the historical development of a primary school pedagogy, in M. Woodhead and A. McGrath (eds) *Family, School and Society.* London: Hodder and Stoughton in association with the Open University.

Walkerdine, V. (1981) Sex, power and pedagogy, *Screen Education,* 38: 14–25.

Whitney, I. and Smith, P. K. (1993) A survey of the nature and extent of bullying in junior and secondary schools, *Educational Research,* 35(1): 3–25.

Willis, P. (1977) *Learning to Labour.* Aldershot: Saxon House.

10 Some neglected issues of transfer

Identity, status and gender from the pupils' perspective

Jean Rudduck and Isobel Urquhart

In our education system the continuity of pupils' school careers is interrupted by the necessity to move, at least once, to another school – for example, from infant to junior, or primary to secondary, or middle to high school. These are strong academic and social markers of change and, not surprisingly, the transfer[1] points become sites of considerable anxiety and excitement for pupils, and opportunities for cajoling and threat by teachers: 'My teacher says I've got to know *everything* before I move to secondary school' (Year 6 [i.e. 10–11-year-old] pupil). Transfers are also occasions when pupils' optimism is high but their status and identity can, as they discover, be vulnerable.

In this chapter we discuss data from three transfer studies in the light of Carolyn Jackson and Jo Warin's work (2000) on the importance, at transfer, of gender as an aspect of identity. They argue that moments of transfer produce a predictable disequilibrium: people move into an unfamiliar social context – new places, spaces, people, rules, standards and so on – and that they respond by modifying, often through the process of comparing self with others, their sense of self – and, in the case of pupils in school, their identities as learners. Young people's 'confidence in their ability to control and predict their environment becomes much less certain' (Jackson and Warin 2000: 381) as they move to a new school; but at the same time they recognize that the move marks a step towards the more adult status, activities and responsibilities that they look forward to. They are also having to manage, therefore, considerable emotional dissonance as excited anticipation is layered with anxiety about whether they will manage the change with their dignity intact.

Comparing self with others, Jackson and Warin suggest, may serve to 'confirm self-perceptions, enhance self-concept or ... defend a person's self-concept' (2000: 379). Situations with defined reference groups are those which prompt social comparisons, for instance, when pupils are put into ability-based groups, or, we would add, when pupils hear the outcomes of tests and exams, and when they hear whether they have succeeded in gaining a place in the school they want to go to. Transfer, of course, brings pupils among new references groups, including new friends and classmates, where there are more opportunities for defining and re-defining self as learner in relation to others.

We go on to argue, somewhat more speculatively, that at these moments of turbulence, young people cope with the strains and stresses of change by using a more established dimension of self – which is gender – as a way of organizing the multiplicity of new experiences, but this move can lead to stereotypical behaviours (see Jackson and Warin 2000 for supporting evidence). We use Jackson and Warin's thesis as a lens through which to look at data gathered in three recent studies of neglected aspects of transfer (that we were involved or associated with) and we check out the goodness of fit. One study focused on the transition or transfer from Year 2 (6–7-year-olds) to Year 3 (7–8-year-olds) (Doddington *et al.* 2001). Next, we focus on a study of Year 8 (12–13-year-old) pupils' retrospective accounts of their transfer to the first year of secondary school, looking at what experiences remain vivid in their minds a year later (see Rudduck 1996). Finally we look at the responses of Year 6 (10–11-year-old) pupils to the realization that they have not got a place in the secondary schools they wanted to move to (Urquhart 2001). In the first two cases Jackson and Warin's uncontentious argument that at times of transfer concepts of selfhood and status are at the forefront of pupils' responses to the new situation are undoubtedly confirmed but the suggestion that the participants' sense of gender identity serves as a crucible through which new experiences are made sense of remains unconfirmed as the data were insufficiently focused on gender. In the third study, perhaps because emotions surrounding the news of rejection run deeper, we find some evidence that girls and boys cope by attempting to protect the self but in different, gendered ways.

Pupils' perspectives on the move from Year 2 to Year 3

Both Year 8 and Year 3 have been identified as times where pupils' learning appears to slow down (Ofsted 1999). These two periods represent distinctly different stages in pupils' school careers: Year 8 can be a somewhat 'fallow' period between the excitement of transfer (Year 7) and the 'serious' test and examination years (Years 9 to 11) whereas Year 3 marks the step-over point between the first two key stages of the National Curriculum when pupils and teachers have to adjust to a new set of academic demands. In some cases, Year 3 can also be a point of transfer where pupils move from infant to junior school with all the associated excitements and uncertainties of becoming part of a new physical and social environment.

Chris Doddington, Julia Flutter and colleagues (2001) undertook a small scale study of pupils' and teachers' views of the move from Year 2 to Year 3. Eight schools in each of two local education authorities (LEAs) took part and pupils and teachers in the two target years were interviewed. Selected for interview were pupils judged by their teachers to be above average in their performance, about average and performing below their potential. The research team found that all pupils were keenly aware that the move to Year 3 was important. They talked about their advancement in social as well as academic terms. As going to school is an important step away from childhood, so the move to Year 3 is another big step forward and pupils often have high expectations. Four lines from a poem by Rod Hull (2000) pinned to a teaching staff's noticeboard capture new pupils' disappointment when expectations are not met at the start of their school career:

> My first day at school today.
> Funny sort of day.
> Didn't seem to learn much –
> Seemed all we did was play.

Young students expect school to be different from home, to be about working hard to learn. The Year 2 pupils interviewed had equally high expectations of moving up to Year 3 and among the Year 3 pupils there were many positive responses to what they saw as being in the next stage of education and of enhanced personal status. The first two statements highlight some markers of progress in terms of content learning:

> Since you're a junior . . . we have to call our speech marks just actual speech marks now and in the infants we could call them 66 and 99's but we have to use the proper word now . . .
>
> (Year 3, boy)

> I've noticed something – in Year 2 we didn't count up to 100 because she thought it was too hard and in Year 3 I just sort of learned it straight away.
>
> (Year 3, girl)

The next two statements suggest pride in enhanced autonomy. What is interesting is the assumption that the changes are triggered by the move into Year 3 rather than as an outcome of the normal process of personal and cognitive development:

> In Year 3 you can do more things, you're not treated like little kids, you're treated more grownup-ly and you don't have to be shown about because we can look after ourselves.
>
> (Year 3, boy)

> We have to think for ourselves sometimes.
>
> (Year 3, boy)

Teachers were clear that learning *was* more demanding in Year 3 – and pupils' comments bore this out – but not all were coping well with the new demands. Year 3 was not turning out entirely as they had expected:

> What is hard about the work is that some of it has to be done all in one day – that is tricky.
>
> (Year 3, boy)

> Well, you have loads more writing than in Year 2.
>
> (Year 3, girl)

> The thing I don't like about one of my lessons is the maths because we always have to do like complicated things and it's a bit awkward.
>
> (Year 3, girl)

> Sometimes I don't like English because bits of it are too hard – everyday it gets a tiny bit harder. There's too much writing.
>
> (Year 3, boy)

We did not find any clear differences that the pupils were dealing with the difficulties they were encountering in gender stereotypical ways. A few girls mentioned difficulties with maths and a few boys mentioned difficulties with English and both boys and girls were put off by the amount of writing, but we could not generalize in any way that supported stereotypical patterns of response to these subjects.

In the last four quotations the difficulties were handled fairly lightly – things were described as 'tricky', 'a bit awkward', 'a tiny bit harder' but there were some sharper indications of strain and stress: pupils' confidence in themselves as learners in the more advanced stage of education that they had looked forward to was already being stirred, if not shaken! These small indicators of strain reflect the pressure on Year 3 teachers who see their task as very different from that of Year 2 teachers, in terms of both academic and personal development. In Year 2, says a Year 3 teacher, 'they're mollycoddled and they can get a lot of attention whereas now, in Year 3, they have to cope on their own more'. Year 3 teachers seemed eager to distinguish their work from that of their colleagues' teaching of the Year 2 children by emphasizing that learning is tougher, more demanding in Year 3. So, while Year 3 pupils like feeling more grown-up and enjoy the status of knowing that they are now doing more advanced work, the learning curve may be too steep for some of them.

One factor in what Ofsted (1999) identified as a fall off in progress in Year 3 may be that some parents (as we learned from the interviews), hearing that pupils are expected to be more independent in Year 3 and that the work will be harder, offer less support – either because they feel the content is beyond them or because they feel that pupils should be learning to work without their help. Clearly the dips in progress, whether at Year 3 or Year 8, cannot just be attributed to poor teaching; the situation is more complex than that and needs to be looked at through the eyes of the pupils.

Schools that have a clear awareness of what the transfer or transition can mean for pupils can plan support strategies to help them cope with the new demands and sustain a positive sense of self as learner. For example, Doddington *et al.* (2001) found that where schools gave careful consideration to introducing and explaining the new aspects of learning required by the Key Stage 2 curriculum, pupils across the ability range were more confident and robust. In contrast, where liaison between Year 2 and 3 teachers was haphazard, there was no systematic preparation for what lay ahead and less confident learners were vulnerable to losing ground in the face of a faster, tougher pace of learning. Some pupils – both boys and girls – were, at this early stage in their school careers, beginning to see learning as a burdensome struggle and there were expressions of self-doubt and anxiety. And, as Woods (1987: 120) points out, negative views of learning, acquired early on in pupils' school careers, can have serious, long-term repercussions:

> Life-chances are determined or constructed for many people in the early years. The channels of their educational potential which is realised at secondary school are already formulated before they arrive there ... the 7–8 age group is a crucial one in the development of those attitudes, abilities and relationships that go into the making of educational success at that level. In this sense the transition is not only of infant to junior. Like joined-up writing and the second set of teeth, there are other ultimates here, and they lay down the means for the next transfer to secondary, and indeed for later life.

The move into Year 3, whether an experience of transfer or transition, clearly has an impact on pupils' identity as learners but (and this may be because gender was not a main focus of the study) there is insufficient data to allow us to speculate on any gendered differences in response. However, it should be noted that various factors, such as social class and ethnicity, as well as gender, are likely to influence children's experiences of transfer to a new school and also the construction of their social and academic identities.

Pupils' retrospective accounts of their transfer to Year 7

Research studies that have focused on transfer as a rite of passage draw attention to the myths that sharpen anticipation, the challenges that new pupils often have to endure at the hands of older pupils and the intense anxieties about coping – with harder work, new rules, travelling to school more independently and, in some cases, with having to wear, and learn to knot, a school tie! There is a mix of emotion:

> However hopeful our anticipation, we also harbour fears about the future. It is the nature of the beginning that the path ahead is unknown, leaving us poised as we enter upon it between wondrous excitement and anxious dread.
>
> (Salzberger-Wittenberg *et al.* 1983, in Morrison 2000: 47)

Going to 'the big school' marks a significant move from one stage in the life course to another, and the expectation among the young people involved is that they will be treated 'more like an adult' and that 'work will be harder' in the secondary school. Sadly, the expectation often outstrips the reality. Pupils who have been prepared for the move by very challenging work in Year 6 of their primary school may find themselves repeating work in the first year of secondary school rather than enjoying the excitement of the new challenges that they had been expecting (see Galton *et al.* 1999). But disappointment is perhaps more commonly engendered by the realization that in the new setting, the transfer pupils will be the lowest in status, an experience that is reported in other countries with similar transfer arrangements. For example, Kvalsund, from Norway, says that 'seen through the eyes of the pupils, it is not just a great transition, but also a great fall – in the feeling of social mastery, status, power, and security – that occurs almost overnight' (2001: 11). The author quotes (in translation) a Norwegian pupil: 'Think of it, here we are, used to being the biggest – and after the summer holidays, hey presto, we're the smallest' (p. 10).

There is plentiful evidence in our interview data (from 80 pupils in three very different schools in three LEAs in the north of England) that issues of status and identity are very much on pupils' minds at transfer. We talked to them a year later to see what kinds of experiences were still remembered and most were to do with aspects of identity and status. Their sense of diminished status after being the biggest and the most senior members of their primary schools are reflected in their comments on the size of the school in relation to their own size: they often use telling imagery. Their related observations are echoed in Morrison's (2000: 47) later interviews in an East Anglian school with Year 7 pupils (11–12-year-olds):

> I felt like an ant in the middle of a football pitch.
>
> (boy)

> All the pupils seemed really large. I thought I was going to suffocate.
>
> (girl)

> I was used to being the biggest in the school but now I had shrunk. [And] there were about 200 people waiting round the bus stop – this was a big change compared to my 59-pupil school.
>
> (girl)

A Year 7 boy in Urquhart's study makes a similar comment:

> In primary school before I left, you know, you're all keen and everything, but when you get here, you're like one of the little babies, so you're at a disadvantage . . . You never know what can happen around the corner.

Year 8 pupils recalled with great vividness, a year after transfer, particular incidents where their attempt to appear socially at ease in their new school and to impress their new teachers and peers failed. For example, the naivety of one group of young women was exposed at the first school disco: 'We ended up wearing jeans and a nice top and we wore high heels. And everyone else was in like trainers and shell suits and we just felt so out of place'. Other pupils remembered turning up late for lessons 'and white-faced' because they had lost their way, being confused about the new rules, not understanding how to set about homework, realizing that they had forgotten to bring the right books or equipment to school, and knowing that they were behaving like novices when it came to coping with a journey to school by bus instead of walking.

Jackson and Warin (2000: 379) suggest that the social comparisons that are triggered by encounters with new reference groups can affect identity in different ways 'so as to confirm self-conceptions, enhance self-concept or to defend a person's self-concept'. Here, the likelihood is that comparisons are quickly unravelling the enhanced self-image that pupils expected secondary school to grant them. But there is also contrasting evidence of attempts at defending the self-concept: the Year 8 pupils' backward glances at their old schools suggest a reassuring restructuring of experience. Most recalled feeling a sense of loss at leaving their primary school where, so they claimed, they knew everyone – an exaggeration perhaps but nonetheless a statement indicative of the familiarity and security of the past as against the uncertainties of the present. But, at the same time, they also remembered responding positively to changes in the organization of learning. While they were still at their primary schools they were probably unaware that they were largely confined to one classroom for most of their lessons or that they were taught much of the day by one teacher. But looking back with the wisdom of hindsight they commented on the lack of variety in the primary school day (quoted in Rudduck *et al.* 1996):

> That's what I like about this school. You have a different teacher for a different lesson. You don't get like bored with the same teacher.
>
> (p. 22)

> You don't have to stay in your own classroom all day . . . looking at the same four walls.
>
> (p. 22)

> It's better now. You can go round different lessons. It's more interesting, isn't it? Used to be just sat in one classroom like, listening to one teacher blabbering on about one thing all the time . . . Used to be boring.
>
> (p. 23)

Another Year 8 student, also engaging in a retrospective restructuring of experience, says that the work she did in primary school 'wasn't real learning . . . we just used to paint and things like that'. Real lessons, she now claims, are things like science and doing experiments. On the whole, students were expecting, and most were ready for, a new intellectual challenge, which they didn't always find.

These recalled experiences of new Year 8 pupils suggest that transfer to secondary school is indeed a time of personal reorientation when young people are re-shaping their self-image as they encounter new situations, new teachers and a new peer group.

The Year 6 / Year 7 transfer: pupils who fail to get into their preferred schools

Isobel Urquhart opened an article (2001) with the following extract from a newspaper:

> It's two days since 11-year-old Frances heard she'd got into the secondary school she was hoping for, and she's still walking on air.
>
> (*Guardian Education*, 20 March 2001)

She comments:

> By celebrating the successes of those individuals who achieve places at popular and high achieving schools, press reports often draw readers' attention to the emotional highs of choosing a secondary school. And yet, for many children, the experience of choosing a school is one of protracted anxiety and ultimate disappointment.
>
> (Urquhart 2001: 83)

Lucey and Reay (1999) also studied the disappointments of transfer from the pupil perspective; Urquhart's study, commissioned by one inner-city local education authority, replicated the research on a smaller scale. Both studies gathered data from pupils in multi-ethnic inner-city schools in socially disadvantaged areas. Urquhart interviewed 22 predominantly working-class pupils from three primary schools; a small number were followed up into secondary school. Both studies were undertaken 'against the backdrop of a pervasive rhetoric of "freedom to choose" which is silent about the growing evidence that increasing numbers of children ... are being refused places at the school of their choice' (Wolchover 1998, in Lucey and Reay 1999: 5).

Urquhart's study (2001) suggests that at transfer from primary to secondary school, issues of status – in this case, in relation to acceptance or rejection – are deeply felt by both boys and girls and social comparisons are being made, as Jackson and Warin (2000) suggest, which affect the individual's sense of self. Moreover, there was some suggestion in the data that gender might be influencing boys' and girls' coping strategies in the face of the turbulence of transfer and feelings of rejection but the disappointment and pain seemed to be felt more or less equally by both girls and boys. Urquhart quotes one Year 6 girl who said, 'Well I don't think it's fair really because my cousin, yeah, she got ten choices and all ten she failed. She's like me. I feel like an orphan' (Urquhart 2001: 84). Lucey and Reay comment: 'These children's voices reveal just how traumatising and demoralising the business of choosing a school can be to those who fail to be selected by their first choice of school' (1999: 11–12).

The pupils' early experience of rejection – at a time when they were enthusiastic about 'getting a good education' – was difficult for them to come to terms with. Girls were inclined to see *themselves* as the problem rather than to blame the system, with the consequence that their self-esteem seemed to be more directly diminished in relation to their more successful peers:

> I was a bit sad when I got the letter – my mum didn't want to show it to me . . . I just thought I weren't that good at things really.
>
> (Year 6, girl)

> I think people do sometimes get upset when they think they're the only one who haven't got in and they start to think they're not smart or they've done something wrong.
>
> (Year 6, girl)

> Why did they pick them not me? . . . You think you must be bad.
>
> (Year 6, girl)

Previous research (Spender 1982; Stanworth 1983; Walkerdine 1990) suggests that self-esteem is experienced differently by boys and girls, with boys tending to be over-confident and over-optimistic about their ability, and with girls tending to be under-confident. In our study, however, boys – and this does not mean that the hurt was any less for them, merely that their way of responding was different – tended to externalize the problem, venting their anger on the shortcomings of the transfer process itself. Their logic is persuasive and their commitment to learning is, in the circumstances, ironically impressive:

> I done a test and my head was aching . . . and I don't care if it hurts my head . . . the more education I get the more I'll learn . . . They should take the ones who haven't (got) more education – they need more.
>
> (Year 6, boy)

> I didn't really like choosing schools . . . they shouldn't be able to make you do tests because they're just looking at answers and it's not going to tell you much about you, is it, so I would say interviews are best; tests [only] tell you about what work they can do and how smart they are.
>
> (Year 6, boy)

Another Year 6 boy attributed his failure to win a place at his preferred school to national policy, describing the irony of a situation where he and some of his mates live near the school they want to go to but haven't been offered a place, while pupils who come from farther away are: 'Why can't we go to our local schools? If they haven't got a school, why don't they build one?'

However, in apparent efforts at self-protection (one of Jackson and Warin's categories of response to comparing self with others), two of the girls interviewed rationalized the grounds for rejection in ways that avoided self-blame:

> I probably didn't get in because I don't go to church – it's a church school isn't it? I don't go to church often.
>
> (Year 6, girl)

> I know why [school] rejected me – we had to take a test but they never wrote down my test scores. They never wrote down my test scores – I don't know why.
>
> (Year 6, girl)

A third girl adopted an 'it doesn't really matter' stance which we tend to think of as more typical of boys:

> All the schools do the same work really so it doesn't really matter what school you go to because you just do the same thing there whatever school you go to.
>
> (Year 6, girl)

A sense of rejection elicited a similarly ambivalent response in one of the Year 6 boys: he fluctuated between concern and a contrived nonchalance which is, in our experience, typical of the discourse of older groups of alienated boys:

> It kinds of makes my work go down because it's like, because . . . I don't really care because I've only got a school that's rubbish. I don't really care.

There is some evidence, then, to support Jackson and Warin's (2000) thesis that gender stereotypical behaviours are a predictable response to disorientating situations: the outcome is a tightening of the 'us and them' gender affiliations. This tendency is apparent in the aspects of boys' behaviour that girls (and their mothers) choose to talk about. For example, Year 6 girls reported their mothers as having strong opinions about some of the schools in the area, and these often featured 'boy trouble':

> My mum doesn't want me to go there at all because in the school even when she got in there some boys were jumping over the gates and the girls they were like playing about with boys – there was the gate there and a fence yeah and there was a big hole there and boys would be going through in and out and I don't think none of the teachers noticed there and when my mum just reached the gates [she] turned around: 'We're not going to that interview.' Turned around and went away.

Another Year 6 girl reported a 'boy trouble' incident that had occurred in a secondary school:

> Some boys, they tried to get into the school, and everyone was running about and everything. They tried to climb over, they tried

to come over the fence and the teacher, the headteacher, had to come and tell them to go away. And one boy, he comes into the school and he covered his face and he went up to this girl, she used to go to my school in my class, and he tried to take her bag. She said he punched her, I think, and then just ran back out the school.

Not surprisingly in the face of these boy-centred horror stories, some Year 6 girls said they wanted to go to a single-sex school – one reason being their *own* perceptions of 'boy trouble':

Girl 1: I don't want to go to a mixed school – boys pick on you
Girl 2: They're disgusting
Interviewer: Boys are disgusting, they pick on you – do you mean call you names?
Girl 2: Not really – more like watching you when you are getting changed. And teasing.

One Year 6 boy, quoted earlier, said that he felt at a disadvantage at transfer because 'you never know what can happen round the corner' and it seemed from Urquhart's post-transfer follow-up interviews that boys adopted more combative ways of gaining or regaining physical ground and social status in the new environment. Boys seemed more concerned about territory and more aware of the threats to territory (see Askew and Ross 1990; Connolly and Neill 2001). Jackson and Warin (2000) suggest that boys' response to challenges in the environment is to become more challenging themselves. Certainly some evidence from the Year 7 boys point to a kind of 'continuous power play' among boys – what Askew and Ross (1990: 47) describe as 'an ongoing process of positioning and a continual seeking of status and prestige'. This often involved 'play' challenges with older boys which could easily turn into something more serious:

the Year 9s and the Year 8s . . . they chase the Year 7s in our class, but then we turn back and chase them and we get people, put them somewhere and if any of their friends come, we beat them up instead of them . . .

(Year 7, boy)

I make jokes with some [older boys], yeah, and some, you know, have a poor sense of humour . . . so they chase me around . . . I just run away from them . . . and I get someone bigger than them to come and help me . . .

(Year 7, boy)

The sense of power in relation to territory can extend to where you sit:

> A boy tried to get on my nerves by sitting in the chair that I normally sit in. And I told him to move and he said, no, so I grabbed him by the throat and chucked him away. I got my own seat and then I went to the referral room.
>
> (Year 7, boy)

Being sent to the 'referral room' seems not to have muted the boy's pride in getting his own seat back!

Most of the Year 6 and new Year 7 boys' discourse was about positioning themselves in relation to boys, girls did not come into the picture: 'We don't know about the girls because we don't talk to the girls much' (Year 6, boy). It is important however not to pathologize this as a strategic withdrawal on the part of the boys or the girls or as a re-assertion of gender-typical behaviours in the changing and uncertain world of transfer. Rather, it is the norm for both boys and girls to form same-sex friendship groups at this stage. Indeed, the girls in the sample who went on to a girls' secondary school experienced older *girls* as the threat to their security in the new environment. However, their responses to the threat *were* different from those of the boys: they did not seem to indulge in baiting games but instead tried to avoid the predators:

> I stay out of their way . . . When I go to the toilet, they're all smirking because they're smoking.
>
> (Year 7, girl)

> The girls here do several fights and especially the big girls. You look at them to see what they look like and [they say] why you looking at [us]?
>
> (Year 7, girl)

Indeed, one girl said that she wished she had gone to a mixed school because there girls were less threatening than they were in a single-sex school. It seems that in some single-sex groupings, familiar cross-sex roles are in fact maintained because dominant boys assign female and subordinate positions to the less macho boys in the all-boy group and in some all girl settings some girls take on what we have tended to see as boy behaviours. Power play may, after all, be a stronger dimension than gender in these situations.

However, in the all girl settings, the older girls had a more varied set of relationships with the younger girls (although it is possible that boys in a mixed school chose only to talk about the combative relationships with older boys). For example, some girls attended clubs where older girls taught the younger ones, and some accounts of older girls suggested a warmer, friendlier relationship: 'The Year 11 girls are like mothers. They call us their babies. If we don't know something, they say, "Come on, I'll show you" ' (Year 7, girl). So, while the continuous power play between children will coalesce around gender difference where boys and girls are in the same environment, power play itself is not solely structured on gender lines.

Our data do, to some extent, confirm Jackson and Warin's (2000) thesis about the links between gender and identity at transfer and this is interesting, but the more important issue is that some students, both boys and girls – and often from the least advantaged areas – feel rejected or threatened by the system early in their career as learners: their optimism takes a hard knock as they come to feel that *they* are being rejected. Their trust in the rhetoric of education is also likely to be fractured: they believe they had the right to choose a secondary school but instead it was the schools that were doing the choosing, and they did not choose them. As Lucey and Reay commented – and their analysis is confirmed by Urquhart's study – 'a significant number of working class children conveyed the sense that they were on the brink of an event (transfer to the secondary school) which would have identity implications for them far into the future' (1999: 11; see also Reay and Lucey 2000).

Familiar and neglected aspects of transfer

Although the move from Year 2 to Year 3 has received little attention, the turbulence of the move from primary to secondary school has been well documented. Since the early 1980s research on this transfer event has focused on a range of concerns, some reflecting new policy frameworks. Looking back from our current gender-aware vantage point we are likely to be surprised at the relative neglect of gender as a dimension of research on pupils' experiences of transfer – particularly in the dominant research paradigm that conceptualizes transfer as a rite of passage. Gender and social class feature more prominently in the swathe of research on transfer undertaken in the wake of government commitment to market forces and the consequent responsibility of primary school pupils and their families to choose a secondary school and to negotiate acceptance. Initially, interest focused largely on the determinants of choice, but later issues of agency and influence within the decision-making process gained prominence. Carroll and Walford (1997: 170) comment on the parent-child dimension of the debate about agency looked at in the context of social class:

> ... it has been suggested that working-class families are more likely to take account of children's views and actually delegate the decision-making to the child than middle-class families. ... These

authors have been concerned that the decisions of 10-year-olds may be based upon a range of criteria (such as patterns of existing friend-ships, school uniforms, easy access) that are even less related to the quality of appropriateness of educational provision than those used by parents. It has been argued that delegating the decision to chil-dren could lead to a widening of social class differences between schools.

Reay and Ball (1998: 432) continue the debate, clarifying the nature of the class differences. They go along with the earlier studies suggesting that in working-class families 'the destinations of children's friends and the import-ance of locality' were indeed critical factors influencing choice but that among middle-class families the educational policies of schools, particularly the use of setting, were dominant considerations. They also confirmed the greater agency of pupils in the decision-making process in working-class families: pupils were positioned as the educational experts and there was a tendency for parents to defer to their wishes. In contrast, they point out, among middle-class families the impression is given that children share power within the family decision-making process but, argue Reay and Ball, in fact while there is discussion and negotiation, these activities actually 'mask parental control' (1998: 443 drawing on Walkerdine and Lucey 1989: 112). David *et al.*'s (1997: 400) work also focused on agency within the family and their study underlines the importance of the mother in the decision-making process: they concluded that across social boundaries it is mothers rather than fathers who do the *groundwork* necessary for informed decision-making and who deal with the 'ambiguous market place'.

At the present time the key national concern is standards and it is not surprising that studies of transfer (see Galton *et al.* 1999) are focusing on 'dips' in academic progress post-transfer and the balance of social and academic support at transfer. In a climate dominated by the pursuit of grades, schools are in danger, but not of their own making, of defining and presenting learning as a series of 'quick fixes' – intensive bursts of revision for the next test – and students, not surprisingly, see years without tests or exams as unimportant, as 'on the back burner' years, as 'rest years' (Rudduck and Flutter 1998). Policy makers have seen the key challenge at transfer not in terms of the develop-ment of pupils' identities as learners but as maintaining continuity of aca-demic progress from one key stage to another: through bridging units and the passing on, from primary to secondary school, of pupil grade profiles. All this is, of course, well intentioned but the preoccupation with continuities can ignore the importance, for pupils, of some element of discontinuity. Transfer to the secondary school represents a big step in their school careers and their life course and they expect life and learning to be different in the secondary school.

Jackson and Warin's (2000) work extends the familiar focus of transfer studies by looking at *how* pupils cope with the physical, social and personal disorientations of transfer; this approach enables them to bring in the neglected dimension of gender. Interestingly, Reay and Ball (1998: 442, our emphasis) say that 'whether the child was a boy or a girl appeared to make very little difference to internal dynamics of *choice*', but gender may be more influential in shaping the way that pupils *respond* to experiences of transfer.

Studies such as Jackson and Warin's are important in the present grades obsessed climate because they focus attention on the young people themselves and the issues of selfhood that they struggle with at times of transfer, particularly when transfer happens to coincide with the parallel turbulence of early adolescence. Hargreaves and Earl (1990: 26, in Hill and Russell 1997: 170) are among many who argue that young people at this stage in their life course and school career

> are seeking to develop a positive self-concept; are eager to grow towards greater independence; are keen to experience social acceptance and affiliation; are eager to establish relationships within which these processes of growth can take place.

Again, in their review of research on motivation, Anderman and Maehr (1994) argue that early adolescence is a period when autonomy, self-determination, social interaction and image are important to young people and they go on to underline the importance of students maintaining a positive image in their own eyes and in the eyes of their peers. And Wigfield *et al.* (1991) suggest that young adolescents can become more negative about schools and themselves at times of transfer because they find themselves moving into a more competitive setting where, unsure of their strengths in relation to others, they can experience a loss of self-esteem which may lead to disengagement.

In the three small scale studies reported above – all looking at transfer from the pupils' perspective – there were examples of pupils beginning to feel that they were second-rate, unwanted, wouldn't be able to cope, and that school work was stressful rather than fulfilling. It seems that both boys and girls are vulnerable to such feelings. We reviewed the data from the studies in the light of Jackson and Warin's (2000) thesis that transfers affect status and identity as those involved encounter new situations and new people and make comparisons between past and present and between themselves and others. Our data support this aspect of the thesis and we found some support for the idea that at such moments in their school careers young people tend to seek security from the turbulence of change by ordering their world around the relatively constant dimension of gender identity, and in doing so tend to exhibit gender stereotypical behaviours. But what seems to us to matter more is the story of rejection that some of the interviews tell and the disappointment and pain felt by both boys and girls, even though they may deal with the situation in different ways. Finally, it is issues of social class more than gender, we think, that are seriously affecting the learning and life chances of the pupils whom we and our colleagues talked to.

Recommendations

Some of the issues raised in this chapter have their roots in the system of choice at transfer which teachers are not in a position to tackle directly. Again, given the pressures on schools in the present climate, it would also be difficult for teachers to give the kind of support needed by children and families who are disadvantaged by procedures that require higher levels of literacy and social confidence than they have.

There are, however, some smaller things that teachers might do to minimize the sense of failure that pupils experience who do not get their first choice of school, especially if they have visited and been impressed by the buildings, resources and spirit of schools that they wanted but failed to secure a place at. The suggestions do not relate specifically to gender but respond more to the general sense of disappointment and loss that both boys and girls felt in our study:

- Finding some way of identifying the good things about the schools that some pupils are reluctantly going to could help them. In some settings inviting Year 7 pupils back to talk to Year 6 pupils about the good things in their schools and establishing a link between Year 7 and the present Year 6 which might be sustained until they become, respectively, Year 8 and Year 7, could help. Such 'buddy systems' are more effective if there is face-to-face contact but follow-up by email can also help.
- If Year 6 teachers can tune in to rumours about the status of secondary schools and seek to balance the more negative images (see earlier) that are often quickly and unreliably constructed by peer group gossip, this might also help.
- Finding a way of enabling children to discuss, supportively and not competitively, the excitements, anxieties and concerns that they have in relation to transfer could be helpful but as we have seen above, Year 6 pupils who have experienced disappointment and rejection are already finding ways of covering up their feelings – by bravado, by secrecy – and the timing of such discussions could be significant. It would also be important to ensure that such discussions are not occasions when a personal sense of failure is reinforced by hearing about the successes of others.

Note

1   By transfer we mean the move from one school to another and by transition we mean the move from one year to another within the same school. At Year 2 pupils might be moving from an infant to a different junior school or they might, within an all-through primary school, merely be making the transition from Key Stage 2 to Key Stage 3 work.

References

Anderman, E.M. and Maehr, M.L. (1994) Motivation and schooling in the middle grades, *Review of Educational Research*, 64(2): 287–309.

Askew, S. and Ross, C. (1990) *Boys Don't Cry: Boys and Sexism in Education*. Milton Keynes: Open University Press.

Carroll, S. and Walford, G. (1997) The child's voice in school choice, in *Educational Management and Administration*. London: Sage.

Connolly, P. and Neill, J. (2001) Locality, gender and educational aspiration, *International Studies in Sociology of Education*, 11(2): 107–29.

David, M., Davies, J., Edwards, R., Reay, D. and Standing, K. (1997) Choice within constraints: mothers and schooling, *Gender and Education*, 9(4): 397–410.

Doddington, C. and Flutter, J. with Bearne, E. and Demetriou, H. (2001) *Sustaining Pupils' Progress at Year 3*. Cambridge: University of Cambridge Faculty of Education.

Galton, M., Gray, J. and Rudduck, J. (1999) *The Impact of School Transitions and Transfers on Pupil Progress and Attainment*. London: HMSO.

Hargreaves, A. and Earl, L. (1990) *Rights of Passage: A Review of Selected Research about Schooling in the Transition Years*. Toronto: Ministry of Education, Ontario.

Hill, P.W. and Russell, V.J. (1997) Systemic, whole-school reform of the middle years of schooling, in R.J. Bosker, B.P.M. Creemers and S. Stringfield (eds) *Enhancing Educational Excellence, Equity and Efficiency*. London: Kluwer Academic Publishers.

Hull, R. (2000) First Day of School, in S. James (ed.) *Days Like This: A Collection of Small Poems* (Cambridge, Mass: Candlewick Press).

Jackson, C. and Warin, J. (2000) The importance of gender as an aspect of identity at key transition points in compulsory education, *British Educational Research Journal*, 26(3): 375–91.

Lucey, H. and Reay, D. (1999) First choice or second best? The impact on children of not getting their first choice of secondary school. Paper presented to the British Educational Research Association (BERA) Conference, University of Sussex, 2–5 September.

Morrison, I. (2000) 'School's great – apart from the lessons': sustaining the excitement of learning post-transfer, *Improving Schools*, 3(1): 46–9.

Ofsted (1999) *Standards and Quality in Education 1997/98* (the annual report of Her Majesty's Chief Inspector of Schools). London: HMSO.

Reay, D. and Ball, S.J. (1998) Making their minds up: family dynamics of school choice, *British Educational Research Journal*, 24(4): 431–48.

Reay, D. and Lucey, H. (2000) Children, school choice and social differences, *Educational Studies*, 26(1): 83–100.

Rudduck, J. (1996) The turbulence of transition, in J. Rudduck, R. Chaplain and G. Wallace (eds) *School Improvement: What Can Pupils Tell Us?* London: David Fulton.

Rudduck, J., Chaplain, R. and Wallace, G. (eds) (1996) *School Improvement: What Can Pupils Tell Us?* London: David Fulton.

Rudduck, J. and Flutter, J. (1998) *The Dilemmas and Challenges of Year 8*. Cambridge: Homerton Publications.

Salzberger-Wittenberg, J., Henry, O. and Osborne, E. (1983) *The Emotional Experience of Learning and Teaching*. London: Routledge.

Spender, D. (1982) *Invisible Women: The Schooling Scandal*. London: Writers and Readers.

Stanworth, M. (1983) *Gender and Schooling: A Study of Sexual Divisions in the Classroom*. London: Hutchinson.

Urquhart, I. (2001) 'Walking on air?' pupil voice and school choice, *FORUM*, 43(2): 83–6.

Walkerdine, V. (1990) *Schoolgirl Fictions*. London: Virago.

Walkerdine, V. and Lucey, H. (1989) *Democracy in the Kitchen*. London: Virago.

Wigfield, A., Eccles, J.S., MacIver, D., Reuman, D.A. and Midgley, C. (1991) Transitions during early adolescence: changes in children's domain-specific self-perceptions and general self-esteem across the transition to junior high school, *Developmental Psychology*, 27(4): 552–65.

Wolchover, J. (1998) Parent fury as schools reject record number of children. *Evening Standard*, 25 September.

Woods, P. (1987) Becoming a junior: pupil development following transfer from infants, in A. Pollard (ed.) *Children and their Primary Schools*. Lewes: Falmer Press.

Index